Beyond the Lighthouse

MARGARET CROSLAND

Beyond the Lighthouse

English Women Novelists
in the Twentieth Century

Taplinger Publishing Company

New York

First printing
First published in the United States in 1981 by
TAPLINGER PUBLISHING CO., INC.
New York, New York

Library of Congress Cataloging in Publication Data
Crosland, Margaret, 1920–
  Beyond the lighthouse.
    1. English fiction – 20th century – History and
criticism. 2. English fiction – Women authors – History
and criticism. I. Title.
PR888.W62C7 1981   823′91′099287   81–5638
ISBN 0–8008–0734–0   AACR2

For Jennifer and Jon Wynne-Tyson

Foreword

As I look at the present state of the sex-war in Britain, it seems to me that women, the readers more than the writers, having attempted to fight men with emotional and social nuclear weapons, are now fighting about fighting with no real enemy except themselves. Their better organized colleagues in the USA, fortunately for them, still seem to present a united front.

These chapters about twentieth-century fiction by women are not intended as a contribution to feminist propaganda. I am more interested in showing how women's writing is different from men's than in trying to prove it must be better.

Women did not invent the novel, which I define here as a prose narrative, but it seems a natural form for women to use, growing as it did out of letter-writing in the drawing-room, now more likely to be typed on the kitchen table. In some two hundred years, women writers have covered a good deal of new ground and the twentieth century has seen them travelling farther still: beyond the lighthouse.

M.C.
1981

Acknowledgements

Without the advice and help of my editor Elfreda Powell this book would never have been written: thanks to her I have even enjoyed writing it.

Among the many others who have helped me I would like to thank: John Calder, R.S. Collins, Stephanie Dowrick, Dan Franklin, Alice Frick, Anne Harden (Librarian, Oxford University Press, London), Colin Haycraft, Margaret Marshall, Jean Mauldon, Peter Owen, Sue Roe, Jeffrey Simmons, Christine Stockdale, Thomas J. Watson, and Michael Williams.

Contents

[1]

Beginning

❦❦❦

'The nineteenth century did actually end at last. Probably every one over twelve and under seventy sat up to see it out, to see the twentieth in, to catch that elusive, dramatic moment and savour it.' Imogen, in Rose Macaulay's novel of 1923, *Told by an Idiot*, shouted 'Happy new century' to her sister, who did not wake up, and looked out at the clear frosty morning. 'What a jolly century it looked; what a jolly century it was going to be!' Before going on with the story she was inventing, in which she appeared herself, as a young man, Imogen had thought of reading *Treasure Island*, published seventeen years earlier, but decided to go on thinking instead. In a slightly earlier chapter entitled *Last Lap* Rose Macaulay had mentioned some books which appeared in 1898: 'Swinburne publishing *Rosamund, Queen of the Lombards*, Mr Yeats *The Wind among the Reeds*, Mr Kipling *Stalky and Co*, and the *Day's Work*, Mr Conrad *Tales of Unrest* . . . Mr Stephen Phillips *Paolo and Francesca*, Mr Thomas Hardy *Wessex Poems*, Mr H.G. Wells *The War of the Worlds*, Miss Mary Cholmondeley *Red Pottage*, Mrs Humphry Ward *Helbeck of Bannisdale*. . . .' She went on to mention 'bad novels pouring into the libraries with terrifying increase of speed. . . .'

In 1900 the situation was not very different, the same writers were still busy in Britain, Henry James was publishing his 'third period' novels, Edith Wharton was about to publish her first. Even though the year 2000 appears on the horizon now a surprising number of those British titles are still about, but for anyone interested in writing by women the list is disappointing: Mary Cholmondeley is unremembered, even if she had her biggest success with a novel (reprinted in 1968) which attacked the middle

classes, and for those of us curious and courageous enough to read
Mrs Humphry Ward the choice would be surely *The Marriage of
William Ashe* (proving that it is not a good thing for a man to marry
beneath him socially) or *The Coryston Family* which came in 1913
and sadly enough is anti-feminist in part of its theme.

If in this deliberately random list men well outnumber women
there was of course, as Rose Macaulay well knew, no shortage in
Britain of novels written by women, and good ones too. George
Eliot had died in 1880 after publishing seven novels, and it was
about this time that a new generation of women, though not yet a
regiment, began to write novels and did not know how to stop,
unlike the lamented Kate Chopin in the USA who wrote actively
for only six years or so between 1894 and 1899. The end of the
Victorian era produced novelists, both men and women, whose
stamina equalled that of the explorers and empire builders, while
their thousands of readers, mostly through circulating libraries, had
equal stamina for reading and an insatiable appetite. The men,
some of whom are listed by Rose Macaulay, had a good deal of
personal publicity while the women, mostly assisted at home by
hard-working domestics, even if they had no husbands to support
them, could not complain they had no time to write, and it was too
early in history for them to toil miserably in garrets over their
manuscripts; if they needed to support themselves most of them
would do something else, usually teaching the children of people
superior in class to their own and at least earning a roof over their
heads. Once the women novelists had pushed their way into print,
sometimes using an alias, like the American-born Pearl Craigie,
who called herself John Oliver Hobbes, nothing could stop them
and their readers kept them alive. They began to be persons in their
own right, although they tended to be solitary. Mrs Humphry
Ward was not so much solitary as austere, but what else could one
have expected of the granddaughter of Dr Thomas Arnold of
Rugby? When she published *Robert Elsmere* in 1888, a novel which
publicised the need for practical Christianity as against the worship
of the miraculous, its success was nothing short of stupendous and
in the USA no fewer than half a million copies of the one-volume
edition were sold.

'Ouida' had similar successes with her obviously escapist works and wrote 45 novels in less than 30 years. Marie Corelli's outpourings took place between 1886 and 1921 and if the lives of these writers are now more entertaining than their novels there can be no biographies without the novels in the first place. Some of the best things of Marie Corelli are her prefaces, chapters in personal and social history. If ever one thinks of embarking on the 401 pages of *The Life Everlasting* (1911) the 31 pages of author's prologue will do very well instead. From them we learn how the author, with no thought of reward, yearns to help those in the Wilderness to hear the Divine Voice, which is more, she thinks, than the present day Church can do. She refers to her first and successful book *A Romance of Two Worlds* (1886), claims that she had been forbidden to use the word radium and had to use 'electricity' instead. She maintains that her 'Electrical theory of the Universe' in this novel predated an important theory explained in the *Hibbert's Journal* of January, 1905, by a scientist who said '*Electricity* is all things, and all things are *electric*'. She likes to link one book with another, for, after all, that way she can keep her readers close. It was a preface she wrote in 1900 itself which showed what she felt about the professionalism of writers and the brisk way in which publishers were ready to exploit the situation.

'By the special request of the Publishers,' she wrote in her Author's Note to *The Treasure of Heaven*, 'a portrait of myself . . . forms the Frontispiece to the present volume. I am somewhat reluctant to see it so placed, because it has nothing whatever to do with the story which is told in the following pages, beyond being a faithful likeness of the author. . . . Moreover, I am not quite able to convince myself that my pictured personality can have any interest for my readers, as it has always seemed to me that an author's real being is more disclosed in his work than in any portrayed presentment of mere physiognomy.' She had decided to allow publication of this 'authentic' likeness, taken by a photographer unaware of her identity, because 'libellous, fictitious representations' had been circulated at home and abroad by what she called 'certain "lower" sections of the pictorial press'. She ended by saying that 'to myself the personal "Self" of me is nothing' while her work 'and the keen desire to improve in that work . . . constitutes for me the Everything of life'. Worthy indeed, but the authentic photograph is known to have been improved.

Despite her high principles Marie Corelli's many works would not have interested the heroines in any of Rose Macaulay's novels, who read a lot and liked talking about writers mainly if they were highly intellectual or very entertaining, or if they were scientists, controversial theologians or philosophers. But the girls in *Told by an Idiot* might have glanced at Marie Corelli's *Boy* which appeared in 1900 and is worth looking at for its portrait of an adolescent. 'Boy', whose father was an alcoholic, was dragged up by a careless, bohemian mother who did not wear stays and only washed under protest. He was taken up by a loving spinster, Miss Letty, and there is a description of an extraordinary lunch party when Boy, on his way to Sandhurst, upsets a conventional-type major. Britain was fighting the Boers in South Africa and when the Major asks him if he is glad to be on his way to the army Boy replies 'Oh, I don't mind it!' The older man had never heard anyone make such a remark and is even more devastated when Boy says of his colleagues 'You couldn't expect them to *love* work! You see they do just what their fathers and mothers want them to do.' You never know what you are going to find in Marie Corelli.

She has been laughed at, much written about and hardly re-read. Things were different for Sarah Grand, whose long life stretched from 1854 to 1943, for at least one of her books was due for reprinting in 1980, after long neglect. In 1893 she had proved that an author could publish a novel partly at her own expense and win. '*The Heavenly Twins*, the brilliant book which was to make her so famous, had at first failed to attract anyone, and she had had it set up in type at her own expense.' So wrote Frederic Whyte in his 1928 biography of William Heinemann. This enterprising publisher brought Sara Grand luck. She offered him her book in 1893, 'saying he could have the copyright for £100; it looks a small sum in retrospect, in view of the history of the work, but we must reflect that not one novelist in a thousand earns so much money by a first effort'. Heinemann admired the book and agreed, although very doubtful about his investment. The novel came out and was a quite unlooked-for success. In a few weeks' time Heinemann sent for the young authoress, told her that he proposed to tear up their agreement, substituting for it a new one by which she was to be paid 'the most favoured authors' royalties', and concluded by handing her a cheque for £1200, the amount he owed her already upon this new basis.

In 1897 came *The Beth Book*, now due for emergence from neglect, for it is a kind of primer for the women's movement. Nearly every basic theme which is so argued about today is in this novel, from the difficulties of the mother-daughter relationship, the problem of marriage as escape, the question of property owned by women, the difficulties in finding suitable work, the status of the common-law wife, the dangerous business of liberation through writing, and the neglected question of men's need for help and understanding: poor things, it could be said they are still waiting. This long book was 'asked for at Mudie's, suburban, and seaside libraries, and discussed at every hotel table in the kingdom'. (*The Manchester Examiner* on *The Heavenly Twins*.) *The Beth Book* is well worth reading, even if the author may be working through a programme. Most of her younger male characters are either horrible or feeble or both, and in her famous story *When the Door Opened* –? the suspicious husband is something of a joke. The story, like the title, finishes with a question-mark and the reader is left to imagine the end. It was included in the collection *Emotional Moments* (1908) of which the title story is an intriguing mini-analysis of love and sexuality; the heroine is a playwright who found her work revitalized by the love she had given up. Then there is the story of the butcher's wife who suddenly grew tired of being downtrodden by her male chauvinist husband; plus many other curiosities showing that Sarah Grand deserves to be better remembered, even by men, who will forgive the heroines their lonely little battles, for they do not moralize too much.

These later Victorian women thrived on writing: witness Elinor Glyn, her married name rhyming so conveniently with sin and tiger-skin. By 1909, at the age of thirty-six, she had already published seven novels and the immensely silly heroine Elizabeth, married to Lord Valmond, had appeared in several of them before

Elizabeth visits America (1909), all in the form of letters addressed to her mother in England. In tone it is like all the 'high society' and débutante-style books produced in Britain over several decades. The Elizabeth books are also reminiscent of those irrepressible American novels like *Our Hearts were Young and Gay* (Cornelia Otis Skinner and Emily Kimbrough). The first of the 'Elizabeth' books dates from 1900, they are part of social history nowadays and I can recommend a glance at the heroine's lively remarks about America and the Americans.

If Elizabeth was immensely silly Elinor Glyn certainly wasn't, she could not afford to be so, for she had far too many responsibilities. Despite her red hair, a serious disadvantage at the time, the young Elinor Sutherland was able to make what looked like a fairy-tale marriage to Clayton Glyn in 1892, and of course it wasn't. When this caricature of the British aristocracy confessed, after sixteen years of boring wedlock, that he had now spent his capital, what was his wife to do, except earn some money somehow, despite her lack of qualifications to do anything – except write novels. No doubt it was from now on that she developed that 'set mouth' that Rose Macaulay saw in 1920 to be a feature of the lady novelist. For Elinor never stopped writing, brought up her two daughters, set up her sister as a Mayfair milliner and kept an eye on her mother until the latter's death at 96 in 1937. As for her husband, he packed his bag and retired from the scene.

There is not much sin in Elinor Glyn, only a desperate yearning for the happy romantic life that she had so much wanted and failed to find. The phenomenal success of *Three Weeks* (1907) is hard to understand now for most of it strikes us as rubbish: it is the story of an unhappy Balkan queen who has a brief love affair with a very young Englishman in Lucerne and Venice. She returns to her own country and is later murdered by her jealous husband: but she had given birth to a 'fair, rosy-cheeked, golden-haired English child'. The broken-hearted father was allowed to see him when he was five, and heir to the throne. The possibly true story may owe something to the Queen of Roumania's love affair with an Irishman. The anecdotes related by Anthony Glyn, the author's grandson, about the book, are better reading. The Headmaster of Eton wrote to the author to say he had banned the book at the college. The author asked the Headmaster whether he had read the novel, which he hadn't. On doing so he admitted he 'had enjoyed the book and had been misled by its reputation. The ban, however, must stay'.

Everyone who wants to talk or write about romantic novelists should read at least one Glyn novel, and my choice is *His Hour* (1910), later called *When the Hour Came*. Its glamour is not spoilt by effusive vagueness, it includes a fascinating description of the Russian Imperial Court at St Petersburg, based on the author's own visit there the previous year. There is also a sight-seeing trip to the Great Pyramid in Egypt, made of course by moonlight. Those readers interested in the technique of romantic writing will learn something, those who dislike romance will see just how miserably bad the current successful examples of the genre can be, for *His Hour* is readable; and it is amazing to think that with all the later competition Elinor Glyn has had *Three Weeks* was in print in Britain in 1980 with an appreciative preface by Cecil Beaton. She had that extraordinary longevity so often attained by lady novelists and lived on until 1943. That must have been a lonely moment in 1920 when, at the age of 56, she set out alone for Hollywood. Her behaviour there, according to her grandson, belonged often to the realms of fantasy. It can hardly be said that her life achieved the romantic success of her books, for after Lord Curzon had treated her badly there was little in her life except her books and her grandchildren. It is very easy to laugh at her, but she was a professional in her way and even now she is more than a period piece. There is a particularly sad photograph of her, taken when she was a young 70, in a vast drawing room with no fewer than three tiger-skin rugs on the floor. The room, and the décor she presumably chose, emphasize not her success and wealth but her total solitude. The women novelist tends to be something of an actress, and it is a pity that the public stage performance of *Three Weeks* in which she was due to star in 1908 was cancelled, following the Lord Chamberlain's decision on the unsuitability of the play. She might have found more happiness as an actress than as a novelist, but at least in the 1920s she was instructing the young Hollywood stars how to act and more particularly how to make love.

Obviously her yearning for ideal romantic love will seem ridiculous to most people now for it is hardly likely to bring personal happiness; but at least she learnt how to use her yearning to some purpose and brought up her family, which was a more practical contribution than her husband had made.

A most extraordinary feature of the turn of the century and the Edwardian period is not so much the quantity of novels being written by women as the range of styles they offer us. Some writers of course had produced their best-surviving work just before the year 1900 and so escape our catchment area in time. I have only discussed them if they seem to have been unfairly neglected. In addition to *The Real Charlotte* and *Some Experiences of an Irish R.M.* Somerville and Ross (Edith Anna Oenone Somerville and Martin Ross [Violet Martin]) for instance published *The Silver Fox* in 1897 which actually reminded Arnold Bennett (in *Paris Nights*) of Henry James. Elizabeth von Arnim wrote the incredibly successful *Elizabeth and her German Garden* in 1898, and went on writing (as 'Elizabeth') for several decades.

One of the most interesting and often neglected writers of the early century was of course Ada Leverson, different from all her contemporaries with the exception, naturally enough, of Oscar Wilde, whom she and her husband helped so much at his most difficult moment. Her admirers, like those of Jane Austen, Firbank or Saki, feel they could have done with more books to gloat over and yet are deeply grateful for what they have. It is hardly surprising that her dialogue is sometimes reminiscent of Wilde because they met in the same range of drawing rooms, but her writing has more depth, if less neatness and glitter. Her books began to appear in 1907 and the sixth and last came out in 1916. The novelist Colin MacInnes wrote about her with admiring conviction, dwelling especially on the three titles that made up *The Little Ottleys* and stressing that she was universal, by no means merely Edwardian. Yet part of her attraction to the contemporary reader today is the 'atmosphere' in which her people moved: we can almost smell the red plush and see the quivering aigrettes. To read her is to live, superficially at least, in that world where some men occasionally worked and women spent their time organizing social life.

The reader of today with any feminist interest might decide that novels which are all about 'upstairs' with no mention of 'downstairs' have no relevance or reality. But any such decision would be a mistake, for Ada Leverson knew very well what was going on in society and if she was preoccupied with the behaviour of the rich and the would-be rich she did not regard it all as a mere joke. She does not approve the behaviour of Mary Hillier, who starts to write blackmailing letters, but the reader of today is sidetracked when he/she learns how the blackmail is administered. Mrs Hillier is dependent on a working woman, for she engages a 'typewriter', in other words a typist. The reader can do all the 'right' things with the characters, such as going to tea at Rumpelmeyers, but if he/she goes to the Russian ballet on this basis there is no point in expecting a rave review: 'One wants to see it, one is interested, from curiosity, and then, afterward, there's a sort of Dead-Sea-fruitish, sour-grapes, autumn-leaves, sort of feeling! It's too remote from real life and yet it hasn't an uplifting effect. At any rate it always depresses me.' Percy is surprised by Bertha's verdict in *Bird of Paradise* and anyone reading the book for the first time would be further surprised and delighted by the appearance of Signor Semolini, the Futurist painter. His remarks on 'the simultaneity of the plastic states of mind in the art' and his reference to 'Orphic cubism' are too comical to be quoted out of context. In other books Kipling ('so fearfully familiar with his readers') and Shaw are neatly put in their place.

Ada Leverson's most crushing remarks are reserved for these extraneous people or for the minor characters in her story. There is always one young heroine who radiates goodness to such an extent that other people usually improve through knowing her. Bertha Kellynch is so full of understanding that even the pathetic and odious Mary Hillier, a husband-catching heiress, comes round in the end, and the author is ready to allow charm even to a member of the unspeakable *nouveau riche*, such as Mrs Pickering: 'She spoke with a very light Cockney accent. She bristled with aigrettes and sparkled with jewels. Her bodice was cut very low, her sleeves very short, and her white gloves came over the braceleted elbows. She wore a very high, narrow turban, green satin shoes and stockings,

and altogether was dressed rather excessively. . . . She was
certainly most striking in appearance, and a little alarming in a quiet
room, but most decidedly pretty and with a very pleasant smile.'
Her hostess thought she must recently have been 'the principal boy
at some popular pantomime'.

The editors of serious literary reference books tend to find Ada
Leverson beneath their dignity. She may not involve her characters
in the type of problems that May Sinclair for instance liked them to
discuss but for anyone interested in the crucial problem of
husband-wife relationships there is a lot to be learnt, especially
from the conversations between Bruce and Edith Ottley. Although
the author does not write unkindly about men the reader is left
wondering if they are really worthwhile companions for the
heroines. In *Bird of Paradise* for instance Nigel Hillier has married
for money, soon stopped speaking to his wife and yearns for Bertha
Kellynch, now out of his reach. Rupert Denison treats Madeline
badly and can never make up his mind: he also has an eye for any
good opportunity (with a woman) open to him. The author seems to
indicate that these men may be unsatisfactory but there is a chance
that after gentle coaching and example from the women they may
improve. Edith Ottley for instance has to point out to her husband
that it is not always much fun for a wife to be at home all day with
small children while the husband is out 'working'. But Ada
Leverson does not spoil her novels by making the women perfect.
The selfish Lady Kellynch in *Bird of Paradise* seems to owe more
than her name to Jane Austen, and Lady Cannon dressed badly:
'generally a velvet dress of some dark crimson or bottle-green, so
tightly-fitting as to give her an appearance of being upholstered
rather than clothed. Her cloaks were always like well-hung curtains,
her trains like heavy carpets; one might fancy that she got her gowns
from Gillows.'

It is true that the novels deal with what Mr Salteena called 'high
life', but this does not prevent the inclusion of children, who are
seen and heard, brilliantly and amusingly drawn, and the ghastly
adolescent boy in *Bird of Paradise*. Then there are those people who
had formed their own sort of society, like Miss Belvoir, who was
arty, and received her friends in a room which 'had a delightful view

of the river from the Embankment. It was a greyish afternoon, vague and misty, and one saw from the windows views that looked exactly like pictures by Whistler. The room was furnished in a Post-Impressionist style, chiefly in red, black and brown; the colours were all plain – that is to say, there were no designs except on the cciling, which was cosily covered with large, brilliantly tinted, life-sized parrots.' And there is much more, proving that surely nature imitates art.

Ada Leverson, unlike Elinor Glyn, had no need to write for money, and she seems to have written because she enjoyed it. She is essentially feminine, as Jane Austen and Rosamond Lehmann are feminine, seeing everything through a woman's eyes, never pretending to be masculine, but remaining consistently professional within a small world, small, yet microcosmic rather than microscopic.

It is extraordinary to realize that when Elinor Glyn and Ada Leverson were writing such a different person as Katherine Mansfield was producing her first stories and actually publishing a few, even if they were too close to Chekhov to show real originality. Of all the worthwhile women writers of this century she is the one most easily taken for granted, suffering from her melodramatic biography, until suddenly you re-read practically anything she wrote, from the German *pension* sketches to *Je ne parle pas français*. Then one is aware once again, as on the first reading, of a style that is fresh, that makes an immediate impact, that does not try to be 'literary' and succeeds in being literature for that very reason. Her New Zealand upbringing prevented her from being stifled by an English middle-class education, for anyone who was adolescent in the 1900s ran the risk of annihilation from convents, governesses and other menaces.

Mansfield cannot be added to the list of experimenters, because the short story as we know it had not been in existence very long and she did not change its course fundamentally, she merely used its resources to the utmost and handed on a kind of post-Chekhovian tradition which was original enough in her hands but not one which the less talented could follow. As readers we can just succeed in escaping the biography, but of course it went into her stories and that is why her contribution is such a particularly personal one. Her attractiveness to both men and women was only matched by her unlikeableness. Katherine Mansfield was probably tough in all ways except the physical. She needed to dominate and succeeded in many ways, especially since providence had sent her Ida Baker. She needed to succeed as a writer, and she therefore had to dominate her subject matter. Given her poor health she could hardly have dealt with a full length novel, and only left fragments of one; if she had tried to work on it consistently it would have dominated her, she could not have tolerated that.

She was not a 'feminine' woman in the normal sense of the word, for attractiveness to men and women does not automatically make a woman so, but the stories on the whole could not have been written by a man. Of course the narrators in some cases are men, even if we do not realize this at once, as in the famous *Je ne parle pas français*, but the voice is too light-textured for the average English-writing male. So many of the stories pick up the sound of continental or Russian writing, which in view of her friends and her reading, from Chekhov, his translator Koteliansky and one of her lovers, the French writer Francis Carco, is hardly surprising.

Anyone thinking over the history of recent fiction soon sees that women writers find it hard to disentangle themselves from their writing – no wonder perhaps that Cyril Connolly regarded love-stories as 'confessions', no wonder that so many men writers have been suspicious about their women colleagues. Katherine Mansfield used endless incidents and people from life – think of *Psychology* (Ida Baker and probably Murry), or *The Man without a Temperament* (certainly Murry), yet if one does not know the facts behind the fiction one's enjoyment of the work is undiminished, so convincing is the treatment. It is this sureness of touch which gives her work classic status, makes it hard too to realize that she was born in 1888 and died in 1923. And she, who was so deeply embroiled in her own times, has not dated, showed a sense of humour in her work and was not painfully self-conscious for long: which is more than can be said of Virginia Woolf.

Some writers, like Katherine Mansfield, in the early part of the century, made an appearance that was far too brief, but some, in contrast, with that longevity in life and writing that seems peculiar to women, began to publish when Britain was genuinely Victorian and continued well into the Twenties. Marie Corelli lasted a long time and surely May Sinclair, who lived from 1870 to 1946, has been unfairly neglected. Nobody has yet revived interest in her by discovering some secret love-affair, as happened in the case of Edith Wharton, but she *has* been re-discovered as a novelist of particular, but by no means exclusive interest to women.

Once you start reading May Sinclair it is hard to stop, despite some repetition of themes, hard to avoid in a total of twenty-four novels. Of all the women writers who studied Freud early in the century and used his theories in fiction she is the most interesting, even if her applications of them are sometimes a little too obvious. *The Three Sisters* (1914) is not exactly an enjoyable book from any point of view, it describes how a repressive English vicar ruins the lives of his three daughters, and how in their different ways, conscious and unconscious, they attempt to cope with the situation. This situation in fact is based on that luckless family the Brontës, surely the most overworked, as biographical subjects, in British literary history. In fact, May Sinclair wrote a preface to *Wuthering Heights*. The US critic William York Tindall summed the novel up convincingly: he found the sisters 'curiously wanting in tragic significance. Too clear and intellectual to be moving, defining the irrational motives of her people too well, May Sinclair has the air of penetrating mysterious recesses with a guide book in her reticule.' (*Forces in Modern British Literature*, New York 1956).

But when she is at her best her people are alive and her stories moving. Her general style of writing shows affinities with that of Wells, she likes the situation of what one can only call the lower middle class, and her descriptions of life in the London suburbs have now acquired an extra dimension, they have a period flavour in addition to their suburban local colour – think of *The Combined Maze* (1913), with Winny and Ranny sitting in a meadow in Southfields. Winny gathered buttercups and stuck them in Ranny's bootlaces while he thought 'Her position was as good as his, yet she only earned five pounds a month to his eight'. May Sinclair would never have missed such a good opportunity and on the whole does not underline too much. The title of this novel was taken from the name given to a gymnastic display, and this is how Ranny, the hero, explains it all to the girl he unfortunately married, mentioning the girl whom he unconsciously loved but did not marry.

The Combined Maze? That wasn't so easy to explain. . . . It was, he said, a maze, because you ran it winding in and out like, and combined, because men and women ran in it all mixed up together. They made patterns accordin' as they ran, and the patterns were the plan of the maze. You didn't see the plan. You didn't know it, unless you were leader. You just followed.
'I see. Men and women together.'
'Men and women together.'
'Are you running in it?'
'Yes.'
'Does Winny run in it?'
'Rather. We run together. You'll see how it's done.'
Miss Usher thought she saw.

This title shows, like so many other of her books, that she did not limit her understanding to her women characters; the novel is seen almost exclusively through the eyes of Ranny, and if he marries the wrong girl he hates being 'beastly' to women and he learns in the end what love means, especially when he is a deserted father trying to look after a baby and a small child.

May Sinclair really did write about and for men and women, much more so than Sarah Grand, who probably did not think much of men. Rosamond Lehmann reports in *The Swan in the Evening* that she read May Sinclair when young and was 'excited' by her. One of her most memorable books, *Mary Olivier* (1919), is however about a woman and more specifically for women readers. At its heart is the love-hate relationship so many girls experience with their mother. Another part of the story, inevitably linked with the first theme, is the fate in the marriage market of a girl who has real intellectual power, educates herself and is happy living with a man even more brilliant than herself. But he marries someone else because he cannot wait for Mary's mother to die. Mary thought briefly that life was over for her, but it wasn't, because of course she had built up a true life of her own, even if it was a solitary one.

The author herself strikes us today as a solitary person. She was one of the very first people to understand that solitary artist, Dorothy Richardson, and nothing came easily to her, for her own life had been not unlike that of Mary Olivier. She is mentioned briefly by many contemporaries, people as varied as Douglas Goldring and Virginia Woolf, but she never appears anxious to talk too much, she obviously expressed herself more easily in writing. It could be said that she bridged the gap between the late Victorian writers and those who wrote about 'the new woman' in the Twenties. Her later novel *The Life and Death of Harriet Frean* belonged in fact to 1922 and is again concerned with the self-sacrifice of a woman, something which so many of them, even today, cannot prevent, they still move lemming-like towards this emotional death. Nobody wrote about it more convincingly than May Sinclair.

Between 1900 and 1920 there were of course many other women novelists who no doubt ought to be more than names to us, but they are not, even though some have become fascinating characters for the biographers: Elinor Mordaunt, who argued with Somerset Maugham, Amber Reeves, one of the many literary young women who was fascinated by H.G. Wells and had one of his sons, Violet Hunt, whom Ford Madox Ford did not marry, the recently re-discovered F.M. Mayor whose first novel *The Third Miss Symons* came in 1913 and perhaps her best *The Rector's Daughter* belonged to 1924. In that strange, sad posthumous compilation *The Note Books of a Woman Alone* by the unknown Eve Wilson (1935), the editor mentions *The Rector's Daughter* as one of the books to be read as relevant to what Charlotte Brontë had to say about the difficulties of women: 'Old maids, like the houseless and unemployed poor, should not ask for a place and an occupation in the world: the demand disturbs the happy and rich, it disturbs parents'. F.M. Mayor, however, who was published by Virginia and Leonard Woolf, was too interesting technically to depress the reader.

In twenty years or so a great deal had happened, and in the field of women's writing there had been entertainment, experiment, education. Fiction-writing, unsurprisingly, was mainly still an occupation for the middle-class for there were still far too many families living on 'round about a pound a week'. It was to be a long time before women could relax those efforts which were directed into stretching this pound, and do something else. Just before 1920 two very different books were published – *The Young Visiters* (1919) by Daisy Ashford, which she had written as a girl of 9 in 1890, as though perpetuating that moment, and *The Return of the Soldier* (1918), by Rebecca West, one of her most readable novels. It describes how shell-shock in the war that was ending affected a man and his marriage. Proving forcibly the ghastly effects of war on the individual and the family it showed at the same time that if the twentieth century had not been able to stop wholesale suffering, if it was not exactly that 'jolly century' that Rose Macaulay's young heroine had thought of, its people were at least able to come to terms with the suffering and by their own endeavours and discoveries they could make life go on. 1914 had, in fact, been the delayed end of the nineteenth century, and *The Return of the Soldier* was an unconscious forecast of what was in store for Britain and Europe.

Experimenting (1)

❄❄❄

During the nineteenth century women writers were no rarity in Britain or the USA.

The first woman to write professionally in order to support herself and her children was probably Christine de Pisan in fifteenth-century France; Jane Austen began to find money interesting and useful while Frances Trollope wrote in order to keep her family going, after her unsuccessful attempt to settle in America. As soon as women had made the experiment of professionalism they made literary experiments.

Their exploration and achievements in the early part of the century have not yet however been fully assessed. Dorothy Richardson, the earliest, is too easily taken for granted, and from the publicity angle everything about her was wrong, while Virginia Woolf, the second, suffers from the over-glamorous image of the beautiful, neurotic, well-educated woman who fell in love with Victoria Sackville-West, received a marriage proposal from the homosexual Lytton Strachey and wrote perhaps too many acid letters. The principal contribution to fiction-writing by these two women was two-fold in itself, innovation in method, and preoccupation with the psychology of women and their position in society. Few people were better placed than women writers to concern themselves with the reality and the potential of women's status generally in the years before the First World War, and, come to that, after the Second World War.

It seems more practical to mention Virginia Woolf first: she is admired and talked about by thousands of people who may have read only a few of her books while Dorothy Richardson is practically unknown. The American William James had written about the 'stream of consciousness' before 1900 while the French writer Edouard Dujardin had actually used the technique in 1888, for his novel *Les Lauriers sont coupés* of that year is full of 'interior monologues'. Dorothy Richardson was the pioneer in Britain, but still it is Virginia Woolf who leads the curious into that other literature which Elaine Showalter, quoting John Stuart Mill, has called a 'literature of their own' – writing by women.

Without the figure of Virginia Woolf the Bloomsbury Group, so piously remembered half a century after its death in the Second World War, would be as dull as any men's club in London. Bloomsbury made itself into a type of club so avant-garde that a handful of women were life members. Yet how few of those Bloomsbury figures, apart from John Maynard Keynes, have kept a living and controversial personality that can in some way, even today, continue to stimulate young people all over the world whose interest must surely be something other than mere nostalgia or curiosity about sexual gossip.

Few people, even if they are not too much concerned with fiction, fail to respond to Virginia Woolf in some rational or irrational way. The fortunate and happy reader is he or she who reads her when young. For once one can say he or she because men have not been afraid of Virginia Woolf the writer; they probably felt that her femininity was not going to engulf them in any obvious way and her work, supported as it was by the intellectual background of Bloomsbury, was to be respected, like that of Jane Austen. For its maximum impact Virginia Woolf's fiction, like poetry or the ballet, needs readers who have the emotional and intellectual time to relish not the death, but the life of the moth. Her books make many other demands too, they ask not simply for 'young' readers but for readers not too much concerned with a story, not wholly preoccupied with the realistic, social aspects of a novel.

For her creative work Virginia Woolf chose fiction, the art form that has always been the daily conversation of literature, and exposed herself to criticism by attempting the impossible – the creation of prose that was not 'poetic', but poetry in itself, and the use of this vehicle to tell a story through the most apoetic of means, human beings who remain, on the whole, 'real' people. She did infinitely more than this, as we know, but it is worthwhile remembering that she consciously chose what had been, up to the time of the First World War, a serviceable but hardly exciting medium.

In view of Virginia Woolf's unique position in twentieth-century fiction writing it is also worth remembering three things – the principal facts of her life, the range of her fiction and the period when it was produced. She was born eight years later than Gertrude Stein, as far back as 1882, elder daughter of a professional critic and writer, and educated entirely at home. She married Leonard Woolf when she was 30, in 1912, and worked with him on the day-to-day labour of publishing at the Hogarth Press. She saw something of France, but travelled little, dividing her time between London and Sussex. In 1941, when she was 58, she drowned herself. This handful of facts forms the framework of a life that could have been longer and happier, but hardly fuller. Other, infinitely more personal and important facts have reached the public gradually since the early critical studies and the publication of *A Writer's Diary* in 1953, the latter containing only the sections that Leonard Woolf chose to publish at that time. Since then there have been his own deeply moving autobiography and various volumes of letters.

Two more points need to be made. One is the number of novels she wrote – only nine, including *Orlando*, originally a 'biography', now often classified as a 'fantasy', along with four collections of short stories over a long period of time: *The Voyage Out* was written before 1912 and *Between the Acts* was unrevised at her death in 1941. It was a dedicated working life of thirty years, one which saw two world wars and possibly some of the most profound changes that ever occurred in Britain, producing novels in many different keys. This wide range is one of the most intriguing aspects of Virginia Woolf the writer, for there have been only too many successful novelists who reach a certain standard and apparently do not dare to experiment. Woolf's work is all the more interesting because sometimes the links between one book and the next are not obvious, just as motifs in much surrealist work are linked by some intangible thread perceived only in the unconscious mind.

A first book can only be linked forward to the books written later, and backwards to the author's own life. The first published novel by a writer subsequently accepted as great is usually something to be read with special attention, even excitement: it may be the best work he or she ever wrote, it may be the worst, it may be imitative, it may be brand new. *The Voyage Out* is a curiosity, with more to offer the specialist than the general reader.

The plot is simple: a young girl, Rachel Vinacre, brought up without a mother's help, full of romantic ideals and ignorance, meets a young man on a voyage out to South America, becomes engaged to him but dies of a fever. According to Leonard Woolf in *Beginning Again* Virginia Stephen, as she then was, had written the book at least five times by 1912, then she had married, spent two years in a state of mental breakdown and waited until 1915 to see her first novel published. Clive Bell believes that the generally favourable notices it received helped her to recover her health.

A great deal had happened since she wrote it, and in 1920, she re-read it: 'I've not read it since July 1913. And if you ask me what I think I must reply that I don't know – such a harlequinade as it is – such an assortment of patches – here simple and severe – here frivolous and shallow – here like God's truth – here strong and free flowing as I could wish. What to make of it, Heaven knows.' She tried to be fair:

> The failures are ghastly enough to make my cheeks burn – and then a turn of the sentence, a direct look ahead of me, makes them burn in a different way. On the whole I like the young woman's mind considerably. How gallantly she takes her fences – and my word, what a gift for pen and ink! I can do little to amend, and must go down to posterity the author of cheap witticisms, smart satires and even, I find, vulgarisms – crudities rather – that will never cease to rankle in the grave.

From the very start this woman writer was preoccupied with her heroine's mind and it is the women who make the book worthwhile, along with the stray conversations about men-women relationships and the role of women in society. There is a preoccupation with the ideal and a failure to feel any real sympathy with men. The author's deep interest in Rachel, the appearance of the poised Mrs Dalloway, who was to be the central figure of a later novel, the introduction of so many other women, from Miss Allan, the unmarried writer, to Mrs Chailey, the hard-done-by but faithful ladies' maid: this is a woman-dominated book.

The other striking thing about the 'harlequinade' is that it proceeds by two different methods – moments of drama, such as the description of Mrs Ambrose: 'Tall, large-eyed, draped in purple shawls (she) was romantic and beautiful' and the sort of edgy, destructive academic chat the author would certainly have heard in the Stephen home. But the ladies were 'after the fashion of their sex, highly trained in promoting men's talk without listening to it'. The Dalloways join the ship in Lisbon because they had no difficulty in making the 'special arrangements' necessary, 'for they came of a class where almost everything was specially arranged, or could be if necessary.' Mrs Dalloway thought the scene was 'so like Whistler' and three pages later the company are discussing the suffragettes, whom Mr Dalloway, the politician, pities. 'Nobody can condemn the utter folly and futility of such behaviour more than I do; . . . may I be in my grave before a woman has the right to vote in England!'

Although the 1960s and after have alerted readers, especially women readers, to the preoccupation of earlier novelists with 'women's problems', perhaps everyone has forgotten how this novel tries to make everyone face those problems. Rachel, for instance is twenty-four, had been kept in ignorance of sex and seems to have felt or discovered nothing for herself.

She becomes engaged to Terence and they conduct an odd little sex-war which Rachel might have won had she not caught fever and died. The conversations between Terence and his men friends are idiotic and yet interesting because the author makes one say for example that women are 'so stupid' and the other reply reflectively 'are they?'. This may have been one of Virginia Woolf's first written references to the subject which was to preoccupy her so deeply, in and out of fiction, later in life. Other big problems are discussed in a direct manner: 'When I'm with artists,' says Mrs Dalloway, 'I feel so intensely the delights of shutting oneself up in a little world of one's own, with pictures and music and everything beautiful, and then I go out into the streets and the first child I meet with its poor, hungry, dirty little face makes me turn round and say, "No, I *can't* shut myself up – I won't live in a world of my own. I should like to stop all the painting and writing and music until this kind of thing exists no longer." '

The richness and complexity of this first book have understandably attracted literary and academic critics from Winifred Holtby onwards, their theories often moving beyond literature into psychology. There are references which may foreshadow the lighthouse symbol and all that it may signify. Perhaps Virginia Woolf found herself writing the book five times over because she tried to say everything at once, as many writers of first novels do. Did Rachel die because the author could not face the thought of marriage? Was the sailing of the ship down the river unconsciously intended to indicate the sexual act? Was it wishful thinking that made the author introduce a male novelist who professed to be deeply interested in the lives of women? These are some of the questions that academic critics of this novel have asked, and there are plenty more waiting to be examined.

In *The Voyage Out* the author and the characters were all aware of the sex war, and Rachel had told Terence that after their marriage they would certainly argue and fight. At one point she decides that men and women cannot possibly live together, at another she remembers that despite the intimacy of marriage there was a life in her that was 'independent of her, and independent of everything else' . . . 'she was independent of him; she was independent of everything else'. Despite these repeated assertions of independence Virginia Woolf was more deeply preoccupied in most of her work with people in relationships rather than people on their own. In *Jacob's Room*, the third novel, published in 1922, there is no real Jacob, only an amalgam of the many Jacobs whom his friends and acquaintances saw. This and her second novel, *Night and Day* (1919), are in themselves less absorbing than any of the others but cannot be forgotten because they fit so closely into the pattern of her work: they are concerned still with the ideal, the reconciliation of opposites, the male and female principles, absence and death. Only in death perhaps does this reconciliation take place. There is one other way it can occur, in the marriage of the male and female principles within the mind, a concept Virginia Woolf had not yet expressed but one towards which she was unconsciously working. Coleridge's famous remark, inseparable now from a whole area of critical approach to Virginia Woolf, cannot be quoted too often: 'The truth is, a great mind must be androgynous.'

If *Jacob's Room* is not too attractive in itself the author herself became aware that she had achieved as a writer the independence that Rachel had thought about, the independence that could exist even in marriage. On July 26th 1922 she recorded in her diary how her husband had reacted to the book.

> We argued about it. He calls it a work of genius; he thinks it unlike any other novel; he says that the people are ghosts; he says it is very strange. . . . But I am on the whole pleased. Neither of us knows what the public will think. There's no doubt in my mind that I have found out how to begin (at 40) to say something in my own voice; and that interests me so that I feel I can go ahead without praise.

In other words she had become a professional writer, she was confident now not because Leonard Woolf had mentioned the word 'genius' but because there was so much to argue about. The key phrase in Leonard Woolf's 'report' is the phrase 'unlike any other novel', for it is only that kind of novel which is worth reading, whether we admire it or not.

Mrs Dalloway (1925) was a crucial step, essential if sometimes irritating reading. There is a dazzle about this one-day story of a woman concerned almost exclusively with the party she is giving that evening. It is a stimulating book and in some ways undated because a walk through London today in the right circumstances, following Mrs Dalloway's route, can produce the same kind of vibration, but there are two drawbacks – the average reader is convinced that Mrs Dalloway is an unbearable snob and the sub-plot, the story of the war-damaged Septimus Warren Smith, does not 'belong' to the book. Virginia Woolf simply failed here as a story-teller: if she was trying to indicate that society had rejected him, that the medical profession was beneath contempt, she might just as well have written a separate piece on the subject. The author failed too in her attempts to create male characters, a perennial failing of the average woman novelist. The men in the present and past life of Mrs Dalloway are only half-real, and the remembered girl who is now a woman, Sally Seaton, is the only other person in the novel who seems alive.

But the book fascinates through its immediacy, its moment-by-moment development, and the author is achieving such technical skill here that she can be forgiven for using a character she had used sketchily once before, in *The Voyage Out*. Virginia Woolf was attempting now to show her in depth, and only just failing, because she was almost exclusively preoccupied with technique, but she did at least make her the centre of a picture which is not only impressionist but a picture where nothing is ever still, silent or untouched by light for more than a second. It is so far above reality that the Septimus Warren Smith plot has been described as showing something of the alternation between manic and depressive behaviour. But it was the true beginning, and this was 1925, when the author was forty-three, middle-aged.

What was happening in the book world in 1927, when *To the Lighthouse* appeared, causing a *Spectator* reviewer to write that the author's genius was 'at once more difficult and more original' than that of any other novelist of the day? It was hardly a vintage year for English novels, and probably the one that has lasted best was *Dusty Answer*, by Rosamond Lehmann, for it is still read and discussed. No Wells novel, only *Mornings in Mexico* from Lawrence, but a strong American contribution: *Men without Women*, *Death Comes for the Archbishop*, *Elmer Gantry*, *Twilight Sleep* (Edith Wharton) and *The Bridge of San Luis Rey*.

In the first few pages of *To the Lighthouse* there are some scraps of dialogue, a few characters, hints of relationships, and a setting by the sea. But no character, no action or thought is described as though the writer were looking straight ahead.

The whole work is created through and round the figure, or rather the essence of Mrs Ramsay. The stuff of the book materializes about her almost as though she herself were a lighthouse and the beams that sweep round her catch other people and reveal them sharply if momentarily. The light emanating from her passes through several planes and the reader is for a time dazzled not by its brightness but by the clarity and variety of what it reveals. There is no doubt about the author's involvement with Mrs Ramsay as an expression of the feminine principle in all its essential creativity and as a potential expression of the feminine plus the masculine: not bisexual but unisexual, or to use again that splendid and sonorous Greek word, androgynous. As for the female principle itself, in the last fifty years its existence has been analysed and discussed, leading indirectly to some legislation in many countries. The social scene has changed as a result and it is not far-fetched to see *To the Lighthouse* as an important work in the history of this change, principally because its contribution is indirect and less likely to appear dated. Virginia Woolf wrote meaningfully on these subjects in her non-fiction but the reflections of her feelings in the novels are more telling because they appear as instinctive elements in her characters' make-up, they are not conscious urges towards improvement. The indirect method has one other value – it is a hidden persuader, it does not stop men from reading these books and convinces them, as no propagandist could do, that women's artistic achievement and women's social condition are inseparable from each other.

To come back to Mrs Ramsay: she is the focal point of her household and everyone turns to her as a sunflower to the sun. Her beauty exists in an essentially dynamic way, inseparable from her active life, even if it is slightly too good to be true, for 'she knew without having learnt . . .'. In addition to being a mother to everyone, adults included, she had a social conscience: 'She ruminated the other problem, of rich and poor . . . she visited this widow or that struggling wife . . .'. But it was all too much: 'So boasting of her capacity to surround and protect, there was scarcely a shell of herself left to know herself by; all was so lavished and spent.' She was so exhausted that the author could not allow her to go on living, her death seems a protest on behalf of all women who cannot be expected to make such a vast contribution, without any real help from men, to the family and social life generally.

The book is so highly wrought that the reader forgets how sentimental the ending might have been. James Ramsay, now seventeen, goes to the lighthouse with his father, who ten years earlier had not allowed him to go. They are visiting not the building itself but the lighthouse figure of his dead mother, and they are out of touch with reality: they even take the parcels they were going to take ten years earlier and Mr Ramsay solidly reads a book in order to escape the world about him. Lily Briscoe finishes her painting as the boat reaches the island, and fortunately she cannot actually see the landing because there is too much mist. Without this mist – deliberate impressionism, some might say – the ending would have been too contrived. But there is not only the mist to obscure the finality of it all, there is Lily Briscoe's self-punishing remark to herself that her painting would be hung in the attics, as though neither the author nor her character could bear to finish her work, could not bear it once it was done, and could not imagine other people could bear it.

William Bankes, in *To the Lighthouse*, remembered seeing Mrs Ramsay when she was a young girl: 'There he stood looking down the avenue at Hampton Court, as if he could see her there among the fountains'. Immediately one is transported to *The Waves* (1931), and that significant visit made to the same palace and gardens by the characters, and realizes that for the author at least it is a place so beautiful that it is always associated with the much-loved and idealized dead, Mrs Ramsay or Percival. Among all Virginia Woolf's work there is no title – some people do not allow the term 'novel' in this instance – that has caused such cut-and-thrust contradiction between critics as *The Waves*. Stephen Spender has assessed it as her greatest achievement while Dame Rebecca West has condemned it as 'Pre-Raphaelite kitsch'. To like or not to like is hardly the question here: how can anyone pretend to be objective about this strange work which seems to have affected world literature as deeply as those very different books *The Trial* and *Ulysses*?

The complexity of the work is matched by the slow growth of the idea behind it, which can be traced in *A Writer's Diary*. The author began with the title *The Moths*, something one cannot forget while reading the final version since it is impossible not to think of moths fluttering round or towards a source of light, for that is what the characters seem to do, like a set of dancers maintained in relation to each other and isolated from the world in general by light, the luminous atmosphere in which the author keeps them talking, or rather thinking. Perhaps the most interesting note in the *Diary* is the one of 21st February 1927, which preceded any actual writing: 'Why not invent a new kind of play; as for instance:

Woman thinks . . .
He does.
Organ plays.
She writes
They say:
She sings.
Night speaks
They miss

I think it must be something on this line – though I can't now see what. Away from facts; free; yet concentrated; prose yet poetry; a novel and a play.' This idea was never lost, although Virginia Woolf seems to have changed her general approach several times in the course of the work. The idea of poetry certainly came through to Winifred Holtby who wrote to the author saying 'It is a poem, more completely than any of your other books, of course . . .'. In 1931 the intellectuals at least were surprisingly ready for all the newness of *The Waves* and Harold Nicolson pronounced it a masterpiece. It is worthwhile remembering that 7,000 copies were sold in about two months and the author noted that she was 'in danger . . . of becoming our leading novelist, and not with the highbrows only'.

The Waves, superficially at least, stands alone; never had an author, thinking of a new fiction-form that was half way to drama, appeared to move so far from tradition: and yet she noted that it was a continuation of something she had first thought of while writing the end of *To the Lighthouse*. It was her supreme experiment and is important for two things at least outside the basic new form: the central character, with the voice that matters most, is a man, Bernard, and the love of his life has been another man, Percival, loved also by all the other characters, but he is dead. In each of the earlier novels there had been death: Rachel, Jacob, Septimus Smith, Mrs Ramsay, they all die. Percival's death is built into *The Waves* from the beginning, it is the darkness in the book, but not dark enough to quench the all-embracing luminous quality. The author knew consciously that she was thinking of her brother Thoby, just as she had known that *To the Lighthouse* was about her mother's death and her father's widowhood. She had even wondered if she could add Thoby's name and dates to the first page of her book. How much of herself did she write into the voice of Bernard, and how much of a man was Bernard, far though he was from the conveniently sex-changeable Orlando? So the book is the memorial of a brother who died at the age of 26, and it remains in the mind as a book of regret, nostalgia, loss, accepted if not overcome, although the reader only becomes aware of this once he has absorbed the experiment in form, the experiment which in itself was to be the exorcism. The reader who cannot accept this book need not feel lonely: Virginia Woolf had to avoid Roger Fry and Lytton Strachey when it came out, for she sensed they did not like it.

What of the search for a male-female synthesis, for the creative principle that transcends sex? The three women in the book, Susan, Rhoda and Jinny, are sharply contrasted and Susan represents femininity in its simplest form. Yet there is more balance between the men and women characters than in any book so far, as though at the age of 48–9 Virginia Woolf had accepted the fact that men and women can inhabit the same world after all. It may not be a book about women but only a woman could have written it and remained for so long in control of such delicate evocation and interplay of personality. Men, especially in fact creative men, do not have such sustained patience, which among their sex is the gift of the analytic or scientific mind, not the artistic. Virginia Woolf said several times while she was at work on this book that it 'screwed up her brain'. By deliberately keeping the form as rigid as she did the strain was bearable and she was able to keep the book under control. A man might have been tempted to discuss deeper issues, imponderables, something stranger than the 'mysticism' that Virginia Woolf talked about while writing this. The book is a proof, if one is needed, that talent or genius need not be a sexless combination of masculine and feminine, talent or genius can have sex, and can be feminine.

Some of Virginia Woolf's books have dated. *Orlando* for instance, which the author wrote for fun but realized it was too serious or not serious enough, now seems precious, but the biographical background is absorbing, concerned as it is with Vita Sackville-West and the history of Knole House in Kent. Its presentation as a biography, complete with a page of acknowledgements, seems a feeble joke now, although it must have been entertaining to most people when first published, with its photographs of Vita. If the idea was original, the page about the actual sex-change of Orlando is neither interesting nor amusing, although nowadays we can laugh in our own way at the remark: 'But let other pens treat of sex and sexuality; we quit such odious subjects as soon as we can'. The author had written in her *Diary* that it was 'about Vita, Violet Trefusis etc' and she had also written elsewhere 'Friendships between women interest me'. They have interested most women writers, for many of them have found men less interesting than writing and yet needed human love or companionship in order to go on writing themselves. Now these friendships interest everyone, men included, while homosexual lovers, men and women, are out of the ghetto and sex change is a reality, not a fantasy, as in *Orlando*.

On the last page of *The Waves* were the words *O Death*, the words that close the book. Ten years later Virginia Woolf was dead, having completed only two more novels, *The Years*, in 1937 and *Between the Acts*, published after she died. It is the only novel in which there is no death. In the meantime came the longest of her books, and some might say, the dullest.

Average admirers of Virginia Woolf would probably read any of her books rather than *The Years*, which is over four hundred pages long and chronicles the life of Eleanor Pargiter from 1880 to what is called 'Present Day', the 1930s. Eleanor's life draws together the story of her own family and that of two others, but it is far from being a 'family chronicle' novel; it does not attempt to tell the whole story, for Virginia Woolf was obviously not that kind of novelist. But *The Years* was admittedly much more 'accessible' as a novel, telling a story of sorts and inevitably interesting the reader, especially the woman reader, in the figure of Eleanor, who does good works, takes on the housekeeping for her retired colonel father after her mother's death and remains unmarried, as several of the other women do, while the families in general disintegrate.

Many critics have reported with a show of surprise that the book topped the best-seller list in the States for several weeks. It is easy to say, with hindsight, that the American public relished a novel which on the surface at least must have looked like a nostalgic picture of that 'quaint' British society which has always fascinated them. It is no criticism of what is called 'popular success' to say that certain aspects of the novel appeared to fit the formula required by the average reader. By page 9 for instance Colonel Pargiter is going to see his mistress, Mira, feeling guilt as he waits on the doorstep of the poor little house in the shadow of Westminster Abbey. Two pages later he begins his clumsy love-making and the expected 'censorship' operates immediately when 'the hand that had lost two fingers began to fumble rather lower down where the neck joins the shoulders'.

It was part of Virginia Woolf's purpose in writing *The Years* to indicate how slowly nineteenth-century life faded, for obviously people pass on inherited traditions, even if they do not like them or think they are rebelling against them; at the same time change in Britain came slowly until 1918, after which it accelerated a little and then, after 1945, a lot. For this reason the novel is still highly relevant today and anyone involved in amateur social work will sympathize with Eleanor, who wanted a vast amount of change but had to accept that it would not come quickly. She and the women she meets spend a great amount of time observing how 'the poor' live, notably how poor women live, and how the lives of women in general, poor and rich, differ from those of men, being notably unsatisfactory.

The novel may be too long, the pace too even, the style too 'ordinary', because it must not in any way distract from the details which this time the author wanted to describe directly, but its documentary interest compensates for all this. In a curious way the experimenter now wanted to experiment with the ordinary, and was intent on using everyday language because she was consciously writing a propaganda novel and wished to make it readable. 'Eleanor did not like talking about "the poor" as if they were people in a book.' Poor people in this novel were to be real people. Rose notices that her friend Maggie was poor because she cooked her own food and made her own clothes. Eleanor Pargiter's family laugh at her when she does organizational and practical work for the poor, for it makes her irritable, absent-minded and 'broody'.

In no other fiction was Virginia Woolf so preoccupied with the class situation, she was concerned that all details of this sort should be included in a non-obvious way. She also recorded the way in which the poor or the semi-poor looked at the rich. Kitty Malone goes to see the Robson family, who work for their living, and looks at the daughter, Nell. 'As she stood there with her father's hand on her shoulder under the portrait of her grandmother, a sudden rush of self-pity came over Kitty. . . . Did they know how much she admired them? she wanted to say. Would they accept her in spite of her hat and her gloves? she wanted to ask. But they were all going off to their work. And I am going home to dress for dinner, she thought. . . .'

All these painful truths were included in a mosaic so broad that it might have provided material for Wells or Arnold Bennett. In her *Diary* Virginia Woolf records over and over again her exhaustion as she laboured to produce this book and found she had written 148,000 words. Was all the labour worth it in the end? The author decided that it was, and went straight on to write the essay that has been so important to historians of the women's movement and to critics of Virginia Woolf at the same time – *Three Guineas*, which is non-fiction and so outside our scope here. She felt so strongly about the question of women's rights generally that she was compelled to write about it in a creative work, not just in a pamphlet. The two works are linked in ways which are obvious and less obvious, the most interesting theme common to both of them being the preoccupation with money, the money that could come through education, the money that would free women from the prison of

Victorian, male-dominated society. Given her passionate feelings on the subject Virginia Woolf has been criticized for refusing to join organizations and societies for the promotion of anything from women's suffrage to social and educational parity with men. She considered that her status as a writer was enough. Was she then not entirely convinced about her own theories or was she too arrogant and inclined to think that other, non-creative people could do the kind of work that Eleanor Pargiter did? There can be no final yes or no, and before anyone attempts to decide this issue for their own purposes I would recommend that they read carefully *The Years*, the novel that seems so far from the brilliant experimentation of the other work and yet so essential to its author that she was prepared to exhaust herself writing it.

It is hard to enjoy Virginia Woolf to the full without knowing and caring about English literature, particularly Shakespeare and all the poets, and *Between the Acts* proves this to the utmost, for the whole pageant sequence would be meaningless otherwise. One wishes the book could be adapted for television for there are many moments of potentially rich, moving and comic visual effect. Radical experiment seems absent, as though the great experiment now were paradoxically the lack of it. There is also a controlled preoccupation with male-female polarity. Miss La Trobe, the writer of the pageant, is a lesbian, an unhappy one who is unsuccessful both in love and work. Her part in the book is balanced by the inclusion of William Dodge, described by Giles Oliver as a 'half-breed', for he could not bring himself to utter the word, or his personal equivalent of it, homosexual. Isa Oliver is in love with another man but is more than prepared to stay with her husband for the sake of quarrelling and love-making. The book is easy to read, and the author found it comparatively easy to write, despite the many themes she brought into it, varying from the fear of war to the difficulties of the marriage situation. But even plans for more writing could not save her from the puerperal depression from which she suffered after finishing each book. Many writers know this state even after a mild and untaxing labour, and Virginia Woolf had no protection against the threat of war and the destiny of her beloved England. She was mentally too vulnerable and treatment for her state of mind in 1941 was still too limited and risky. She was only 58 and would surely have continued to write novels – she had in fact started one – although at the same time she would probably have developed her brilliant critical work and become the most revered critic in Britain.

She was the most imaginative propagandist for the women's movement who ever existed, and rightly she is quoted every day now. She can hardly be quoted as interested in other writers; she, the great experimenter, who wrote novels and did not care for stories, was slow to understand or accept the experimentation of James Joyce, and was either blind or jealous when she had to deal with the work of Dorothy Richardson.

In 1919 she had been 'irritated' by Katherine Mansfield's review of *Night and Day*, 'I thought I saw spite in it'. Although it was on the same day, November 28th, that she had written about 'friendships with women' she did not always find women writers acceptable as professional colleagues. Women writers she had not met did not interest her, and one whom she clearly did not want to encounter was Dorothy Richardson. The latter's first novel, *Pointed Roofs*, had appeared a few months after *The Voyage Out* in 1915. Virginia Woolf had reviewed *The Tunnel* four years later, but when it came to *Interim* later in 1919 she thought it better to withdraw. 'Today, bearing K.M. in mind, I refused to do Dorothy Richardson for the Supt [*The Times Literary Supplement*]. The truth is that when I looked at it, I felt myself looking for faults; hoping for them. And they would have bent my pen, I know. There must be an instinct of self-preservation at work. If she's good, then I'm not.' It is hard to forgive such pettiness.

Virginia Woolf was not genuinely happy for much of her life yet she had never been solitary, unloved, unsupported, and many people helped her to write and publish. Dorothy Richardson had very little on her side, she had to deal with the whole of life and writing single-handed, and she never had any luck, until it was nearly too late. She lived from 1873 to 1957 and published a series of twelve novels entitled *Pilgrimage* which recount the life of Miriam Henderson, a life which is never far away from that of the writer herself. Any life reflects social change, but a woman's life must inevitably reflect it more deeply at this time because ever since the Industrial Revolution the whole make-up of society had depended on the changed way in which women participated in it. Dorothy Richardson had suffered from a father who aspired to be a gentleman, an almost impossible task for the son of a Wesleyan grocer. Although he bettered himself for a time his final failure left his wife a nervous wreck and his daughters without support. Two married, one became a governess and Dorothy went into teaching, first in Germany and then in London. It was all a middle-class girl could do at the age of 18 in 1891, and it was the start of a struggling, independent life destined never to change. Dorothy was always the one who coped, trying but failing to care for her mentally depressed mother who killed herself in 1895, trying and succeeding to rescue the man she later married from starvation and alcoholism.

Reading and discussing, rather than writing, were her preoccupations when she came to London in 1896, working improbably enough for a successful dental surgeon in Harley Street, living frugally in Bloomsbury, suffering from narrow-minded landladies, but spending time happily in the British Museum and observing all the ideas so much in ferment at the time, notably socialism, whose adherents she found 'narrow and illiberal'. She came to writing through translation, having come to that through the Russian-Jewish immigrant Benjamin Grad, who had taught her how to learn languages. She almost married Grad but could accept neither the role of a Jewish wife nor Grad's offer to renounce his faith. She began to write stories and she met H.G. Wells, who had married a girl she had known at school. In retrospect Wells as a man seems remarkably unattractive, however stimulating his books can still be, but endless women found him fascinating and his second wife coped with a succession of mistresses, many of them writers. To her own surprise Dorothy Richardson could not resist a love-affair with him which ended in disaster. She was going to have his child, and wanted to have it, but Dorothy Richardson never had any luck. One day in 1907 she visited a friend who had been sent to Holloway Prison for her suffragette activities. Dorothy herself was no agitator in the cause, although deeply aware that women's situation in society was miserable. Did her visit to the prison upset her already poor health? In any case she had a miscarriage. The affair was over but fortunately later the friendship with Wells and his wife continued.

After this episode Dorothy's friends encouraged her to try creative writing and said she should write a novel. A novel? Other friends, including Wells, discouraged her, for they felt that the orthodox fiction plot did not interest her, so often the case with a novelist destined to break new ground. In Virginia Woolf's later novels plot is minimal, with facts stated tersely as in the *Time Passes* section of *To the Lighthouse*. Neither is it a lengthy job to summarize the 'plot' of *Ulysses*. But Dorothy Richardson's perennial trouble was that she had to buy every minute of time she spent writing, and buying it with hack writing has usually been unsatisfactory for poets and novelists, with the possible exception of Apollinaire, who at least produced entertaining erotica when he needed money.

The name of J.D. Beresford may not be known to many people now but he was a successful novelist and editor. Perhaps he most deserves to be mentioned as the friend of Dorothy Richardson who persuaded her to come to Cornwall and live in a nearby cottage, once a ruined and apparently still haunted chapel. There he hoped she would begin the writing he felt was ready within her mind, and he was right; unlike Virginia Woolf she was not basically unsure of herself, she was unsure only of how she would achieve the new elements in writing, the only aspects that really preoccupied her. Plot was so unimportant that she would merely use the facts of her own existence, but not with any intention of drawing attention to herself and her problems. Her heroine was admittedly herself but she was a heroine who channelled the existence of other people through herself, those people existed because of her. The approach may sound indirect, as Virginia Woolf's was indirect, but there is one enormous difference: every sentence Dorothy Richardson wrote is clear and straightforward, she writes as someone who looks always ahead and is never caught in a complex play of light and sound and literary imagery as was Virginia Woolf. The present day reader can be disappointed in Dorothy Richardson because of course there is nothing specifically new in her method now, since so many novelists have adopted it, but at the beginning of the First World War nobody had yet used it, with the exception of Joyce.

It was Edward Garnett, after reading *Pointed Roofs*, this first novel, for the firm of Duckworth, who used the phrase 'feminine impressionism', misleading perhaps, because it sounds vague and limiting. Dorothy Richardson, as we have seen, was not a great feminist, but she had chosen to write from her own experience and therefore she wrote of a woman's experience. When J.D. Beresford wrote an introduction to the novel on its first publication he reported a change of mind when he read the book for the second time. 'This, I thought, is the most subjective thing I have ever read. The writer of this has gone through life with eyes that looked inward; she has known every person and experience solely by her own sensations and reactions.' He wanted to prepare the reader for 'a peculiar difference which is, perhaps, the mark of a new form in fiction'. Miss Richardson was neither realist nor romantic. 'The romantic floats on the surface of his imaginings, observing life from an intellectual distance through glasses specially adapted to his own idiosyncrasies of taste. The realist wades waist deep into the flood of humanity, and goes his way peering and choosing, expressing himself in the material of his choice and not in any distortion of its form.' This novelist was different: 'Miss Richardson is, I think, the first novelist who has taken the final plunge; who has neither floated nor waded, but gone head under and become a very part of the human element she has described'.

There is today endless discussion of Dorothy Richardson's work in purely literary terms: did she, as even Virginia Woolf claimed, devise a new sentence, a new 'feminine' sentence, one which came close to the way women speak? Jane Austen is said by some critics to have made a similar invention. Literary criticism is meaningless here, for once she had found her method Richardson did something which is outside literature, or at least certainly was so in 1914–15, she wrote *naturally*. Virginia Woolf hardly ever did so in fiction outside certain scenes in *The Years* and *Between the Acts*. Every sentence is highly wrought, like so many bejewelled ornaments lining the long road towards death that she walked with hardly a sideways glance. There was nothing natural about the author, her upbringing, marriage, her attitude to writing. She and her work fascinate us because together they had an intellectualised glamour.

Dorothy Richardson had none, just as she had no luck. Her biographer John Rosenberg has dwelt on the charisma she obviously possessed when young, attracting and influencing both men and women, although she was obviously more drawn to the former. Virginia Woolf could probably never have developed fully as a writer without her husband's help, whereas Dorothy Richardson's husband, Alan Odle, an artist as unlucky as she was, leant heavily on her and died comparatively young. There was nothing masculine nor androgynous about Dorothy Richardson herself, although she came to believe in the bisexuality of the artist. She wanted to invent, she had no ambitions for fame and she was not afraid of criticism. Her influence on the much younger woman Winifred Elliman, who became known as the writer 'Bryher' was remarkable, for Bryher saw her as a social historian and a campaigner for women. 'I have always told my friends abroad,' she wrote in *The Heart to Artemis*, 'that if they want to know what England was like between 1890 and 1914, they must read *Pilgrimage*, and Dorothy Richardson has often been more appreciated on the Continent than in her native land. People do not want to know what really happened in that epoch that they persist in calling "the golden years". Miriam's England was the England that I saw. I never identified myself with her because she was twenty years older than I was and I was full of the revolutionary spirit of my own generation. We had faced the same reproaches, however, and shared the same fury that social conventions were considered more important than intelligence. Perhaps great art is always the flower of some deeply felt rebellion. Then there was the excitement of her style, it was the first time that I realized that modern prose could be as exciting as poetry and as for continuous association, it was stereoscopic, a precursor of the cinema, moving from the window to a face, from a thought back to the room, all in one moment just as it happened in life.' And Bryher also remembered that when Dorothy Richardson had to send her first MS from Cornwall to London she gave up eating for two days – otherwise she could not have paid the postage. It is Bryher's account of the visit to Paris by Mr and Mrs Odle in 1923 that makes us realize that in this long, impoverished life there were some moments of happiness. In

Paris Dorothy Richardson met such writers as Gertrude Stein and Hemingway and realized that she was valued by other writers at least for her original contribution to literature.

Although Dorothy Richardson wrote a long series of novels based closely on her own life, she could not indicate how much of it she gave to others. She even interrupted her own hackwork in which – like every hack – she was working against time, to help H.G. Wells edit his *Experiment in Autobiography*: he went to Russia, she coped in his absence. No doubt he paid her for her work but he did not acknowledge her help in his book. He made one reference to her as he described his life in 1896–7, just after his second marriage:

> Among others who stayed with us was Dorothy Richardson, a schoolmate of Jane's. Dorothy has a very distinctive literary gift, acute intensity of expression and an astonishingly vivid memory; her *Pilgrimage* books are a very curious essay in autobiography; they still lack their due meed of general appreciation; and in one of them, *The Tunnel*, she has described our Worcester Park life with astonishing accuracy. I figure as Hypo in that description and Jane is Alma.

This passing praise was typical of Wells but even more typical of how people in general reacted to Dorothy Richardson – they admired her, thought about her and did very little more than that. Her novels, crowded with the wide variety of people she had encountered, are waiting for an equally wide audience.

In order to attract these potential readers, how can one convey the richness of texture, the particular flavour of Dorothy Richardson's writing? The richness is neither heavy nor artificial, and the lapses from it so touchingly human that one can be not only converted but carried away and especially, if you happen to be a woman, absorbed into the persona of Miriam Henderson.

If Miriam goes no further than to different parts of London – Bloomsbury, Wimpole Street, Hampstead, various southern suburbs and a particular school in Germany, she is aware of a multi-layered world that exists all round her, waiting to be discovered, she

wants to convey this existence and identify her discovery of it with
her own achievement of personal freedom, even if this latter is no
more than a cheap bare room in Bloomsbury. Each novel of
Pilgrimage describes the stage of a journey but in no over-planned
fashion, and each novel can obviously be read on its own. The
fourth title of the original thirteen, *The Tunnel*, published in 1919,
half way along the road, is no more, no less stimulating than any of
the others. The first chapter describes in detail how Miriam comes
proudly to the small top-floor room not far from Euston station, a
dingy room where the bed smelt of dust. But nothing mattered, for
in this rented room of her own Miriam was free, she was aware of
more than mere details about the blind and the washstand. She
knew she had done what she *had* to do, and she was aware of
present, past and future all at once. 'She was surprised now at her
familiarity with the detail of the room . . . that idea of visiting places
in dreams. It was something more than that . . . all the real part of
your life has a real dream in it; some of the real dream part of you
coming true. You know in advance when you are really following
your life. These things are familiar because reality is here.' And the
chapter ends with her first morning of real freedom: 'St. Pancras
bells were clamouring in the room. . . . The bells climbed gently
up, made a faint dab at the last top note, left it in the air askew above
the decorous little tune and rushed away down the scale as if to
cover the impropriety. . . .'

A visit to friends, a brief discussion about church-going ('Smart
people go to show their clothes'), then Miriam played the piano,
thinking about one of the men present. 'But he could not be really
happy with a woman unless he could also despise her. Any interest
in generalities, any argument or criticism or opposition would turn
him into a towering bully. All men were like that in some way. They
each had a set of notions and fought with each other about them
whenever they were together and not eating or drinking. If a woman
opposed them they went mad. He would like one or two more
Mendelssohns and then supper. And if she kept out of the
conversation and listened and smiled a little he would go away
adoring.' This is all calm enough in the end, and let no reader, male
or female, think that the book is a feminist tract. It is feminist by

implication only because no intelligent woman writing in 1919 could be otherwise, it was impossible to avoid seeing the extraordinary differences between the life-styles of men and women. Conversation in 1919, as heard and shared by Miriam, touched on endless aspects of man-woman polarity: men were free. Women did not want freedom. Men 'take the hearthrug', make judgements, pass sentence. It is implied that women want none of these things.

Half the interest of the book comes from the way these discussions grow naturally out of talk in many different milieux, and Miriam, despite her bored impatience with conventional unadventurous behaviour in any group, is not concerned with propaganda, she is reporting what happened in the situations where a single woman found herself.

As for Miriam's 'professional' life at the dentist's establishment in Wimpole Street, this little world comes truly alive with its varied, over worked characters, some with a sense of humour, some without. Miriam has too much responsibility and too little pay, but these related facts are never stated, they are only too obvious. There is talk of the professional life she could dream about, the life of a writer, and the meeting with that not reliable but intriguing writer Hypo Wilson, whom her friend Alma had married. Every detail about Wilson-Wells, based on fact, can be relished.

In 1954, in his short critical history, *The English Novel*, Walter Allen wrote about Dorothy Richardson and came to a disappointing conclusion: '*Pilgrimage* is a remarkable achievement, and yet, having read it once, it is not, I think, a novel one wishes to return to. In the end, one is bored, bored by Miriam and by the method of rendering her.' He thinks the novel begins well but deteriorates. 'Miriam's momentary perceptions are often delightful; her aspirations are not; they are dull even in their worthiness.' He was aware that Miriam, like her creator, lacked glamour, but his decision is not based on prejudice or superficial reading. 'One feels, indeed, that for Dorothy Richardson, as sometimes for Virginia Woolf, the world exists only to provide fodder, as it were, for the voracious sensibility of her character. Of *Pilgrimage* it might be said that if one robbed Miriam of her sensibility there would be not only no novel and no Miriam but also no world at all.' This last remark could be made of a great many other writers and their characters. Perhaps Miriam is boring to some readers simply because she is not exceptional, she is like many thousands of other women who remained inarticulate without her creator's unassuming but original talent. A quarter of a century has passed since Walter Allen made this judgement; one wonders if he would be likely to revise it today.

Dorothy Richardson and Virginia Woolf were the two experimenters among women novelists early this century, but they were so different that it is impossible to compare their achievements. 'O Death', says Bernard on the last page of *The Waves*, and Virginia Woolf said it to herself far too often. This shadow gives the same sort of fascination to her work that haunts the best creations of Cocteau. Through all her problems Dorothy Richardson clung to life, which, to those who are alive at least, seems more natural than death. The search for something new can easily take one down destructive, death-bound slopes. Virginia Woolf lived dangerously in all ways except that of the practical day-to-day. Dorothy Richardson surmounted the dangers of poverty and never dazzled anyone, but what she wrote and the way she wrote it is a vital chapter in the history of women's achievement in the early part of this century. She may have written the story of one woman, herself, but in each novel that very heroine saw more of life and people than did the whole of Virginia Woolf's characters put together. Both writers were absorbed by experiment, which became a way of life for them, a mingling of an inner and an outer existence; Virginia Woolf was more solitary than she seemed, Dorothy Richardson in the end less so. They complement each other and when Dorothy Richardson is read even half as much as Virginia Woolf it will be possible to assess the first-stage contribution by women to experimental writing in Britain. No one reading any of their books would ever think they were written by a man. If these authors had been men they would have led totally different lives, for most women still had no room of their own. Dorothy Richardson had struggled to pay the rent of such a room, and Virginia Woolf had theorized about the need for its existence. The women's movement needed both kinds of pioneers.

[3]
Laughing (1)

꽃꽃꽃

There can never be enough laughter in any century and when it comes to the female novelists who inhabit this one it must be said that only too many of the ladies have unwittingly invited people to laugh at them and have tended to be a desperately earnest lot. This is hardly surprising, because they had a good deal of campaign work to do. Rose Macaulay was certainly born a lady; she reported more about the female mind than the male one, she did not worry too much about form and laughed her way through novels while preoccupied with immensely serious matters.

W.S. Gilbert's executioner in *The Mikado* would not have dared include Rose Macaulay among all the other fated people:

. . .

> He's got 'em on the list,
> And they'll none of 'em be missed –
> And that singular anomaly, the lady novelist,
> I don't think she'd be missed,
> I'm sure she'd not be missed –

but she had a list of her own and was one of the few women writing fiction in the Twenties whose first truly memorable novel *Potterism* (1920) already put the lady novelist, called here Leila Yorke, in her place and used her family to express all her own satiric warmth about most subjects from sensational journalism to the higher education of women. The portrait of Leila Yorke should be of great help to many women novelists because it tells them precisely what to avoid: 'She was pink-faced and not ill-looking, with the cold blue eyes and rather set mouth possessed (inexplicably) by many writers of fiction. If I have conveyed the impression that Leila Yorke was in the lowest division of this class, I have done her less than justice; quite a number of novelists were worse. This was not much satisfaction to her children. Jane said, "if you do that sort of thing at all, you might as well make a job of it, and sell a million copies. I'd rather be Mrs Barclay or Ethel Dell or Charles Garvice or Gene Stratton Porter or Ruby Ayres than mother. Mother's merely commonplace; she's not even a by-word – quite".' She preferred her father's achievements with the Potter press.

Mrs Potter's novels, as a matter of fact, sold quite creditably. They were pleasant to many, readable by more, and quite unmarred by any spark of cleverness, flash of wit, or morbid taint of philosophy. Gently and unsurprisingly she wrote of life and love as she believed these two things to be, and found a home in the hearts of many fellow-believers. She bored no one who read her, because she could be relied on to give them what they hoped to find – and of how few of us, alas, can this be said! And – she used to say it was because she was a mother – her books were safe for the youngest *jeune fille*, and in these days (even in those days it was so) of loose morality and frank realism, how important this is.

She hoped she was as modern as anyone, but saw no call to be indecent. However, she evolved: 'It is only fair to record here that in the year 1918 she heard [the call] herself, and became a psychologist. But the time for this was not yet'.

During fifty years of professional writing Rose Macaulay herself may have developed 'rather a set mouth' but she provided entertainment for many different kinds of readers and the guerilla warfare of the women's movement has only made most readers find her more entertaining still. She has never been short of admiration and respect while the passage of time has made her work seem even richer in its pseudo-casual way and nobody now can fail to be amused by her own awareness of the sex-war. On page 5 of *Potterism* we read about Jane and Johnny Potter, the twins, of whom Jane was 'just a shade the cleverer'. At Oxford Jane's first was safer than Johnny's.

Both saw every reason why they should make a success of life. But Jane knew that, though she might be one up on Johnny as regards Oxford, owing to slightly superior brain power, he was one up on her as regards Life, owing to that awful business sex. Women were handicapped; they had to fight much harder to achieve equal results. People didn't give them jobs in the same way. Young men possess the earth; young women had to wrest what they wanted out of it piecemeal. . . . Women's jobs were, as a rule, so dowdy and unimportant. Jane was bored to death with this sex business; it wasn't fair. But Jane was determined to live it down. She wouldn't be put off with second-rate jobs; she wouldn't be dowdy and unimportant, like her mother and the other fools; she would have the best that was going.

She almost succeeded, and found it not so easy as she had hoped.

Twins are a useful device for novelists, as Iris Murdoch has since discovered, for twins can demonstrate between them characteristics which are almost too complicated to 'fit' inside one character. But there was only one Rose Macaulay, a complex person indeed, who wrote no less than twenty-three novels in addition to many other books and much journalism, and most people will remember the Rose of their choice. Most middle-aged members of the London Library remember the tall figure who could be seen, inevitably wearing an unbecoming hat, talking to Harold Hobson in the entrance hall. Everything about her, from her odd clothes to her bicycle chained to the railings, from her voice to her Anglicanism, was so English that her compatriots were delighted and mere foreigners could hardly believe it possible that one woman could embody so many aspects of Englishness without turning into a caricature.

Rose was the only one of the six Macaulay daughters to receive higher education, which had only recently become available to women. An uncle paid for her years at Somerville College, Oxford, and she came down with an aegrotat degree in 1903. The idea of teaching did not appeal to her and at a time when Marie Corelli was pouring out her virtuous novels, when Ivy Compton-Burnett was fourteen and Virginia Stephen twenty-four, when Edith Wharton had recently published *The House of Mirth*, she wrote her first novel, *Abbots Verney*, and John Murray, a friend of her father's, published it at once in 1906.

Eight more novels appeared before 1920, all somewhat gloomy and earnest, very different in tone from the later, well-known work, although *What Not* of 1918 showed her turning towards satire. She also found her way out of agnosticism and into Anglo-Catholicism, the faith that influenced the rest of her life. During the First World War she worked in the Ministry of Defence, where she met Gerald O'Donovan, a married man who had formerly been a Roman Catholic parish priest. The couple fell in love and their relationship was a lasting one.

Shortly after the war Rose Macaulay began to publish a novel every year. The first of the batch, *Potterism* (1920), deals with a subject that does not go out of date: newspaper tycoons. *Potterism* was probably one of the earliest novels in which they figure and even more probably the first on such a theme written by a woman. But it is typical of Rose Macaulay that she did not write a well-constructed novel with a concentrated attack on 'Potterism', the name given by the Potters' twin son and daughter to intellectual and moral hypocrisy, which they intended to expose. The author allowed herself to be cheerfully side-tracked, into presenting and discussing the many problems of Jane, the intelligent daughter, and Clare, who was less intelligent but more obviously feminine. One ought to care that the eligible newspaper editor, the Canadian Oliver Hobart, preferred Jane to Clare, and to care why the marriage decayed; one ought to wonder who threw Oliver downstairs, but one doesn't much. One is also slightly surprised perhaps – for 1920 – to find Jane so much in love with Arthur Gideon after her husband's death but before she had produced the latter's baby, although since the end of the 1950s we are quite used to this situation in fiction. In reality even odder things happen but reality does not always make good fiction.

But the picture of Britain just after the end of the First World War is intriguing, especially of course for the woman reader of today who can laugh cheerfully at the novelist Leila Yorke and mull over the obviously serious interest shown by Rose Macaulay in the

psychology and social situation of young women. The characters in
the novel are ostensibly concerned with fighting Potterism but they
find plenty of time to think about that inevitable difference. 'It
wasn't fair. If Johnny married and had a baby it wouldn't get in his
way, only in its mamma's. It was a handicap, like your frock
(however short it was) when you were climbing. You had got round
that by taking it off and climbing in knickerbockers, but you
couldn't get round a baby. And Jane wanted the baby too.' Women
novelists are still saying the same thing sixty years later.

Men are so different, thought Jane. Johnny was the same at
Oxford. He would flirt with girls in tea-shops. Jane had never
wanted to flirt with the waiters in restaurants. Men were perhaps
less critical; or perhaps they wanted different qualities in those
with whom they flirted; or perhaps it was that their amatory
instinct, when pronounced at all, was much stronger than
women's, and flowed out on to any object at hand when they were
in the mood.

Arthur Gideon, who was deeply in love with Jane, also made
little speeches about the whole thing, slightly pompous perhaps.

Men usually have, as a rule, more sex feeling than women, that's
all. Naturally. They need more, to carry them through all the
business of making marriage proposals and keeping up homes,
and so on. Women often have very little. That's why they're
often better at friendship than men are. A woman can be a man's
friend all their lives, but a man, in nine cases out of ten, will either
get tired of it or want more. Women have a tremendous gift for
friendship. Their friendships with other women are usually
much more devoted and more faithful than a man's with other
men. Most men, though of course not all, want sex in their lives
at some time or other. Hundreds of women are quite happy
without it. They're quite often nearly sexless. Very few men are
that.

But the book was called *Potterism* which could, can, be found everywhere, and the Potterite Juke, in his journal, makes a point of mentioning some of its more awkward manifestations, in the Christian church, for example: 'an organisation full to the brim of cant, humbug, timid orthodoxy, unreality, self-content, and all kinds of Potterism – one doesn't see how it can overcome anything whatever.' And at the very end of this section – different characters recount each section of the book: – one of the saddest statements of all is about the failure of the Church: 'It is the Potterism in all of us which at every turn checks and drags it down. Personally, I can forgive Potterism everything but that.' No wonder Rose Macaulay subtitled the book A Tragi-Farcical Tract; it went through five impressions between May and December in 1920.

The novels that followed knew much success and none knew failure. Through her friend the novelist Naomi Royde-Smith the author met a good number of literary celebrities, major and minor, while her love-affair with Gerald O'Donovan remained constant and secret. The relationship obviously brought the couple a kind of half-ideal, extra-mural happiness, and that is already more than marriage can do for a great many people. The novels continued to sound flippant on the surface, but only on the surface, they dealt entertainingly with major social questions: the importance of further education, the dangers of psycho-analysis and of course, all the time, the problem of careers for women, and marriage versus living together.

Dangerous Ages of 1921 is about four generations of women, all coping with the ages that are most dangerous to them – all ages in fact, except great old age. It is impossible not to note at this juncture that this group of titles, nearly sixty years after they were written, appeal very strongly to two types of people: middle-class women, like so many of the Macaulay characters, and professional writers. Sometimes these two groups overlap, obviously, and they will enjoy the many references to people busily reading, writing, reviewing and publishing books.

At 63, for instance, Mrs Hilary (before she turned to psychology) had 'looked into Freud, and been rightly disgusted', but Grand-mamma, who was over eighty, read Chekhov's letters 'because she had read favourable reviews . . . by Gilbert and Nan', who happened to be her grandchildren. Mrs Hilary is useful to the author in her wish to toss harmless fireworks about, aiming them at writers and readers: '*Writing* . . . . Mere showing off. . . . Throwing your paltry ideas at a world which doesn't want them. . . .' And her daughter Neville, after asking 'What *is* a good book?' goes on to say that 'Writing's just a thing to do. . . . A job, like another. One must *have* a job, you know. Not for the money, but for the job's sake.' And when Mrs Hilary mentions that Barrie, the man with whom her younger daughter Nan appears to be in love, writes books on 'education and democracy' Neville replies that 'it might be worse. It might be poetry or fiction or psycho-analysis'.

In fact Mrs Hilary, like the novelist Leila Yorke in *Potterism*, turned to psychoanalysis in the end, after first doubting how it could cure so many terrible things – 'Shell shock, insomnia, nervous depression, lumbago, suicidal mania, family life, anything'. She wondered 'how *can* they cure all those things just by talking indecently about sex?'. Along with the Church psycho-analysis was an obvious target for the novelists of the Twenties, who were anxious to be thought up to date, even if they laughed at themselves on account of this very anxiety.

Gerda, aged twenty, went to work for the organisation where Barrie, her aunt Nan's admirer, needed a secretary. The Workers' Educational Association had been started as far back as 1903 and Rose Macaulay's description of it – worked through Gerda – is part of its history: 'But the W.E.A. was a practical body, which went in for practical adventure. Dowdy, schoolmarmish, extension-lecturish, it might be and doubtless was. But a real thing, with guts in it, really doing something; and, after all, you can't be incendiarising the political and economic constitution all your time. . . . Work for the Revolution – yes, of course, one did that; one studied the literature of the Internationals; one talked. . . . But did one help the Revolution on much, when all was said? Whereas in the W.E.A. office one really got things done; one typed a letter and something happened because of it, more adult classes occurred, more workers got educated. Gerda, too young and too serious to be cynical, believed that this must be right and good.'

Later on Gerda refuses the reactionary status of marriage. She found it 'so Victorian. It's like antimacassars.' She held out for a long time, and her discussions with her mother are both timeless and amusing, which is more than can be said for most of the earnest talk on the subject that has gone on ever since the 1920s. But Gerda gave way in the end. All the women characters in this novel are intriguing, particularly Neville, Gerda's mother, a partly-trained doctor who wants to begin her medical studies again at 43 after her family have grown up. Her problem is affected by the attitude of her husband, who 'wasn't altogether pleased, though he understood. He wanted her constant companionship and interest in his own work.' Neville had to tell him that he had had a better time than she had. 'You've had twenty-two years of it, darling. . . . Now I must Live my own Life, as the Victorians used to put it'.

Her husband, Rodney, had to be reminded of one thing, for he seriously believed that she 'wouldn't have time' to practise, because of all the other things she did. Neville told him what a high percentage of wives are still telling their husbands: ' "It's the other things I shan't have time for, old man. Sorry, but there it is. . . ." ' And a little later: ' "After all, Rodney, you've your job. Can't I have mine? Aren't you a modern, an intellectual, and a feminist?"

'Rodney, who believed with truth that he was all these things, gave in.'

Surely nobody could ever talk about 'problem novels' and Rose Macaulay in the same breath, yet there were few problems she did not write about. She introduced her ideas with no prejudice and the minimum of discussion, just enough to whet the reader's appetite, and then stopped before she could be accused of causing boredom. The nature and status of women fascinated her, a preoccupation she showed in endless ways. For instance, like Iris Murdoch so much later, she enjoyed giving her heroines names which were either masculine (part-reflection of a Twenties fashion) or else sexually mysterious – like Derham in *Crewe Train* (1926), who could accept neither social convention nor basic femininity. Stanley in *Told by an Idiot* (1923) has been described by Raymond Mortimer as expressing a disbelief in any innate differences between the sexes. This latter entertaining book demands to be read for its presentation of social and literary history between 1879 and 1923, and for its deeply contrasted women all in one family: Stanley herself, a suffragist who suffered the humiliation of divorce, Rome the cynical and Imogen the romantic, for its incredibly amusing picture, with the usual serious undertones, of how religious belief could preoccupy a man like the girls' father, Mr Garden, who spent most of his life losing his faith and immediately finding a replacement.

Orphan Island of 1924 contains surely the maximum of social fantasy which can be extracted from the classic wrecked-on-a-desert-island situation, while *Keeping up Appearances* (1928) had a dual-personality heroine, Daisy/Daphne, who together turned the book into a light-hearted formal experiment and continued discussion of such topics as the work of popular women journalists and novelists, the frustrating loneliness of housework and the (implied) unsatisfactory behaviour of men.

Those who are addicted to Rose Macaulay in general will obviously enjoy everything she wrote and if the atmosphere of her work changed after 1930 this is hardly suprising. She was too intelligently creative to spend the rest of her life producing what is regarded as light fiction, even if it was obviously not as light as all that. *Staying with Relations* (1930) and *Going Abroad* (1934) contain a travelogue element and the heroine seems closely identified with the author. *They were Defeated* of 1932 was a historical novel set in the seventeenth century, introducing her admired poet, Robert Herrick. For those interested in the author's religious attitudes and her return to the church, it obviously must be read, but how much more accessible, how much more movingly readable is *The World my Wilderness* which appeared in 1950 after ten years devoted to journalism and travel writing but empty of fiction.

The new novel was not a mere continuation of what she had written in the 1920s, but the themes which had always preoccupied her now came to the surface. The technique was highly professional and it was not intended to amuse. The author had lost her companion Gerald O'Donovan in 1942, she had lost her apartment and all her possessions in the London blitz, and this novel shows her concern at the collapse in moral standards which had begun in the

1930s. Family life had broken down, and the behaviour of the young people in the book, who become adept at stealing in the ruined city of London, reflects the mentality of the French collaborationists. The crazed priest who celebrates mass in the bombed church is too much of a 'symbol' but in 1950 there was every reason for using symbols, even obvious ones, for most serious writers felt that western civilization was in danger.

Her letters to Father Johnson, published after her death, are of significance to those who wish to understand the complex personality of Rose Macaulay. For those concerned only with her fiction they would not have been particularly meaningful were it not for *The Towers of Trebizond*, her last novel, published in 1956, and in some ways perhaps not a novel at all. It is of course possible for totally secular readers to enjoy this unique book, but how much more does it mean to those concerned with all aspects of religion, including the faiths practised in various Middle Eastern countries and the whole question of Anglo-Catholicism. It is fitting that this should be the last published novel because it is an epitome of all her styles and enthusiasms.

The narrator of this travelogue, which is also a sort of love story, a celebration of certain Middle East architecture and a satiric attack on people writing books about Turkey, as well as a jubilant exaltation of the Anglo-Catholic faith, is called Laurie, and some critics have believed that the sex of this young person is concealed until the very end of the book, when it is revealed as feminine. The author believed that nothing gave her game away, yet Laurie is surely feminine from first to last, the cadences of her voice are feminine. She is like a personification of Rose Macaulay when young, going off cheerfully to rendezvous with her married lover and in her excitement, after meeting him, driving too fast – as Rose Macaulay had once done while on holiday with Gerald O'Donovan. As for Aunt Dot, the elderly lady who travels about on a camel, accompanied by a priest, Father Chantry-Pigg, there is a lot of Rose Macaulay's eccentricity about her. She no longer talks very much about how women should behave, she does as she likes and does some very strange things. Aunt Dot and her creator seem intoxicated with life and with each other. One might wish both of them were a little less intoxicated with Anglo-Catholicism, because the subject becomes almost boring by the end of the book. It is hard to accept the fact that Laurie cares so much about this particular form of Christian worship, but there would have been no story without it, and it is no doubt the author's rediscovery of faith that gives such vitality to Aunt Dot and the whole book. *The Towers of Trebizond* is a dazzling performance, but it is not truly moving – that is why *This World my Wilderness*, with its deeply-felt, interpretive concealed emotion, is a more satisfying book, and without doubt the author's best.

Rose Macaulay saw the early struggles of women (individuals rather than the members of a movement) as preoccupied less with votes than with living, more with the possibility of love-making outside marriage than with the Married Women's Property Act. She spent middle and later life travelling, but the longest journey she undertook was from her early family life to those years of deeply spiritual existence, involving retreats and confession, that she crystallized in her last book. Only someone so immensely English could have entitled a volume of her articles 'A Casual Commentary'. Her novels also might seem casual on the surface, but they are still some of the most stimulating fiction written by anyone, and not only by women, this century.

The search for a successor of some kind to Rose Macaulay leads me, to my own surprise, into an apparent digression about religious themes in twentieth-century fiction and even in fiction earlier than that. *The Towers of Trebizond*, as I have indicated, does not send the average reader rushing to the nearest Anglo-Catholic Church, fascinating though it is to readers concerned in some way with Christianity and the spiritual life generally. It could send readers to Rose Macaulay's *Letters to a Friend* and its sequel and it will surely make many others speculate on the intriguing question of religious themes in twentieth-century fiction, for there is no shortage of writers who have handled them. As far as women writers are concerned one quickly remembers Marie Corelli and Mrs Humphry Ward, just as quickly stops reading Marie Corelli, if one has ever started, and if one perseveres with Mrs Humphry Ward it is because her deeply moral purpose, however unattractive her message, is conveyed in a professional enough manner. She had of course been brought up as a Victorian Protestant and in many of her books expressed the attitudes which she had learnt in childhood and accepted. This seems to be the Protestant way among novelists, they do not desperately want readers to be converted from other religions to Protestantism; perhaps they assume they are all Protestant already and they merely want to point out that there is a lot to be said for actually following Protestant teaching as they see it. This is particularly the attitude of women novelists who express in this way the practical sense which women are said to possess more commonly than men. Harriet Beecher Stowe, after all, who wrote *Uncle Tom's Cabin* and so upset the whole of the United States, could hardly have written it had she not been a convinced Protestant. In several of her books Mrs Humphry Ward was concerned with the practical aspects of Christianity, which she thought had been neglected. Women on the whole have not been much concerned with doctrine, they have obviously felt that such abstractions can safely be left to men.

In the early part of the twentieth century women (and women novelists) who believed that their social status needed immediate improvement, tended to see the established church as a natural enemy. Such different and equally professional novelists as Virginia Woolf and Ivy Compton-Burnett convinced themselves without any difficulty that the church was of no interest or value because the life of the spirit in its relation to a Christian God was meaningless to them – Virginia Woolf was conditioned by the intellectual fashions of Bloomsbury and Compton-Burnett by her devotion to classical mythology and drama. It was obvious in any case that a whole generation brought up in the Victorian and Edwardian tradition of rigid churchgoing would reject it – how strange if they had not done so.

As the century advanced however, as Fabianism and the Left Book Club waxed and waned, a new avant-garde appeared, an intelligentsia who took an increasingly deep interest in the philosophy, sociology and even the practice of religion. Rose Macaulay was a member of this highly individualized movement, one of the rare women members to have a personal status of her own. Other women writers preoccupied with some form of spiritual life tended to be poets – Alice Meynell, followed by Kathleen Raine, Anne Ridler and several others. Men writers in whose work religious themes were inextricably part of the plot were not Protestants – they were Roman Catholics, usually by conversion, notably Evelyn Waugh and Graham Greene. Part of the latter's success seems to be due to this perpetual drama – for it always looks like drama against the undemandingly orthodox English scene – of the convert's fervency and his simultaneous perpetual moaning about his own lapses. It is a very strange thing that the 'Catholic' novel in England, if such a genre can be said to exist, has not had much of a Christian message. Everyone behaves rather badly and everyone is rather unhappy, nowhere can be seen the glowing light of Good.

Goodness in itself is of course undramatic and can only become exciting when there is struggle, discovery or miracle. For these no novelist has equalled the writers of the Gospels or, say, John Bunyan or Tolstoy. In the twentieth century these message-bringers have not been joined by any women, although there is an undercurrent of fervency in various writers of many different kinds – in Mary Webb, for instance, while the ironic humour of Barbara Pym cannot, does not intend to destroy her belief in human goodness and her devotion to the Anglo-Catholic church, two traits which link her obviously with Rose Macaulay.

It was a pity that Simone Weil, one of the greatest women writers of the century, distrusted fiction, but anyone who studies her personality and work can see clearly that she could not have believed otherwise. Again she was a convert – from her non-religious Jewish background to total belief in the church of Rome, except that her belief ended in a colon and not in a full stop. She could not go through *la porte étroite*, she could not enter the Catholic Church because she felt in that way she would be abandoning everyone who remained outside it. So after a search for women novelists who are remembered particularly for their comedy, and for one woman who is somehow reminiscent of Rose Macaulay, we are left with another convert, Muriel Spark.

She is a particularly interesting example of what religious

'conversion' can do to and for a writer; in this case it caused her to leave dull work and emotional insecurity behind and earn success on many levels with what contemporary critics just after the Second World War saw as innovation in *Robinson*, or *Memento Mori*, an apparent combination of religious awareness and great wit. I myself have searched for years in an effort to find why I could not agree with the judgements of the mandarins and the thousands of book-buyers who agreed with them – lucky, happy author. The apparently inventive and black-comic devices seem to be a set of gimmicks, differing from those of the detective story writers and the surrealists mainly because they had this inbuilt theme of religious belief, Roman Catholicism, and most people found this combination vastly entertaining.

I concluded I had been mistakenly looking for depth both of character and thought, and had been disappointed at finding none. I had of course been looking at everything in an old-fashioned way and was perhaps resisting the danger that I too might be converted to Rome. Eventually I discovered why the books failed to entertain or interest me. The stories are of course patterns, intellectualized square dances in which there is a semblance of progression but no real development, presumably because none was intended: it would have spoilt the dance. It seems strange that some one who has been so deeply affected by religion should work so hard to prevent the reader from being affected in the same way. I assume that Dougal in *The Ballad of Peckham Rye* (1960) is supposed to work evil and possibly he is a kind of devil, but he fails to be entertaining, because he is neither real nor fantastical. He is one-dimensional and I wish I could find something interesting in him, he does not lead me to laugh and to speculate on the human condition at the same time. There are only two enjoyable qualities about the book, the great zest in the dancing, that is the pattern-making of the story, and the obvious glee with which the author writes of the situation between Mr Druce and his mistress Merle, inevitably ending in murder. The author can be very good at dealing briefly with real life relationships like this but does not seem to want any further development of them. This is a pity but it is wise of her not to attempt too much in one book which wins readability through high-speed writing.

The deepening of character is something the author does not particularly care for, I think, even in the longer books. Like Miss Brodie, probably her best character, she likes things her own way and if she were to write about people who are convincingly human they might take her over, something she would not want in any way; *she* must take over, *she* must remain in the driver's seat, nobody else. One has the feeling that she could talk to her characters, but they are never allowed to talk back to her. She would not, like Jane Austen, wonder what happened to them in later life, for she does not sufficiently care. This attitude is reflected very clearly in the way the characters assume they love God and are loved by Him. God is a very safe being to love – concept, ideal, however one sees Him – because one can never say He does not love those who love Him. He will never point out if our love is inadequate and He will never stop loving.

In her fiction Muriel Spark obviously believes that God is in his Heaven and so all's right with the Roman Catholic world. All this makes for tremendous confidence and of course confidence is a great part of comedy. But how I wish I could find a book like *The Abbess of Crewe* entertaining in any way at all. The unfortunate thing is that if one looks for a feminine quality in this writing one can find only the one which women try to live down and can't: the useful, invincible quality of bitchiness, one of those traits which prove, if any proof were needed, that women are different from men. Men's aggressions are cruder, larger-scale but on the whole more bearable because they are more straightforward. Bitchiness is an enviable quality because after all it cannot be learnt, and that is another reason for the extreme confidence of the Spark heroines. In *The Mandelbaum Gate* Barbara Vaughan shows some insecurity because she was brought up neither as a Christian nor as a Jew, but of course conversion to Roman Catholicism changed all that. It is hard for the non-Roman to see the reason for all the fuss about marriage within the church, it seems a waste of a novel, but for those who appreciate bitchiness there is the splendid letter from Ricky to Barbara with a photocopy of her fiancé's birth certificate showing that he is not only illegitimate but a Catholic who has once been married. And Catholics do not admit divorce. At least the novelist can point out through this letter that the Moslems are more broad-minded, but somehow all this indirect comment seems superficial and the whole novel, like the whole body of work, suffers so badly from a lack of warmth. But bitchiness can only be total and successful if it remains ice-cold, and it does.

The humour that comes from lack of confidence, so often partnered in the music-hall with over-confidence, invites a warm response and in fact arises from a need for some sort of love. Those who need love, and respond when they find it, would be better advised to read Rose Macaulay than Muriel Spark, especially if they are also interested in the social problems related to the status of women.

This chapter was entitled *Laughing (1)* and was about two writers whom most people find amusing. Both of them, in various books and to various degrees are noticeably preoccupied with some of the deepest known problems, those of religious belief and observance, while Rose Macaulay is concerned also with related moral issues, not forgetting the status of women in society and various other psychological and social problems. It may sound paradoxical, but anyone who has studied either theories of humour or merely the personalities of memorable humorists – mainly men, so far in history, at least in Britain – knows that the merely funny is neither funny nor interesting for very long, it soon becomes boring because it is not far removed from schoolboy horse-play, like the much-quoted scene in *Lucky Jim* when the hero sets fire to the bed. True clowns tend to be sad, and humorous writers who last, who acquire any reputation beyond their own country, have always a dram of poetry, however slight, in their make-up, and humour without imagination is a short-lived, journalistic enterprise. Both Rose Macaulay and Muriel Spark have written poetry, even if they are known principally for their fiction. From the 1920s to the 1950s otherwise there was only too much unconscious humour among women writers who were incapable of seeing many obvious jokes because they were forced into a desperate earnestness by the way they were conditioned to live and work. Some who were especially gifted and lucky could stand outside all these problems, including notably the too-soon forgotten Nancy Mitford, who began to write during the 1930s. The best of her later work, particularly *The Pursuit of Love* (1945), *Love in a Cold Climate* (1949) and *The Blessing* (1951), was infinitely more than a succession of mere 'funny' books. The best final judgement on the first of these was made by Rosamond Lehmann's granddaughter Anna, as she reported in *The Swan in the Evening*: after 'recurrent lapses into quiet laughter' the young girl decided it was 'a very sad book'. Fortunately, by 1980, Nancy Mitford's novels had made a successful comeback.

The extrovert humourist is confident and boisterous, of the afore-mentioned schoolboy type, and Britain could not have produced an Anita Loos or a Cornelia Otis Skinner, just as the witty Dorothy Parker or the exuberant Erica Jong could hardly have been native Britishers. But after the 1950s women felt freer, in some ways at least, and soon there was no shortage of writers whose humour had depth and power. The humour of Beryl Bainbridge and Fay Weldon is not much concerned with the theory or practice of church-based religion, but they are preoccupied, unconsciously perhaps, with the new problems of a society with no obvious religion at all. The deeper the humour the blacker it seems to grow, but that is another story and a later chapter.

[4]
Loving

✺✺✺

It would be a long task to make a complete list of the efficient women novelists writing in Britain during the 1920s, 30s, 40s and after who wrote stories of love. I use this phrase to indicate that the content and treatment of such books have more depth than is usual in a 'love story' or romantic novel, although the latter may be written with extreme professionalism and earn comfortable incomes for their authors. Among the women writers this century who tell these stories of love two names are outstanding and at least two generations of readers, women and men, have been addicted to them. The writers are, obviously it seems, even with so many other names clustering fairly close to them, Elizabeth Bowen and Rosamond Lehmann, separated in age by a few years only and in fact close friends for a long time.

Elizabeth Bowen, born in 1899 in Dublin, Eire, came of a family who had originally lived in Wales and in the late eighteenth century built themselves, in County Cork, a too large uncomfortable house which nobody could afford to complete. Elizabeth Bowen spent her summers there and later inherited the house, Bowen's Court. Boarding school in Kent, adolescence and girlhood during the First World War, an early engagement soon broken, and then life-lasting marriage to a man who was probably more of a protective, organizing companion than a lover.

Elizabeth Bowen spent her life writing, entertaining both in Eire and in London, having love affairs with men, married and unmarried, and turning away, most of the time, it appears, ardent lesbian admirers, travelling, and, after her husband's death, there was even more travelling, some intermittent work in American universities. It was a writer's life, in which everything depended on writing, and everything – people met, observed, loved or disliked, houses, towns and parts of towns – went into writing. Without the writing she would probably have been an average autocratic member of the Irish ascendancy, and despite charm and a certain 'style', as uninteresting as the rest of them.

She was however one of those lucky women whose sensitivity was matched by controlled strength; she knew about this strength and seems to have realized when she was young that she had some sort of creative power and spent two terms at an art school. But she soon realized that words were her medium and moved on to a course in journalism. She was lucky in other ways: soon after she herself began to write stories she met the successful novelist Rose Macaulay, who recommended the young author to the publishers Sidgwick and Jackson. Elizabeth Bowen's first stories, *Encounters*, were published in 1923, when she was 24, and since then she published eighteen fiction titles, twelve novels and six volumes of stories, in addition to ten or so other non-fiction books. She worked extremely hard and never seems to have been short of ideas, admiring critics or readers.

Her fiction is especially intriguing now because so much of it, like Lady Latterly's bedroom in *A World of Love*, seems 'a replica, priceless these days, of a Mayfair décor back in the 1930s', yet it has a classic quality, the sort of quality that went with an obviously stable personality born into a stable society, one which not even the troubles in Eire had dislocated utterly by 1920. Society may never be stable again, but it is safe to say now that no novelist can be described as the 'new Elizabeth Bowen', for such a description would be unrealistic. Fortunately she herself was born with a sense of artistry that could turn the will to write into a creative force and, at the time when she was writing, artistry, for many readers and critics was all. Women writers were not expected, on the whole, to explore far outside what was regarded as their own territory, individual relationships either within the family or on its fringe. Elizabeth Bowen, like Rosamond Lehmann, and like her part-contemporary, Colette, whom she admired, is a fascinating example of how a woman novelist achieves artistic success by continually using and expressing qualities always described, if vaguely, as 'feminine'. Her work proves that these qualities are in no way the mark of a lesser order of beings.

It might almost be possible to think of her work as a 'world of women', although by no means exclusive of men, because the women characters are always at the centre of the stories, it is the girls and the women whom the author cares about. Indirectly she asks the reader to care for them as much as she does, she seems constantly aware that there is never enough caring, never enough love. This is obvious in the well-known novels, in *The Death of the Heart* for instance where the young Portia seems to 'belong' to no one and tries so hard to find affection. In 1938, when this was written, the problems of the teenager did not preoccupy the professional novelist (or anyone else, for that matter) to the extent they have done since 1945 or 1950. Young children appeared in many novels for many reasons, as ornaments, pawns, light relief or chorus figures, but the complex frustrations and fantasies of a chrysalis-figure had not been too popular in English fiction. One has to go back to Tom and Maggie Tulliver to find a sympathetic yet unsentimental study of children growing up and then, at a lighter level, a novel like *Ordinary Families* by E. Arnot Robertson. Men writers of the twentieth-century, such as Arnold Bennett or H.G. Wells, had been preoccupied with other problems, and in Britain at least it seemed natural for women writers to adopt the teenager. In the USA teenagers had been more or less invented along with the word itself by writers as different as James T. Farrell and Carson McCullers, in France they had interested such different people as Romain Rolland and Colette. But who would forget Portia, the appalling yet unforgettable Theodora in *Friends and Relations*, plus of course the 12-year-old Maud in *A World of Love*. Eva Trout herself also appears first as a schoolgirl and again in her own way she looks with melodramatic yearning for love, because she had never had it as a small child.

Although it is a sad fact that Elizabeth Bowen apparently saw herself as a novelist first and a woman second one hardly regrets in the end the *déformation professionnelle* because if she had no children herself she was an excellent mother to her characters, especially these young ones, for she loved them without idealizing or falsifying them in any way. She is concerned with them only as individuals, for that was her approach, typical of her times and the only way in which she herself could deal with them. These characters were not revolutionaries. They only *think* about running away, as young people must often have thought when the author herself was young. If Elizabeth Bowen had described active breakout conduct, and not even Eva Trout quite achieves this, then she would have been reporting on social change or disintegration before it had actually happened, in the middle of the century. This, in most of her work, was not her ambition, and since she clearly did not want it to happen she made no effort to look for it, at least until the end of her career, when she could hardly escape it and noticed non-middle class behaviour in various short stories.

Her solitary young girls who fall in love too easily with unsuitable men or become over-devoted to slightly older women are no doubt modelled partly on herself when young, especially as she must have been after her mother's death, but it would be a mistake to think her case was unique and sad. A few generations ago families were larger, most women did not work, all middle-class families had servants, somebody, usually a single woman, always appeared when children seemed in danger of being left alone. Women have always succeeded in keeping life going, by occupying a variety of roles, and it is no surprise to find Elizabeth Bowen's books so full of them, it was they who made the world of love.

What happened to these girls as they grew up, looked for and acquired husbands and/or lovers? In the outer world at least they were not so solitary and in several novels, however different the plot, there are at least two contrasted women of the same generation, like the sisters Laurel and Janet in *Friends and Relations*, Naomi Fisher and Karen in *The House in Paris*, or the three heroines in *The Little Girls*. In *The Death of the Heart* the two characters who are close and contrasted are the young girls, Portia and Daphne, with whose family she stays at the seaside. In *The Heat of the Day* Stella Rodway is on her own, in full limelight, contrasted with the cockney girls Connie and Louie, of whom more later. In *A World of Love* the author uses two middle-aged women for her pairing system, Antonia and her dead cousin's ex-fiancée,

Lilia. The limelight is kept for the young girl Jane, whom one thinks of not as Lilia's, but the author's idealized dream-daughter, but even she has a subordinate partner, her young sister Maud.

The contrasting characteristics of these paired women obviously determine the plot. There is another recurring character who also contributes in varying degrees, the 'older woman', solitary and influential: Mrs Kerr in *The Hotel*, Lady Waters in *To the North*, and very obviously Madame Fisher in *The House in Paris*. In *A World of Love* the part is less obvious because it is modified and also shared between Antonia and Lady Latterley, whose appearances are brief and reminiscent of those of Lady Elfrida in *Friends and Relations*. In *Eva Trout* the pattern of character and plot is much more complex but there is still the slightly older Iseult, whom Eva loves as Sydney had loved Mrs Kerr in *The Hotel*.

In the rooms the women come and go: not for a moment talking of Michelangelo but simply about themselves and their feelings, which are concerned to some extent with each other but basically they are concerned with men. Few of the women described by Elizabeth Bowen do much in the way of work, although Stella Rodway, in wartime London, could hardly have avoided it and Antonia, in *A World of Love*, has been a famous photographer. Although there was something of herself in Antonia Elizabeth Bowen, a supremely professional writer, showed no interest in professionalism among women, the psychological and social problems it raised, she was much more concerned with women's totally feminine existence as it was seen traditionally: they existed as sweethearts, wives, mistresses, mothers, sisters, friends, she watched them carefully and sometimes implied how mistaken they were in what they were doing, indicating through the older women how one generation tried to hand on certain notions of behaviour, sometimes traditional, and often from motives of selfishness or revenge.

So these women looked for men, and what kind of men, one asks, would become involved in an atmosphere which sounds so claustrophobic, full of women's voices and the swish of petticoats, in the rooms so full of flowers? The men are there because they need and want these women, they are drawn to them naturally, attracted by *their* own obvious need for men. Two facts emerge: the men are remarkably convincing characters, so rare in the work even of competent women novelists, and most of these men behave badly. Before the Second World War there was a clear-cut terminology to describe them: they were bounders, rotters or cads, words which belong now to the world of P.G. Wodehouse and are used mostly in the atmosphere of public schools and clubs whence they presumably came. But the type has not changed. There are still plenty of seducers like Markie in *To the North*, plenty of men like Rodney in *Friends and Relations* who becomes his sister-in-law's lover. Of course men behave like Max in *The House in Paris*, who deserted the girl he has loved and his child, and like Guy, who was involved with at least one other girl when engaged to the hero-worshipping Lilia (*A World of Love*). Men still betray their country, like Robert, telling lies to Stella, who loved him. These are the Elizabeth Bowen men, not heroes, not 'anti-heroes', but cads, if only one could think of a contemporary word to use.

In her principal novels Elizabeth Bowen was more of a realist perhaps than she knew, more than she is given credit for now. She wrote of a women's world, for that was the world she knew, but she liked men and depended on them personally. In her novels she saw the best qualities in everyone, idealized only a few young people here and there, and if there are nostalgic moments occasionally – as when she described the castle in *Eva Trout*, mirrored in the lake – they are not exclusively linked to human behaviour and regret. Human beings make their own destiny, they destroy themselves and each other only too easily and Elizabeth Bowen tells moral tales – by presenting a story with believable characters in the most realistic manner possible, keeping a certain suspense through her indirect, subtle approach. To women she says, 'don't expect too much, love when you get the chance, don't devour men for you need them, and you could do much worse, if you are a Lilia, than marry a Fred, a realist who understands his situation and offers what love he can.' Her young men, like Markie and Max, are all credible, and the adolescent Eddie is a triumph, the reader is told enough to see how he came about and one feels sympathetic against all odds because nobody had taught him how to learn about the existence of love.

In fact Elizabeth Bowen wrote fiction as though remembering all the time what Rosamond Lehmann said in her story *The Red-haired Miss Daintreys* – 'take two or three people. . . '. Elizabeth Bowen herself, writing about plot in a piece included in *Collected Impressions*, revealed ideas that would delight the traditionalists – she believed that plot should proceed through some kind of spontaneous combustion. She never wrote without a plot, although some critics have found her narrative either too weak or too melodramatic. Both criticisms seem unjustified, since a good deal happens or at least has happened in each novel, and as for melodramatic incidents, such as a car crash, an illegitimate baby, a suicide or a shooting, these things, unfortunately enough, happen every day. In the Bowen novels the incidents are the direct result of character.

For this author the plot was thickened by what can only be called atmosphere, a word as inadequate as 'magic' for the way in which she gave the reader just enough detail to spark off his/her imagination. There is never any surfeit of detail, she cannot be boring because like Colette she favours the barely-noticed entrance from the wings, the evocation of a person through the minimum of description. Authors who enjoy giving a maximum tend to go out of date quickly, especially women writers who like to dwell lavishly on dress and hair-styles. The old ball-dress which Jane in *A World of Love* discovers in the attic is not described in detail, although we know it is yellow. And we can only guess what Stella Rodway, in *The Heat of the Day*, actually looked like. Our guess is helped by the detailed descriptions of two very different women characters in the same novel, Connie and Louie. The latter's appearance in particular is conditioned by the war, like her life itself. Her warden's uniform and her bobby-pins intrigue readers today, because few descriptions in Elizabeth Bowen's novels are long enough to bore anyone, she is too concerned that they should be telling.

The mention of Louie and Connie involves another particularly interesting aspect of her work. Was she capable of emerging from her essential Irish ascendancy background and describing people who belong to a 'lower' class? These two women are obviously there to relieve the tense atmosphere surrounding Stella, her son, her

lover and the mysterious Harrison. Also at the end Connie is the
horrified witness of Robert's suicidal fall from the roof and the
reader, when he has recovered from the shock of this death, thinks
back to Connie's meeting with Harrison at the start of the novel. It
is significant that the disorientated grass-widow Connie should
interrupt that uneasy dinner *à deux* when Harrison is trying to
convince Stella of Robert's guilt. The interruption is all the more
effective because such an odd trio could only have come together in
wartime London, they are unlikely to have met in peace time.
Those unexpected social encounters which cut across class barriers
were the start of a quiet revolution. Connie then is vital to the novel,
but the descriptions of Connie and Louie together are efficient
while the author's slight sneer is repellent. The famous scenes at the
seaside villa 'Waikiki' in *The Death of the Heart* are genuinely
funny, with brilliantly accurate detail, but the two London girls in
the later novel are treated like music-hall comedians and the result
almost spoils the novel.

Elizabeth Bowen's description of how Stella Rodway enjoyed her
war is a classic:

She had had the sensation of being on furlough from her own life.
Throughout these September raids she had been awed, ex-
hilarated, cast at the very most into a sort of abstract of
compassion – only what had been very small indeed, a torn scrap
of finery, for instance, could draw tears. To be at work built her
up, and when not at work she was being gay in company whose
mood was at the pitch of her own – society became lovable; it had
the temperament of the stayers-on in London. . . . These were
campers in rooms of draughty dismantled houses or corners of
fled-from flats – it could be established, roughly, that the wicked
had stayed and the good had gone. This was the new society of
one kind of wealth, resilience, living how it liked – people whom
the climate of danger suited, who began, even, all to look a little
alike. . . . There was a diffused gallantry in the atmosphere, an
unmarriedness: it came to be rumoured about the country,
among the self-banished, the uneasy, the put-upon and the safe,
that everybody in London was in love – which was true, if not in

the sense the country meant. There was plenty of everything in London – attention, drink, time, taxis, and most of all space.

Anyone who lived through that time in London can judge that Elizabeth Bowen had missed no detail, Rose Macaulay remembered a good deal of it in *The World my Wilderness*, published in 1950, and Henry Green used it in his novel *Caught*, which came out in 1943, when the situation was still current. Elizabeth Bowen perpetuated the life of an oddly privileged class of people in war-time London: they had a very good time, and if they were brave in some ways they were far from unhappy, they lived a heightened glamorous life which many of them have regretted ever since.

She will be remembered for her portraits and caricatures and for her writing about Ireland in *The Last September*. Her descriptions of houses, streets, and gardens have a delicate colouring which only a woman writer could have achieved, for these exteriors are never separated from the feelings of her characters.

Elizabeth Bowen possessed one quality which no enemy can deny her, and it is hard to describe. Not fantasy, but an ability to relate the real and the unreal in a way which no writers on occult or larger-than-life themes could equal. Many of her short stories and she published several volumes of them have become well known through anthologies of the supernatural, but in reality they are more 'natural' than most readers realize, stories like *The Apple Tree*, in which a young girl commits suicide, show people taking just one step beyond reality, their minds moving unconsciously backwards or forwards out of control. Something of the same atmosphere spreads into *A World of Love*, and the reader wonders on at least two occasions if he is reading a ghost story after all – Jane almost 'sees' the dead Guy at Lady Latterley's dinner table, Lilia 'sees' Guy, once her fiancé, only to find her husband Fred: but a ghost-story would have been too ordinary, too contrived. The interplay of memory, hope and nostalgia is infinitely more compelling.

Even if she was Anglo-Irish Elizabeth Bowen was of Celtic origin, and she admired that remarkable Irish writer Sheridan Le Fanu; her interest in the non-material and her handling of it in fiction more than compensate for her occasional over-attachment to the material in life. It is an elusive quality that sets her apart from other novelists, men and women, and writers who have dealt in the quasi-supernatural, even sophisticated ladies like Vernon Lee.

Elizabeth Bowen spent her writing life of fifty years examining and describing people, especially women, and never pretended that any of them were entirely invented, she used friends, acquaintances, people seen by chance and herself as well, making them more real than real. She did not invent any obvious new technique of fiction and she had no happy anticipation of life in post-war Britain. Bowen's Court, the house in County Cork, was her romantic, egotistical dream. What a comically sad situation that was, when royalties from one of her novels had allowed her to equip it with bathrooms (one is reminded of Virginia Woolf doing the same thing at Rodmell) but she was incapable of managing the house after her husband's death and had to sell it. It was promptly pulled down but at least Elizabeth Bowen, accompanied by friends, found the courage to revisit the site. This destruction symbolized the end of a particular type of world, and the start of a new one, in which the inhabitants of seaside villas called 'Waikiki' were to be as meaningful socially as people like Elizabeth Bowen herself, dividing life between an uncomfortable mansion in Eire, a Regency house in London and the hospitality of publishers and universities in the USA. New younger readers may label her as permanently middle-class and middle-aged in her preoccupations, her stories may be about women of all ages but they deal with depths of emotion so often left unspoken or unexplained, and it is not surprising that in her reticence she has sometimes been bracketed with Jane Austen. Novels by young women today, presumably for young women, include as though by necessity descriptions of sex, birth-control, pregnancy, miscarriage, abortion, childbirth, puerperal depression etc. Such descriptions do not occur in Elizabeth Bowen's work because her characters found them less interesting than that infinitely complex 'world of love' where the physical element cannot be independent of emotion.

Fortunately she did not outlive her own reputation. As a classic novelist she will be remembered not only for descriptions of

London and its inhabitants in the Second World War. If she broke little new ground as far as form was concerned, and she cared deeply about form, her achievement in *Eva Trout*, published in 1969, showed that she *could* break away from what might almost have become a formula. Its subtitle was *Changing Scenes* and the change from earlier Bowen books was big. Eva herself was very far from being a romantic heroine, even in Bowen terms, for where she went, trouble happened. This last novel was not the book one would have expected from a woman of seventy, it is long, complex and full of power, it convinces the reader that Elizabeth Bowen was much more than a survivor from the 1930s, she had made her own interpretation of the current 'changing scenes' in Britain and the USA, concentrating, as she had always done, on individual women, and notably the individual young woman on her own. And nobody in any of the novels had been so much alone as Eva.

I have written about Elizabeth Bowen as a novelist concerned principally with love, and caring deeply for the women and girls in her stories. Many women novelists of this century have written intense stories of love in all its aspects and only a few of the truly unforgettable ones can be mentioned here. In *The Love Child* (1927) Edith Olivier showed how a woman's desperate need to give and receive love led her to create an imaginary child who became 'real' until a genuinely real man fell in love with her. Some years later came two minor classics – Antonia White's *Frost in May* (1933) which told of a young girl's equally intense struggle with convent life and family feeling, and *Olivia* (1949), a portrayal of overwhelming adolescent emotion, more 'crush' than lesbianism. The author, 'Olivia', was Dorothy Bussy, sister of Lytton Strachey and translator of André Gide, while the book is dedicated to 'the beloved memory of Virginia Woolf'. Later again came *The Ha-Ha* (1961) by Jennifer Dawson, set in a mental hospital where the heroine is undergoing treatment for depression. The love story, a 'normal' situation in psychotherapy, is of necessity short-lived, but the novel is a minor classic.

But surely the only other novelist of the 1930s and after whose stories of love can match those of Elizabeth Bowen is her contemporary and friend Rosamond Lehmann.

She was born in 1903 and educationally had the best of both possible worlds, private tuition first, followed by three years at Girton College, Cambridge. In 1927, the same year that Virginia Woolf published *To the Lighthouse*, she published *Dusty Answer* and experienced what she herself has called in her autobiography *The Swan in the Evening*, a 'smash-hit'. At least half the background to the book was a women's college at Cambridge, the rest was set in the home counties during the First World War. It showed extraordinary mastery of dialogue between children and, as they grow older, among adolescents and students. The author seems to have overcome all the difficulties of novel-writing without any failures, at least any published ones. Judith, the young heroine, is perpetually in love with the wrong young men – wrong because they do not respond the right way, if at all – but the deeply emotional experience which turns her into an adult occurs at Cambridge when she falls in love with the exciting and fickle Jennifer, who of course lets her down. Fifty years after its first appearance it is still intensely readable, dated only by the author's reticence, which might not be so popular now. 'It seems comical in retrospect', wrote Rosamond Lehmann later, 'that this impassioned but idealistic piece of work should have shocked a great many readers: but it did. It was discussed, and even reviewed, in certain quarters as the outpourings of a sex-maniac. Of those who had known me as an innocent child some were utterly dismayed. How could I have so upset my mother?'

Her mother was indeed 'startled and torn in her feelings'. Rosamond Lehmann had been brought up in the traditional way: 'Girls should be pretty, modest, cultivated, home-loving, spirited but also docile', and of course they must wait for the 'right man' and live happily ever after. At the time Rosamond Lehmann was unhappily married but did not think of herself as a professional writer who had given up hope of normal happiness. At this point in her autobiography she quotes those well-known words of Mrs Gaskell, the nineteenth-century novelist who feared that perhaps women had little hope of taking up a career outside the home: 'a woman's principal work in life is hardly left to her own choice; nor can she drop the domestic charges devolving on her as an individual, for the exercise of the most splendid talents that were ever bestowed.' Fortunately Rosamond Lehmann found married happiness and continued to write, although in a long life she has not published as much as Elizabeth Bowen. She has written of her 'love-hungry nature' always influenced by the 'rectitude, stern puritanic principles' inculcated by her mother, and her books are in fact full of 'love-hungry' girls and women.

The young Judith in *Dusty Answer* looks everywhere for love:

She went dancingly down the garden, feeling moon-changed, powerful and elated; and paused at the river's edge. . . . She took off her few clothes and stepped in, dipping rapidly. . . . It was exquisite joy to be naked in the water's sharp clasp. In comparison, the happiness of swimming in a bathing-suit was vulgar and contemptible. To swim by moonlight alone was a sacred and passionate mystery. The water was in love with her body. She gave herself to it with reluctance and it embraced her bitterly. She endured it, soon she desired it; she was in love with it. . . .

The naturalistic school of writers would say it was too lush, too 'feminine', too easily voluptuous, but such criticism would miss the point. This kind of writing, and there is no shortage of it in Rosamond Lehmann's early work, is not intended as a straightforward description, it takes its colour from the heroine, expressing indirectly all she feels and longs for. In a similar way the emotional drama of the book might seem stifling until one realizes it is the product of the Cambridge environment. Judith's yearnings seem so spontaneous that one almost forgets the artistry needed in order to make them seem so. Rosamond Lehmann seems to be aware of her characters' feelings as from within, which is no doubt why so many of her readers assumed she was writing from her own experience and wrote to her, especially it appears from the USA and later from France, offering her either a share in a lesbian home or else infallible methods of learning heterosexual happiness.

Rosamond Lehmann has an extraordinary capacity for conveying the feelings of young people who are not yet aware that their

yearning emotions are taking them rapidly towards the reality of
sex, and for this reason young people today, who discover that
reality early, may find it hard to accept her books as easily as their
grandmothers did. But the social context of the 1920s produced a
different kind of young person, suffering unconsciously from the
aftermath of the 1914–18 war and the social change that followed.
The basic plot of *Invitation to the Waltz* (1932) could hardly be
more simple: the two teenage daughters of an early-retired mill-
owner, living in a typical English village in 1920, have been invited
to a ball given by members of the local aristocracy. The story is told
entirely through Olivia, who is just 17, and the author's skill is such
that despite the third-person narrative we feel everything through
Olivia's feelings as though she were speaking in the first person. At
first glance the whole level of the story appears to be exclusively
feminine, with interminable details of clothes and hairstyles – for in
1920 girls still put their hair 'up' when they 'came out' – and Olivia's
reactions, moment by moment, dance by dance, to the behaviour of
all the men, young and old, with whom she danced or failed to
dance.

Martin Seymour-Smith has summed up Rosamond Lehmann's
work as 'increasingly misandrous' and if this seems something of an
exaggeration it is true that from the start one feels desperately sorry
for these sensitive plants, these delightful, well brought up girl
heroines, because the only young men they meet are hardly up to
their standard. They are boorish, selfish, destructive, critical,
incapable of affectionate response. The men of course would say
that they were merely protecting themselves against the sentimental
dreams of the girls. The author is not so much prejudiced against
them as realistic. How many middle-aged and older women of
today, as they look back at their teens and twenties remember their
first encounters with men in just these terms – the girls so hopeful,
so eager to give, emotionally, and the young men already cynical,
especially if they had been to university, immune to those touching
feminine appeals, aware, in the aftermath of the First World War,
that there was a shortage of men, that they were at a premium in the
marriage market and that in the English middle-class at least it was
marriage or nothing as far as most girls were concerned. The

aristocracy could be 'fast' and the working-class depraved, but the middle class must be respectable.

This does not mean that Rosamond Lehmann neglects the wider social scene. We may hear a good deal about green stockings, pink powder, lily of the valley scent, but we also hear all relevant details about Olivia's family, starting with the reason for her father's early retirement – he had been overworked during the war. As for the frills and furbelows, they are less important in the end than the description of Miss Robinson, the 'poorly', on-the-shelf spinster who makes Olivia's red silk dress. She is so funny, so pathetic, that we can visualize her life with her aged interfering mother practically as a novel within a novel. It is the same old story: what happened to women who did not marry and had to care for their mothers? They survived as Miss Robinson did, through underpaid dressmaking work.

There is also Major Skinner's wife, taboo because she was twice divorced, dyed her hair and smoked. There is the disturbing visit to the Curtis household of the girl who sells handmade lace in order, she says, to buy some comforts for her elderly mother, and the ghastly Wainwright family who acquire a new baby each year (last year's then becomes the 'owld biby') and are all very sickly, but this does not make them any better-behaved. While the self-centred young men even include, for good measure, a poet obsessed with the merit of his own work and talking like any young poet of today, except for the fact that poetry is no longer a hobby among young men who go to balls at country houses. Any reader interested in sociological speculation will find this apparently light and delicate novel full of unsuspected documentary material. The indirect approach is as far different as possible from that of Doris Lessing, who will in her own way hammer a point home until we really have to notice it. Everything about Rosamond Lehmann's attitude and style could be described as 'feminine' in the way some people call old-fashioned: there is harmony, grace, warmth, affection for characters, especially women characters, but not too much of anything. Under the old-fashioned rule a 'lady' had to dress in a way that would attract no attention to herself. Even Beau Brummell, in the early nineteenth century, felt he could not have been well dressed if the Prince Regent noticed him. As far as fiction by women is concerned, we have now reached the stage when understatement is so rare that it *is* noticeable, and this is what lends an air of distinction to the writing of Rosamond Lehmann, which has always been outside fashion.

My Penguin edition of *Invitation to the Waltz* is forty years old at the time of writing, since it belongs to 1941, and the blurb-writer was determined not to launch it as a book for women. After a four-line summary of the plot he added: 'The most blasé even of male readers must succumb to the attraction of so delicate and truthful a study of a young girl's mind.' The majority of these blasé male readers would at that time be sitting in Nissen huts or fire stations or many more uncomfortable, sexually segregated and extremely boring places. Beneath an unflattering photograph of the author is a laconic potted biography: 'She was born at Fieldham in Buckinghamshire. Her father was a Member of Parliament, a contributor to *Punch*, and also known as one of the best oarsmen in England; she is the sister of John Lehmann . . . and she is related to Liza Lehmann, famous in Edwardian days as a pianist and composer. She herself is an absorbed student of music. She is the wife of a well-known painter; they spend much of their time in Wales, or in a country place not far from Oxford, he busy with his painting, she with her writing.' *Par excellence* the life of a happy woman and a dedicated writer. In 1932, the year that Elizabeth Bowen published *To the North*, and the year after Willa Cather's *Shadows on the Rock*, three impressions of *Invitation to the Waltz* sold out in three months.

Unlike Elizabeth Bowen and so many successful novelists Rosamond Lehmann, in a long life, has not published a long list of books. There is a distilled, deliberate quality about her novels which could not have been achieved by rapid writing. After reading the short stories in *The Gypsy's Baby* one can only wish she had written more of them, or even expanded *The Red-haired Miss Daintreys* into a novel. It ends on a nostalgic note, describing how two young children would 'grow up to look and behave much like other people: but not in the least like their relations of the two former generations. Product of an expanding age, the mould is broken that shaped and turned those out. Forced up too rapidly, the power in them, so lavish and imposing as it seemed, sank down as rapidly and faded out. There will be no more families in England like the Daintrey family.' The author was all the time conscious, like Elizabeth Bowen in her later work, of those 'changing scenes', and this is obvious again in the much praised novel of 1944 *The Ballad and the Source*. Many critics have found it her best, and it is certainly a *tour de force* in many ways, revealing the contrast between two versions of a woman's life, the way she likes to see it and recount it to a typical Lehmann young girl, and the way it really was. The story is brilliantly worked out, but somehow exhausting to read, it is as though the author had allowed technique to take over almost for its own sake.

Surely however *The Echoing Grove* of 1953 is the most highly developed of the novels even if it seems slightly overlong. Again two contrasted sisters as in *Invitation to the Waltz* and this time the most detailed portrait of a man that Rosamond Lehmann ever wrote. Again, love is all, Madeleine and Dinah both love Rickie with different kinds of desperation, but is he worth loving? When the novel first appeared London gossip linked him with a well known English poet, and those who read the book at that time could hardly escape this possible identification. Perhaps we have been too conditioned since then by the existentialist insistence on commitment, but one does so wish that Rickie would make up his mind. In life, and especially in emotional life, however, people do not always make up their minds and stick to their decision, they drift, until the passing of time allows decisions to happen without their intervention. The book seems essentially to be about the weakness of men in contrast to the fidelity and strength of women, a natural development from the situation described in embryo in *Invitation to the Waltz*. There are good descriptions of life in the 1930s, with young men going out to Spain and refugees arriving from Germany, equally good descriptions of London in wartime. There are technical innovations, when sometimes one does not realize for a moment whose thoughts one is following. But most of all there is the unexpected diagnosis, by Dinah in conversation with her mother, of how Rickie came to be as he was. He came of a different class.' 'We weren't conditioned like him,' says Dinah, 'not deeply, by ruling class mentality . . . I couldn't be more thankful for the good sound upper-middle stock I come of. It's meant a sort of solid ground-floor of family security and class confidence that's been a great stand-by. But Rickie hadn't got it. He was a romantic orphan boy, irrevocably out of the top drawer. He was never at home in his situation . . . I mean the contemporary one, the crack-up – not just the general human situation of wondering why you're born.'

The book tells the story of a triangular love affair, but the triangle is far from simple, and all its lines are extended. Those who read stories of love simply for the love-scenes will probably not think this complex book a great success, but its social dimension is continually fascinating, Rosamond Lehmann goes into details of behaviour and class that Elizabeth Bowen only hinted at, or treated in indirect fashion. It would not be fair to make a choice between these two writers, whose material is similar in so many ways, and it would be impossible ever to think one page of one of them could have been written by the other. They are essential reading for younger women novelists with new ideas about 'realism'. They are classics of the mid-century, and less out of date than might be imagined.

In his preface to *Horizon Stories*, published in 1943 in Britain, Cyril Connolly wrote 'Two kinds of story have been deliberately avoided by *Horizon*. One is the love story, which is not a story, but a confession, and the other is the reportage which masquerades as fiction. The object of these stories is to entertain and give pleasure. . . .' This seems an easy way of disposing of many stories by many people, as though feelings were so infinitely less important than events. Yet many events would surely never have happened without the existence of love. Of Connolly's eighteen authors four were women: Elizabeth Bowen, Eudora Welty, Antonia White and Diana Gardner. Men too have written 'confession' stories about love, men such as Hemingway or Fitzgerald. Perhaps Englishmen are less ready to 'confess'. If women 'confess' more readily than men, and write about love, they are not merely proving what Byron said about its being 'woman's whole existence', they are, as Elizabeth Bowen and Rosamond Lehmann have proved, greater realists, with a greater sense of responsibility.

[5]
Hating and Partly Hating

❦❦❦

It would be hard to find more gruesome reading among twentieth-century fiction than the novels of Ivy Compton-Burnett. Murders, mysteries, ghost stories, spy stories, the genre known generally as spine-chillers, all these are infinitely less painful, and probably the only documents equally realistic are psychiatric case-histories. The Compton-Burnett addicts, who invariably assure me I am in a minority of one because I find the work so repellent, will respond with cries of Oh! and are unlikely to show any further reaction to such an eccentric statement. But how else can one respond to the nineteen novels, excluding the early *Dolores*, of which the titles, with their basic duality of relationship, appear so closely inter-related, written in the same language and introducing people who must surely all belong to one big unhappy family? The truly horrible thing about the inhabitants of these books is the way they feel themselves forced to accept their wretched lives, spend years doing things they hate, conduct loveless love-affairs in secret and walk as though inexorably driven by forces they cannot fight into incestuous marriages and other odd relationships. They are exceptionally vain and emotionally sterile. Many of the characters express, indirectly, a great deal of dissatisfaction as they suffer under some appalling tyranny but prefer to remain in that state because they cannot escape: if they have contemplated escape in any way – there are few signs of it – they have finally chosen to stay where they are, presumably for two reasons: they prefer the *status quo* because at least they are used to it and they dare not run away from home because they would not know what to do. Inevitably one returns to this problem while reading the novels. Not even the men would have been able to earn a living and not all the women would have been acceptable as governesses and companions, the only posts open to them at the period to which the books relate.

These novels are possibly the greatest indictment ever made of late Victorian and Edwardian society, for that is what they are about, and the worst thing about that society, so dependent on inherited wealth and a hierarchy of servants, is its power of survival, for the author was still deeply conscious of it until her death in 1969 and enough people have accepted its attitudes to find these books amusing. The other section of happy readers seems to consist more of those who are overwhelmed with nostalgia than those who are delighted to have escaped. And lastly of course one should not forget those who are unconsciously as destructive as the characters in the books but do not quite know how to satisfy these urges to kill or at least hate.

The first person in the Compton-Burnett universe who failed to escape was of course the author herself. She did not even escape an unfortunate Christian name because if she had not been called Ivy then her hangers-on would not have talked about her – in fact they still do so – as though she were some kind of female pet. Hers was no easy life, as her biographers have had no difficulty in showing, and the saddest aspect of it is that she cannot have been a happy person, let alone a happy woman, until she had the second-class success of being a successful novelist. The addicted reader is happy enough: he receives a thrill which is unequalled by his reaction to any other writing, a thrill due to his admiration of the unclassifiable wit involved in this work. It is as though a new taste had been invented. Yet surely there is only a limited reason for rejoicing, limited to the technical achievement. But in the case of Ivy Compton-Burnett biographical data are more than usually valuable because, like her dialogue, they have an oblique relevance to the general plot of her work. She told interviewers and biographers that her life had not been interesting, that she had not done much, that very little had happened.

This non-action on her part is in fact crucial, because all the 'action' occurred in a negative way, and the action was death. Since we know that in the midst of life is death everyone of us experiences the deaths of other people and reacts in one way or another. Ivy

Compton-Burnett's reaction was one of stoicism, occasional depression and mostly inaction, and she had a great deal of death in the midst of her early life. Her father died when she was seventeen, her two brothers died, and later two of her younger sisters very probably committed suicide. Her response to this series of tragedies was not to travel or to take up professional work, which she could have done, thanks to her degree in classics. As the eldest daughter she was responsible for the upbringing and education of the younger children and she tried to do the work as responsibly as she could. The strain and suffering she obviously must have felt was repressed, as it was in most women of her social background, especially among those who had received a higher education. She allowed something of this unhappiness to show through in the early novel *Dolores*, published in 1911, and then for fourteen years she published nothing. This silence was surely her period of mourning, well concealed from the world yet obviously failing to exorcise all those family ghosts. She had suffered emotional deprivation from her girlhood onwards, combined with too much responsibility, and no close relationship developed to fill this gap until Margaret Jourdain appeared in 1919, after which the two women shared a Kensington apartment for as long as 32 years. Not until she was an established author – to the surprise of Miss Jourdain and others – did Ivy Compton-Burnett emerge a little from the shadows in which she had obviously preferred to live.

But it is the unsuccessfully suffocated unhappiness that appears with obsessive repetition in most of the books most of the time. Readers who are unsophisticated enough, or perhaps sentimentally over-romantic, to react with horror to the themes of family strife are not alone: Professor Mario Praz, author of that intriguing book *The Romantic Agony*, was even reminded, on reading Ivy Compton-Burnett, of the Marquis de Sade. Before becoming aware of such extremes we can surely see in this work one aching gap: chapter after chapter, book after book, and all the time this frightening lack of love. All these people who talk incessantly of social differences, snobbery, money, sexual 'accidents', deception, cruelty: they have apparently never known anything of love and do not realize the fact. They do not expect love, and seem convinced that it can only bring disaster. It is extremely uncomfortable in every way. Sexual love is only mentioned when it results in some unfortunate illegitimate child who of course appears or re-appears at the crucial moment in the story and inherits the money and possessions that other people had assumed to be their right. It is a convention of the Compton-Burnett world that partners in these sexual adventures, sometimes 'normal', but often breaking social rules or the taboos of family relationships, should feel no more than a moment of nostalgia (which does not convince the reader) in their memories of what so unexpectedly happened. Nobody hearing of the partners' doings envies them or feels they were justified in such behaviour – any such reaction would have been cheaply romantic, 'common' perhaps, and therefore doomed to exclusion from this world which is equally guilt-ridden, secretive, dark and airless both above and below stairs. Nobody ever opens a window – and of course they would have had to ask the domestic staff to do it – because they were presumably frightened that fresh air might come in, or possibly a bird might have been heard singing.

Stoicism was not enough protection for the author. She did however twist and transfer the considerable stoicism she possessed into a new kind of artifice which her admirers find highly comic. This is the way in which her characters consistently show no surprise or shock when learning of disastrous or totally unexpected events, for in reacting like this they probably reflected the attempted self-protection and emotional inertia of their creator.

The word stoicism seems unavoidable in any discussion of Ivy Compton-Burnett, and in its classical associations it has always been thought of as a masculine virtue. Yet Victorian women, and the author was brought up as a Victorian, were well schooled in it. How would a man have reacted to the problematic situations traversed by the author? Probably he would have avoided them, since men at that time, when it came to bringing up a family, did little more than provide money and issue general instructions. If a man had transferred an equal amount of resentment into writing he would surely have shown more obvious anger and violence, a man would have been incapable of such continued repression. The whole question of femininity and feminism probably interested Ivy

Compton-Burnett more than she realized. She called her first book after its heroine and the titles she gave to at least five more, especially early in her career, emphasized sexual polarity: *Brothers and Sisters*, *Men and Wives*, *Daughters and Sons*, then later came *Manservant and Maidservant*, *Mother and Son*, while one published in 1933 indicates an inevitable preoccupation of the decades after the First World War – *More Women than Men*. Ivy Compton-Burnett once referred to herself and Margaret Jourdain as 'a couple of neuters' and discussions in print about this personal relationship have varied from the vague remarks made by Jane Rule in *Lesbian Images* (1975–6) where she referred to their 'celibate relationship' to the statement by Martin Seymour-Smith in his *Guide to Modern World Literature*: 'She was lesbian by inclination, a condition which she accepted but which she knew, with her withering intelligence, that the crass post-Victorian world did not.' There was surely no woman writer this century whose sexuality was more totally sublimated and dedicated to the service of writing.

The books are of course obsessed with family situations and it is fascinating to see how the author deals with the sexual elements which create these uncomfortable households. It looks as though her relief at being out of a family situation was so great that she could hardly believe in it and felt bound to create a family in nearly every book she wrote. Family seems to have meant tyranny, to which she seems to have been particularly sensitive, she is so preoccupied with it that she leaves no aspect of its inherent sado-masochism unexposed. She seems keen to make it clear that she herself is now a novelist, no longer a woman, and has escaped, something her characters cannot do. Duncan Edgeworth, in *A House and its Head*, has been described as a masterly creation by a woman novelist, remembering as usual that women novelists are supposed to be inadequate in the creation of male characters. Duncan is perhaps not too convincing for the younger generation today who have done so much to force the permissive society into being. Maybe for them he is just funny, maybe they find it hard to understand why every single member of the Edgeworth family did not just break the windows and go away. At the risk of sounding repetitious it has to be made clear that in those early twentieth-century days people did not just walk out one summer morning, they were always capable of eating the food offered to them on silver dishes by uniformed servants and there was not much chance of thumbing a lift once the runaway had gone down the drive and out of the main gates. Young women could at least run away into some sexual encounter, almost invariably unsuitable, but it was better than nothing. As for the tyrant's wife, there was no hope at all.

The author was not prepared to limit her examination of tyranny to the behaviour of husbands and fathers, although this may have been something she remembered with particular clarity from her youth. When she dealt with tyrannical mothers the result was even more chilling. *Mother and Son* of 1955 has been described by Rosalie Glynn Grylls as one of Ivy Compton-Burnett's 'easier' novels; the plot is not too complicated and the light relief is lighter than usual. The novel is particularly relevant in any discussion of the author's preoccupation with the feminine character, the behaviour and treatment of women generally. The mother-tyrant Miranda is more alarming than any mere breadwinner-husband-father who bangs the table when angry and forces his sick wife to come down to the dining-room, as in *A House and its Head*. The way in which Miranda directs her son Rosebery to take sugar in his tea, and even more so the way in which she questions him as to why and how he had apparently broken a long-standing habit (by not taking any) without her permission is agonizing to read. Miranda's probing is rather like that of a dentist equipped with a particularly sharp instrument. On the other hand when the reader can bear it no longer he can at least put the book down, but Miranda's son Rosebery, known as Rosebud, has to go on being her son.

This title is recommendable for many reasons and the 'light relief' comes partly from the unforgettable portrait of a cat-ridden household, a female one, needless to say. If the people had been masculine they would surely have been homosexual. Nobody else would have been capable of the dedication to cats that appears here. Since the mentality of cat-lovers, or rather cat-slaves, has always been a mystery to me, I cannot judge how these latter react to the descriptions of that ghastly but accurately observed ménage where the cat, here named Plautus, is the tyrant. There are also sporadic appearances by Tabbikin, a different class of cat whom Miranda would like kept in the kitchen, but the cat-tyrant wins against the human one. *Mother and Son* in fact won the James Tait Black Memorial Prize in 1955 and to anyone re-reading it some twenty-five years later it is found to reveal a particularly feminine slant and a great deal about the author, who here deals with four women plus a maid or so, two men plus a tutor (for the maids and the tutor are not of the same class as their employers, naturally, and they do not share the same class themselves) and three children, not forgetting the cats who from time to time bring the characters together.

All the books bristle with quotations and aphorisms to meet every possible situation and this title is no exception, apart from the fact that the characters seem more than usually preoccupied with what they consider to be specially feminine virtues and problems, many of them connected with essential aspects of family life. Miss Wolsey proposes to take over the carving, which had always been done by Miranda, whose tyranny of course is never forgotten.

' "I always think it is a woman's business. It was once regarded as such. It was late that feminine helplessness came into fashion." '

The author includes domestic details in this novel as though she were determined to show the non-British world how the British behave about the minor but inescapable problems of inviting people to tea. It is a shameful thing to take out better quality china for the guests, and even more shocking to feel ashamed of the fact. It would be better to use good, old, darned table linen, but if there is none one could use new tablecloths, although they must not look as though they have been bought specially for the occasion. These minutiae, introduced with such dead-pan irony, amuse both the English and the non-English for related reasons: the English seem proud of their own ritualistic behaviour and the non-English, provided they do not run away screaming, can only marvel that such things happen, either in life or in books. It seems a pity of course that someone who was so obviously intelligent, one who gave new lamps for old as far as family life fiction is concerned, should choose to put such effort into the reporting of such abysmal pettiness, which appears in most of the novels in some form or other. But this is after all the gossip and light relief of social history, and who could resist it? Only a woman novelist could have done it well, just as men leave the small-change of tea-parties to women in any case. But in the Compton-Burnett world men often had to come to tea anyway, there was no escape.

The author *could* escape when she wished from the internecine strife between her characters and talk through them about things other than tyranny, hate and lack of love. In *Mother and Son* for instance there are some amusing discussions about writing and publishing. No wonder that this title has been regarded as more accessible than many of the others, and although the family in it, including the dead Miranda Hume, succeed, with the help of one scheming maiden lady, in rejecting the two others who almost joined it, one feels aware that a window has been opened somewhere, perhaps because the Hume family keep no butler and somebody, unconsciously, had acted on his/her own initiative.

In fact it could have been one of the children, because here as in so many other novels they are the second form of escape for the reader, the great letters-in of light. These children are usually frightening, nonetheless, they are in no way naïve or sweet and charming – for where would they have learnt or inherited such talents? – but they are not yet full of hatred and hypocrisy, even if they have acquired the same habits of oblique remarks without which few of their elders, including the servants, could manage at all. The children are often more grown-up than the adults, for they have not had the chance to play the destructive games which occupy their parents and grandparents. In *Darkness and Day* for example the children's voices are particularly fascinating because they are both childlike and at the same time so clairvoyant as to be positively sybilline: Sir Ransom has died, and the children are told to remember the 'happy part of it'. ' "What is the happy part?" said Viola.

' "There is none," said Rose, on the stairs. "Why do people talk as if they were glad, when someone is dead? I think it must mean there is a little gladness somewhere."

' "Perhaps it is because of what they inherit."

' "No, that is something apart. I mean gladness in their sorrow. As if it was good to have something ended and complete. It is not when they really love someone." ' '

These children had already decided they were 'not actually unhappy'. "Not like children in books. People don't seem to write about happy children." '

It is in fact intriguing to realize that spinster-type women writers of the Edwardian generation, who saw children at a convenient distance, notably Ivy Compton-Burnett and Rose Macaulay, for instance, tend to write about them with aunt-like understanding, while the post-Second-World-War regiment of women writers (those described as the Liberated Mum school of English fiction) really do not understand or care for them at all as entities separate from themselves and much of the time apparently wish they did not exist. The Compton-Burnett children are both real and unreal. Anyone who grumbles about the behaviour of schoolchildren today in large classes will have to work out for themselves whether the tutors in these novels – Mr Pettigrew in *Mother and Son* or the enthusiastic amateur governess Mildred in *Darkness and Day* – have a better time than harassed teachers in British comprehensive schools: I should say not, for the children destroy them utterly. The children are chorus-figures in several of the books, often explaining what is going on in the minds of their surrounding adults before the latter fully understand themselves.

In *Mother and Son* there is a revealing conversation about whether the children should go to their grandmother Miranda's funeral, and the author makes interesting use of the situation:

' "Francis can come with you and me," said Julius. "Adrian is too young, and I should not take a girl."

' "I think you are right that it should be a masculine prerogative. If that is the word; and in the sense of privilege it is. Miss Wolsey, may we hope to have you with us? Do your qualities put you above the feminine level in such things?"

' "They will put me with the children. The feminine level is sometimes the one to be observed." '

Most characters in these books are very much aware of the feminine world and the particular characteristics of its inhabitants. The creator of that world was more preoccupied with femininity than might appear at first to most readers, because of course there are so many qualities to attract these readers, including the way in which the author pleases the addicts by appearing to re-write the same book many times over but in fact never doing so. The tyrants vary a little, occasionally one novel may be concerned with a school and not a family, occasionally too there are a few lines of external description. Her interest in the lot of women, individual and general, comes through in practically every book, and no aspect of women's status is neglected, although the average reader would probably not realize just how many references she makes to this complex question. She and her characters seem aware that women do not have the best of any possible world. They do not have enough to do: ' "Women walking, women talking, women weeping!" said Duncan (in *A House and its Head*). "Doing all they can do. I will thank you to let me pass, as I am to catch a train this morning. Otherwise I would ask less. Your chatter may wait, as it is what the day holds for you." ' Some women are inclined to run down their own intelligence. Anne, in *Darkness and Day*, is not interested in the newspaper. ' "I suppose my mind is so feminine that it does not function like a mind. The paper acts on me as a sedative." '

Women have not much to look forward to, whatever role they play in life, and even some men are aware of this, like Gaunt in *Darkness and Day* who remarks sadly, ' "I often wonder if women would marry, if they could foresee the future."

' "I often do too," said Emma. "But I should have thought it was the woman's point of view rather than the man's." '

Neither is there much consolation to be found in professional life, if that is what it could be called, an attitude made clear in *A Father and his Fate*:

' "She is perhaps hardly educated enough for a governess." '

' "Well, if she was, she would not be one." ' '

It is not easy however to think of any Compton-Burnett female character who is anxious to reform the lot of her kind, although most of them complain about it in a resigned, even dignified way. Some kind of odd masochism prevents them from doing anything about it and they talk as if they had not the energy to try. Most of them of course are too tightly locked within the family power-struggle to look outside, and prefer to use their energy in viperish personal ambition, like Sybil in *A House and its Head*, than in any furtherance of women's cause. Naturally, as late Victorian or Edwardian ladies they are fully occupied with domestic and social duties. On the whole of course mothers have little to do with young children, who are much happier in the organized care of nannies, housekeepers, maids, governesses, tutors and butlers, and they often appear in the books because their parents are dead or absent for some reason. But some mothers, like Miranda Hume in *Mother and Son*, do not allow their sons to grow up and if nobody discusses homosexual relationships in any detail neither is anybody surprised by their existence, as in *Two Worlds and their Ways*, but on the other hand no opportunity is missed for a 'loaded' aside: ' "Men who live together talk like women." '

References to social problems occur here and there and are always shrugged off as a kind of joke, which one assumes to be the author's way of indicating the irresponsibility of her characters. Selina, in *Darkness and Day*, means well, for instance, she is knitting for the whole village. But she is not too much concerned about people who have no chance of eating breakfast. On the whole though the Compton-Burnett characters do not have much time to think about good works, who should do them, if in fact they should be done at all. They are too busy expressing their own bad thoughts, of which they are often unaware, and this curious kind of joke kept the author busy writing nineteen novels between 1925 and her death in 1969. Has the contemporary reader the same energy to apply him/herself to absorbing them? Sales show that plenty of customers buy the books. The density of these novels is exhausting, and the equally intense way in which the dialogue is conducted, a lack of differentiation sometimes in the upstairs/downstairs characters makes them even more difficult and you cannot obviously read Compton-Burnett if you are merely looking for relaxation. You have to concentrate. And if you dislike a preoccupation with materialism, pettiness, repressed family feeling and prefer reading about warmth rather than hate, if you are not particularly interested in the themes of Greek tragedy which have impressed so many critics, then, however sincerely you admire her technique, you will not like her books very much.

She may have exorcized a large amount of hatred through her remarkable application to technique, she may not have been so 'neuter' as she thought. She is remembered, as the late Elizabeth Sprigge told, as being deeply concerned with the values offered by various Kensington shopkeepers. She always slept in an unheated bedroom. Which is probably one of the reasons why the characters in her books behaved as they did.

Ivy Compton-Burnett could never have had a successor in the direct line, but there is one person who can be mentioned on the same page, as it were, for the vast family of characters she created all enjoyed viperish talk of minutiae, even if the talk has no deeper overtones.

Angela Thirkell was born two years before Ivy Compton-Burnett and died nine years earlier, living that is from 1890 to 1960. They had more in common perhaps than their nearly-coinciding life-span, both produced work that fascinates horribly and shows great skill. If the Compton-Burnett characters hate each other those of Angela Thirkell are not exactly brimming over with love and are not so much hateable to the reader as irritatingly dislikeable, their middle-class chat sets the teeth on edge like the juice of raw lemons.

There was nothing raw about the author but she sometimes behaved in life as though she might have liked to be that way and, having failed, she had to be content with producing some thirty novels, all possessing a savour infinitely more bitter than sweet. Ivy Compton-Burnett had little on her side except the important things that money cannot buy: high intelligence, stoicism, artistry and a capacity for hard work. Angela Mackail, as she was born, later MacInnes and finally Thirkell, had as many brilliant relations and friends as Virginia Woolf, perhaps in fact more. Her father was Professor of Poetry at Oxford, her grandfather was the painter Burne-Jones, her cousin was Rudyard Kipling and her friends included E.V. Lucas, novelist and critic. She was also a beautiful young woman; unfortunately she could not enjoy life without telling other people what to do. She seems to have been an easy prey for the life-force, to use Bernard Shaw's phrase again. There seems to have been no other reason why, when she was twenty-one, she insisted on marrying a good-looking singer who might previously have been something of a homosexual, who fairly soon took to drink and even beat her. Perhaps secretly she did not want to go on living the genteel cultured life to which she had been brought up and despite her highly feminine aura she wanted a man she could dominate, falling in love with him in March and marrying him in May, ignoring family disapproval. She was feminine enough to want children but she could not go on living with James MacInnes after the birth of her two sons. Not content with one doomed marriage she embarked on a second and as a result went to Australia, as far as humanly and socially possible from the native Kensington she never left in spirit. She began to write for money, and this most terrifyingly English of English lady novelists began her writing life in Melbourne.

The further an exile is away from home, the stronger perhaps the pull of nostalgia, and apart from the reportage of *Troopship to the Southern Cross* the first of Angela Thirkell's novels, and every succeeding one, was about England. She began this writing before her journey back to London leaving Mr, formerly Captain Thirkell, in Melbourne. Marriage no longer meant anything to her, although she now had three sons and did all she could to keep them close to her. By 1934, writing quickly and determinedly, seeking advice from her professional friends, she had published four books, three of them novels, as though in straightforward compensation for her loss of personal happiness.

Everyone interested in the Thirkell phenomenon may choose any one of the later books in order to indulge their addiction but these first three are an essential part of the case history, the equation author + experience = book. *Ankle Deep*, the first published, is accepted as being about her own love affair with an unknown man and although it is easy to dismiss the novel as utterly silly the average woman at least who has read the story of Angela Thirkell's life will be thankful that she had this romance, because it must surely have made her happier than marriage ever did. Marriage seems to have meant wild attraction followed by neglect and near-alcoholism on the husband's part. How capable Angela Thirkell was of deep feeling is not clear and it may have been something beyond her, but she and her self-heroine Aurea in this book decided that there could be a happy form of love which had nothing to do with marriage. She dealt with it lightly, refused to think it might any longer dominate her and kept it all in books. In some ways Angela Thirkell never grew up and she was still an inexperienced novelist. She was however an ambitious one and in *High Rising* (1933) she included herself as she obviously intended to be several years ahead – a successful and envied lady novelist. She allowed her heroine to be no great writer, no twentieth-century George Eliot, but someone who knew her limitations and never tried to exceed them. Even the reader who hates the unbearable and over-selective quasi-reality of her books, and the painful persistence of that reality in present-day Barsetshire, must give her credit for presenting the reality of her own position.

She seems to have taken up Barsetshire rather as Anthony Trollope himself did originally, without being aware of what was happening, although one could perhaps define the area as stretching from Kent to Wiltshire in the south of England and going as far north as Hertfordshire and Oxfordshire. It was, is, in fact, a convenient amalgam of the home counties and just beyond where in the 1930s, and during and after the Second World War, everyone had a nice house, was dependent on a good income, which sometimes meant having a job but by no means necessarily so, and of course most people with status (and these people, from the owners of the Big House to the doctor and the vicar, fitted neatly into the social jigsaw) had servants, all very useful in the plot. Not only has Angela Thirkell been sanctified by Margot Strickland's biography but first editions of her books are sought out now by collectors. There are various obvious reasons for her success: if her continual references to the social pattern are intended to be ironic, only a fellow ironist is likely to notice. Tea at four with the silver teapot (Lady Waring put hers away during World War II – see *Growing Up*) is totally natural and never to be missed, as far as the inhabitants of Barsetshire are concerned, and in 1980 in Britain there are still, in Barsetshire at least, plenty of people who agree. Most Thirkell readers presumably 'identify' with the characters in the books – mostly women – to an amazingly close extent. The collectors of these novels are presumably those people who approve of and cling to this way of life, or else, never having experienced it, they read with deep nostalgic sighs and wish they could have lived like this.

To the professional reader and writer however Thirkell is as fascinating as she is irritating. She situates the heroine at the centre of the novel – nearly always a heroine who organizes everything and everybody – and suitable men are not very far away, varying from the local landowner to the station-master ('the abolition of first-class carriages struck to his heart' – Mr Beedle in *Growing Up*). There is throughout that sort of Englishness which foreigners, once they have stopped being frightened or puzzled, find fascinating: it is like early man to the anthropologist. There is for instance the same talent for understatement and stiff upper lip which is taken to inhuman lengths by Ivy Compton-Burnett. In many novels by Angela Thirkell there are melodramatic events, such as the poison-pen incident in *High Rising*, but we know absolutely that the story must end well, at least for the characters we like most. The author rejected the realism of things going hopelessly wrong, as they had done in her own life. There are no characters whom we can actually dislike, for at all costs the serious side of life must be avoided; some of the people are silly and some are caricatures, like the Provençal scholar in *What did it Mean* (1954), but most people are intended to by *sympathique*, none are much more than cardboard. It is known that she based many of her creations on real-life people, and that Lady Wemyss became Lady Leslie in *Wild Strawberries*, for instance. The author was very fond of Lady Wemyss, apparently, but her way of showing her feelings was to make her into a highly eccentric, brave but irritating comic character.

Angela Thirkell seems to me of great interest to the professional writer for she herself became professional with remarkable speed and stayed that way for a long writing life. *High Rising* is particularly rewarding because it contains portraits of two writers, one of them a self-portrait as has already been mentioned. Women writers not given too much to envy and snobbery will be fascinated by Laura Morland's good ideas, good luck and hard work. Most novels about writers are tedious, but writers in fiction are beset with unsolvable problems. Not so Laura. When her husband died she was left with four sons, one 'only a few months old, and there was very little money'. Writing occasionally in magazines was no longer any use. 'She had considered the question carefully, and decided that next to racing, murder, and sport, the great reading public of England (female section) liked to read about clothes. With real industry she got introductions, went over big department stores, visited smart dressmaking friends, talked to girls she knew who had become buyers or highbrow window-dressers, and settled down to write best-sellers.' Laura Morland found the formula workable enough and educated her sons on the proceeds. Success did not go to her head. 'She was quite contented, and never took herself seriously, though she took a lot of trouble with her books. If she had been more introspective, she might have wondered at herself for doing so much in ten years, and being able to afford a small flat in London, and a reasonable little house in the country, and a middle-class car.' It sounds a little smug, but at least one can find Laura to some extent *sympathique*. She is presented with more depth than most Thirkell characters because she was of course Thirkell herself at the start of her career, her creator knew her well and cared about her.

High Rising even contains a male character with some slight depth and he is a writer too, George Knox, said to be modelled on E.V. Lucas. George is allowed to have a 'colourful personality' which is explained by the French blood he inherited from his mother. He is successful, for Thirkell characters usually are, he is a good father but very stupid about women. He is different from the usual run of Thirkell people because, as a writer, he is allowed various eccentricities and even makes a speech which goes on, with minor interruptions, for more than a page, giving the much quoted recipe for success in the literary world: one must write Awfully Dull Novels, with 'a strong philosophic vein'. In some ways Thirkell was a prophet about the future of the novel, the future of adult education and the way that the latter would strike the average *Daily Telegraph* reader in Barsetshire:

My hero shall be an ardent student of philosophy, a follower of Spinoza, Kant, Plato, a Transcendentalist, a Quietist, what do I know – one can read that up with the greatest of ease thanks to the appalling increase of cheap little books about philosophy edited by men with famous names who do not scruple to pander to this modern craze for education, which is, in sum, only a plan for helping people not to think for themselves. Now, mark me, Laura. What really interests novel readers? Seduction. . . . Novel readers by thousands will read my book, each asking her, or in comparatively fewer cases, him, self: Will seduction take place? Well, I may tell you, Laura, that it will. But so philosophically that hundreds and thousands of readers will feel that they are improving their minds by reading philosophy, which is just as harsh and crabbed as the dull fools suppose, until it is made attractive by the lure of sex.

Laura Morland professes not to understand, but Angela Thirkell could follow perfectly, and there was little that she did not learn, and very quickly too, on how to seduce an immense readership. She is a highly efficient example of how women novelists in particular seem able to succeed because they have the facility of transferring to paper unlimited amounts of idiotic conversation, doing it well enough in fact for it to lose something of its idiocy. The social historian may find some parts of her books more entertaining and just as precise as the study of contemporary newspapers, for there is a horrid accuracy beneath the bird-like chirpings on the surface. In *What Did it Mean?* for instance the celebrations for the coronation of Queen Elizabeth II as arranged in the local village were not too different from those arranged in the rest of Barsetshire, and allowing for local variations, all over Britain. The only drawback is that the reader is sometimes reminded of the pageant in *Between the Acts* and must choose between Virginia Woolf and Angela Thirkell. The changing fortunes of the Pomfret family are far from unrealistic: they close their enormous rooms at Pomfret Towers and move into the servants' wing, having installed central heating and bathrooms, surprised to find that the servants had managed without either for so long. There is a conducted tour of the now uninhabited stately home which Lord Pomfret cannot even afford to demolish, and the details are to be relished, if one can bear a catalogue of the ugly and useless, such as the weighing chair which came from the London club called Black's (the reference is all too obvious). Surely only a middle-class author could have written in this particular tone of voice about the decline of the upper classes: anyone whose background is truly U could never have uttered such a hard laugh without the hint of a sigh.

The comedy situations throughout the book are like scenes from those West End farces which do not seem to have changed in fifty years, and the jaded reader cannot cope with them too often. It is however always worthwhile picking out the dominating women – there is at least one per book – and passing quickly over most long conversations with men, for the male characters are rarely half as interesting as George Knox in *High Rising*, even though he too is partly caricature and partly a portrait from life. It is unfortunately possible that Angela Thirkell became a novelist because she needed men in her life only for a short time: she did not seem able to accept husbands because like so many characters in her books she *had* to tell most people, and certainly men, what to do. It is better that women like her direct their energies into writing rather than into life, and when they quickly develop a remarkable professionalism, as she did, everyone is happier and even a good deal richer, especially the author and her publisher. Thousands of readers enjoy themselves hugely with a predictable story in a predictable setting. The social observers have an entertaining and rewarding time, for Angela Thirkell recorded the Barsetshire scene for over three decades. It is true that Trollope looked much more deeply into the human heart, but any reader who can tolerate the twitterings of Thirkell's female characters can have, to borrow that measured title-phrase used by the Canadian novelist Mavis Gallant, a fairly good time.

[6]

Forecasting

❈❈❈

If nobody is afraid of Virginia Woolf I suspect quite a number of people are, have been or will be afraid of Doris Lessing, starting with the former government of Rhodesia (as Zimbabwe was then called) which in 1956 decided that she must not come back to the country ever again. Individuals are afraid of her (although they will not admit it) because she forces them to look at situations they do not like: personal, social, political; she writes of 'the mortal storm' that surely if gradually has been leading a whole continent to be in truth 'darkest Africa', dark in the sense that violence and suffering will obscure the singing grass in a poisonous dust cloud. And as with that mortal storm of the late 1930s the dust is not likely to remain at a convenient distance, it will blow all round the world and meet, with unforeseeable results, other clouds which have been specially manufactured in order to counteract it.

But it would be wrong to think of Doris Lessing merely as a writer who wrote from long, deeply-felt personal experience about that vanished Rhodesia or Africa in general and condemned what was happening there. Other writers, men and women, have written about various parts of the continent and through their writings have achieved more than a thousand political statements, speeches and pamphlets have done. Doris Lessing's personal life was not limited to her upbringing as a white settler in Africa, for she could remember something of an earlier life, and neither did she make merely romantic or journalistic visits to the places which led to her earliest writing. It was her father who has been described as 'romantic', for he was a Britisher who went to Persia as a senior bank official and then fairly soon afterwards tired of banking. His daughter was born there in 1919 and was five when her father decided to give up his career and move to Rhodesia. There, in a veld farm, the family lived not too happily, Doris went unwillingly to a convent school in Salisbury and later worked there as a telephone operator. The biographical facts continue with two marriages, both unfortunately broken, the birth of three children, and the author's journey from Rhodesia to London with the manuscript of a novel in her suitcase. But most of Doris Lessing's readers will think now of her heroines, whose lives may obviously owe something to that of their creator but who have distinct existences of their own. Mary Turner, that fated protagonist of *The Grass is Singing*, proves how from the very beginning that no Lessing character is straightforwardly good, bad, black, white, but a truly living person with all the shades of meaning and orientation that this indicates.

Immediately here is the proof that before 1950, when this book was first published, Doris Lessing was preoccupied not only with the complex Rhodesian social and racial landscape but with the situation of women in *their* social scene, which is basically *vis à vis* men. Five years after the end of the Second World War was still early for talk about 'women's liberation' and in fact many women in many countries thought they owed some freedom to the war, as their mothers had done nearly thirty years earlier after the First. 'She had inherited from her mother an arid feminism, which had no meaning in her own life at all, for she was leading the comfortable carefree existence of a single woman in South Africa, and she did not know how fortunate she was. How could she know? She understood nothing of conditions in other countries, had no measuring rod to assess herself with.' And immediately the complexities of the scene around her are described. She was 'living in much the same way as the daughters of the wealthiest in South Africa, could do as she pleased – could marry, if she wished, anyone she wanted. These things did not enter her head. "Class" is not a South African word; and its equivalent, "race", meant to her the office boy in the firm where she worked, other women's servants, and the amorphous mass of natives in the streets, whom she hardly noticed. She knew . . . that the natives were getting "cheeky". But she had nothing to do with them really. They were outside her orbit.'

These two significant paragraphs show that this was no

pamphleteering novel, and that is why its message, meaningful in itself, comes through so clearly.

What made Mary Turner the woman she was? Not just one thing. Life with her drunken father, her embittered mother, and her solitude after the deaths of her elder brother and sister, but also the life of Southern Rhodesia itself, its contrasts: love of the land, yet anger at its domination of humans; the typical attitude of whites to Africans, which included a certain appreciation of them, and yet tyranny over them, the top-dog feeling: Mary Turner grew out of all these elements. In the city she was little troubled by the outside world and if she did not suffer from 'class' problems she was 'of course' afraid of the 'natives'. 'Every woman in South Africa is brought up to be. In childhood she had been forbidden to walk out alone, and when she had asked why, she had been told in the furtive, lowered, but matter-of-fact voice she associated with her mother, that they were nasty and might do horrible things to her.'

She was afraid not only of 'natives', she was afraid of sex and marriage. When she married Dick Turner she found that sex was 'not as bad as *that*. It meant nothing to her, nothing at all. Expecting outrage and imposition, she was relieved to find she felt nothing.' She had lived outside realism and realism included the whole business of being a woman. 'If she disliked native men, she loathed the women. She hated the exposed fleshiness of them. . . . Above all, she hated the way they suckled their babies, with their breasts hanging down for everyone to see. . . . The idea of a child's lips on her breasts made her feel quite sick. . . .'

She had not grown up. When she quarrelled with her husband she was speaking 'in a new voice for her. . . . It was taken direct from her mother, when she had had those scenes over money with her father. It was not the voice of Mary, the individual . . ., but the voice of the suffering female, who wanted to show her husband that she just would not be treated like that.' Her ungrown-up attitude was responsible for her strange and crucial relationship with the servant Moses: it was not overtly sexual: he was both the mother and father that the immature Mary still needed.

Does it seem melodramatic that she is killed by Moses, whom she had once struck with a whip? If so, this is a small price to pay for the suspense element of a story which points with such sureness of touch the complex problems of life in Southern Rhodesia – and points them through the presentation of a universal psychological problem and a doomed marriage. Nearly all her states of mind come back to the basic African problem. When she was angry 'She cleaned and polished tables and chairs and plates, as if she were scrubbing skin off a black face.'

In a first novel written by a woman through the life of a woman it would not have been surprising if the author had failed to present convincing male characters, a conspicuous weakness among women novelists. Yet Dick Turner is a character in the round, full of foibles, even if we know little of his background until nearly the end of the book, when we learn something of his hard childhood in Johannesburg and his attempts to study which were foiled through lack of funds.

He deserves as much sympathy as his neurotic wife, and how far he is from those empire builders who peopled an earlier generation of novels. As for Moses, the novelist does not attempt to present or analyze all that was going on in his brain; she probably could have gone further, but decided not to, leaving this gentle, understanding, primitive but not cruel man as a symbol of the strength and mystery of the African in all his variants. He was a 'Mission boy', he 'knew too much'. How much? That is the unknown quantity. In the nineteenth century Victor Hugo had hinted that the problems of Africa would dominate the century that followed – and perhaps he was right. Doris Lessing, as is now realized, did not in *The Grass is Singing* write a novel 'merely' about racial problems – for such a novel would have seemed too limited to a writer of vision and understanding such as she was from the start of her career; she was concerned with people. After the first highly successful publication in 1950 eleven years went by before a paperback edition appeared in Britain but between 1961 and 1974 there were three editions of it. So much of what she forecast, in a non-propagandist way, was coming true.

This novel was short by British publishing standards, still so depressingly rigid. There was not a wasted page in the book, as though the author had made a distillation of all she wanted to say.

This book however was only a prelude to over twenty years of continuous writing on themes which had little to do with entertainment yet still gripped any readers.

Lessing had a great deal to say, her message was too important to be simple, and she knew she was writing against time. If this impressive body of work could be awarded any one quality at the expense of others it would be that evoked by another overworked word: commitment. It has often been said of women that they find it easier than men do to 'dedicate' themselves to other people, to ideas or work but to 'commit' oneself implies possibly more of an intellectual, not only an emotional decision, as though religious connotations, with an element of subjection, still hung over any words linked with dedication. It is the commitment, uncompromising, and not merely one-track, throughout Doris Lessing's work which has so often frightened people, those who do not like facts, those who read reviews of books rather than books and those who assume that a 'committed' writer must be left-wing, if not 'Marxist', cannot be entertaining or have any sense of humour. Such totality of commitment is rare among writers in Britain, at least among novelists of the older generation, and one has to look to France to find writers as committed as Sartre and Simone de Beauvoir. It would in fact be possible to find some parallels between Lessing and de Beauvoir, who both wrote so passionately about the principles in which they believed and used autobiographical material to such effect both in and out of fiction. Lessing is less afraid of emotion in its raw state, less bigoted on the subject of women's emancipation because she does not deal with it as an isolated part of life – how could it be so? Neither is she much concerned with academic philosophical concepts in fiction and mercifully she has a sense of ironic humour, which even Simone de Beauvoir's more passionate devotees cannot find in any of her work.

Lessing, therefore, surely not aware herself at the age of thirty or so of the area of thought and writing she was going to traverse, embarked not on just another novel to follow *The Grass is Singing* but on a whole series of books, five in all, *The Children of Violence*. At the same time she worked on stories, some short, some longer, such as those published in *Five*, appearing in 1953, mostly about

Africa. If any reader needed to be convinced, the stories show yet
again that the author is no propagandist for black versus white, as
the conservative-minded have sometimes thought, she is, here at
least, an educationalist who presents her entire material as
thoroughly readable fiction peopled by characters whose problems
are not entirely due to living in Africa at any 'level'; their problems
are those of human beings affected by their geographical and social
environment which is a factor no one can escape, in or out of fiction.
And if this were not enough, she published *The Golden Notebook* in
1962 before the series was completed.

Before embarking on *The Children of Violence*, the saga of
Martha Quest, readers should try to find in themselves something
of the stamina evidenced by the author, for it would be pointless to
read only part of the series, although it is uneven and the heroine's
name alone seems far too obvious. Her life in Africa, her life in
London, her emotional, marital, psychological and political problems occupy the series of books and seventeen years passed between
the first and the last, *The Four-Gated City*, in 1969. Important
though these novels are to the author, who has literally put a good
deal of her life into them, they are not likely to be, as a series, the
books her future readers will value most. The solidly documented
experiences described in them seem either too ordinary or too
extraordinary. Readers who are principally interested in the
heroine's political life will find the science-fiction element towards
the end disconcerting and few of these readers have seemed ready to
take up the study of Sufism, as the author has done, in order to
understand more fully the end of the series and the later work
generally. It is a long way from the Communist Party and radical
views generally to a philosophical system – if that term can be
applied to this particular form of Moslem mysticism – concerned
mainly with spiritual ideals. The student of Sufism is not on the
whole likely to read solid fiction with severe messages about
underprivileged societies and individuals. But this series of five
novels is still an achievement hard to match in twentieth-century
fiction. Olivia Manning's Balkan Trilogy and Joyce Cary's political
trilogy published during the 1950s are the only major works written
in Britain which can be compared with it and neither of these

writers have left their emotions in their books. That, say their admirers, is why we value them so highly, we like their reticence: and nobody could say Doris Lessing was reticent.

We read her for her uncompromising courage and her refusal to accept any ready-made, secondhand idea. *The Four-Gated City* is the first of her later writing to show a distinct change of atmosphere. Readers who have read with devotion every book published so far begin to look puzzled here when she writes about extrasensory perception and related powers. What has happened to the lucid woman who was so concerned with reality in all its aspects? Has she experienced within herself that 'breakdown' which had begun to preoccupy her so deeply and how did she come to write *Briefing for a Descent into Hell* and *The Summer before the Dark*? The former is set within a loss of memory situation, the imaginary dream-like adventures of Professor Charles Watkins are described in a strong flowing prose unmatched in any other English writing today, but why did she spoil the whole thing by complaining of disagreements between psychiatrists? Surely one could never pretend that psychiatry, even the kind now described as old-fashioned, was an exact science. Neither could one accept the heroine's problems in *The Summer before the Dark* on the level of reality because on that level Kate Brown does not deal with them in a very intelligent way. Since it is hard for most of us to accept that a Lessing heroine is not intelligent, then we must assume she is operating in unreality.

It is all to do with breakdown, Doris Lessing's concern in all her most serious writing, and it varies from the behaviour of the two main protagonists in *The Grass is Singing* to the complex breakdown in *The Golden Notebook* and the Laing-influenced self-division in *Briefing for a Descent into Hell*. The change in the author's orientation then is not so basic as it might appear, it is in fact not a change but a development, and how could such a writer stand still? Nothing does stand still and the political situation in Africa for example has changed constantly since Doris Lessing began to write and even while this chapter was being written.

Concern with breakdown was very much in Doris Lessing's mind when she was gradually writing the long story of Martha Quest. Between volumes III and IV of *The Children of Violence* came the long complex work which is surely at the heart of her achievement, whether she likes it or not. *The Golden Notebook* published in 1962 was reprinted ten years later with a preface by the author of special importance to anyone wishing to see her as a true professional writer situating her own novel in the landscape of world literature. If the quintet of novels needs stamina in the reader *The Golden Notebook* needs even more of it, over 600 pages and planned in a way that might daunt the reader used only to 'straightforward' fiction, including even the previous work of Lessing herself. Although the book has become a classic eighteen years after its first appearance it is worth quoting the summary, if that is the word, given by the author in her 1972 Preface: 'The shape of this novel is as follows:

'There is a skeleton, or frame, called *Free Women*, which is a conventional short novel, about 60,000 words long, and which could stand by itself. But it is divided into five sections and separated by sections of the four Notebooks Black, Red, Yellow and Blue. The Notebooks are kept by Anna Wulf, a central character of *Free Women*. She keeps four, and not one because, as she recognizes, she has to separate things off from each other, out of fear of chaos, of formlessness – of breakdown. Pressures, inner and outer, and the Notebooks; a heavy black line is drawn across the page of one after another. But now that they are finished, from their fragments can come something new, *The Golden Notebook*.'

From these details of the plan it can be seen that the book is a piece of architecture, a long way from the straightforward plan of *The Grass is Singing*, which begins with a five-line newspaper report of the end of the story, 22 introductory pages and then back to the beginning. To say that *The Golden Notebook* is ambitious is an understatement, it is one of the most ambitious novels of the century. Among novels by women it makes even *Middlemarch* dwindle, as far as technique is concerned, and to read it is to undergo so much experience, to think so hard about so many interrelated topics, that it is no spare-time occupation. It is no rest-cure, and anyone who decides he or she prefers one notebook rather than another, or tries to pick their way through the novel which the 'heroine', Anna Wulf, is writing, is cheating. The punishment for cheating is immediate, for one loses the impact of the book as a whole, which is infinitely more subtle than might appear from its sheer size.

Of the myriad questions raised by the book, two come to the surface at once – is it a 'novel' and is it a success? To the first question the answer is yes, and it gives the form a new dimension. It is not a brand-new departure but it is a bold extension of a known architectural design only practised by experienced and confident writers. The novel-within-a-novel has been used by story-tellers from Boccaccio onwards but it would be hard to find any writer brave enough to fragment him – or herself – into four and yet retain the wholeness of the final and golden synthesis. It is an achievement for any writer and for the 'woman writer', that creature whom so many critics regard as worthy but not necessarily classifiable as 'writer', it is surely a milestone along the road to 'liberation'.

The author was angry, not to say disappointed and puzzled by a major failure of perception on behalf of the critics. 'But nobody as much as noticed this central theme, (i.e. breakdown) because the book was instantly belittled by friendly reviewers as well as hostile ones, as being about the sex war, or was claimed by women as a useful weapon in the sex war.' She then points out that obviously she would support the women's liberation movement for she believed, at least when she wrote the novel, that women were second-class citizens in any case, but that her book *anticipated* a state of affairs in the sex-war and took for granted the situation obtaining ten years ahead. Her book was in no way propaganda intended to lead to this situation.

Later in this absorbing preface, which deals with themes of major import, such as dry-as-dust academic principles in teaching, and a lack of international outlook in literary criticism, the author discusses individual response to the book, the letters she was still receiving after the first ten years of its life. She found it surprising that people would write to her about the sex-war, about politics or about mental illness, each writer preoccupied with only one theme, instead of the amalgam which made up the book different from all other books.

But this seems to prove two things: the book contained so much that many people could only respond to parts of it, they could not see the integration that the author saw. Perhaps one of Doris Lessing's failures is in evidence here: not all the readers of her books are so intelligent as she is, that is one of *their* human failings. It may be due to that old-fashioned concept of education which she so firmly condemns, or it may be that many would-be readers are not so intelligent as they think they are. And it is obvious that in reading through a large and complex book each reader will respond to what interests him or her personally.

Him or *her*. Did the author seriously believe that readers, especially women, would notice the 'breakdown' theme rather the women's liberation theme? She says herself that others had already written so cogently about women writers and their problems, both as women and as writers which, as in the case of women who happened to live in Africa, were inseparable from each other. But nobody had yet written enough.

Thinking about the book after reading it one remembers Anna Wulf and all her experiences, her marriages, her love-affairs in Africa, her political involvement, her successful novel and then the writer's block, her relationship with her son, her love affair with Saul Green – how then could one fail to think onward from her problems to those of a great many other women? After all, most people are aware of some kind of sexual life or orientation, or even the lack of it, within themselves – this is something they know and care about, while they may have no experience of political life in their own country or any other, they may have chosen to ignore it and refused any form of political education. Obviously they are wrong, but this is reality, especially in Britain.

The Golden Notebook is far from being a 'woman's book', i.e. obviously written by a woman essentially for women, but it is very much *about* a woman, and that is at least half the point. Can one imagine the book with a man as the central character? No, for a man would not be involved to the same degree in the complexities of changing social status. Even by 1981 there has not been as much 'role reversal' as might have been expected after a partially improved life became available to women. Change, breakdown, however we see it, the effect on women can only be greater than on men, for another generation or so at least. In her preface to the 1972 edition the author seems to accept the fact that the readers of her book see it differently from the way she did, but in how few cases do author and reader coincide? In a book of such complex construction the gap between their points of view can only be greater than in the case of most novels, and Lessing herself stated that she had learnt a great deal while writing the book. She added that she had learnt a great deal since she wrote it. Not every writer would admit this and I don't think she revealed bitterness when she said that it was now time to pass on to other things. But surely not 'time to throw the book aside, as having had its day, and start again on something new'. She can never forget that she wrote it, and whether she likes it or not it will probably be read, studied and remembered as the most important she produced. If readers still approach it as a book about the sex-war it is because the sex-war, in its wider aspects, is more far reaching than even the author realized.

To the second question, is it a success? the answer is more difficult. As far as sales go there is no doubt about the commercial results, with thousands of copies sold all over the world, and there was the delayed prestige success of the French Prix Médicis (for foreign literature) in 1976. As to critical success, this did not consist wholeheartedly of praise. She found that the theme at the core of the novel had not reached the regiment of reviewers. 'Throughout the Notebooks people have discussed, theorised, dogmatised, labelled, compartmented. . . . But they have also reflected each other, been aspects of each other, given birth to each other's thoughts and behaviour – *are* each other, form wholes. In the inner Golden Notebook, things have come together, the divisions have broken down, there is a formlessness with the end of fragmen-tation. . . . Anna and Saul Green the American "break down".' She then describes in some detail what this breakdown entails and how it is expressed. She points out that 'breakdown' is sometimes 'a way of self-healing, of the inner self's dismissing false dichotomies and divisions' and she does not believe she is the first or only person to write about it. She does believe however that this is the first time *she* wrote about it although she was to write about it again in later books. 'Here it is rougher, more close to experience, before experience has shaped itself into thought and pattern – more valuable perhaps because it is rawer material.'

It could be argued perhaps that if the author has to write such an important preface ten years after the novel itself, then this novel must have been in some ways inadequate. But that would be unfair, surely, for Doris Lessing has so much to say that she could never have limited herself to the 'average' type of novel throughout her career. The complexity of her message, here especially, needed a complex form in which to express itself. *The Golden Notebook* is larger than life, it could not be contained in a conventional literary form.

Altogether then this has been, and still is, one of the most important writing careers of the century, proving that fiction, long novels and short stories, can be a creative force in political and social life. If Doris Lessing did not write with style, colour and rhythm her books would have no literary value and therefore their 'message', complex as it is, would not have come through and reached so many readers. But thank goodness they are not 'literary', to use the word with some unfairness as though literature were necessarily precious, unrealistic and remote. The purely 'literary' novel can make pleasant reading if one is patient enough and could apply one's mind to, say, Sybille Bedford, but it has little relevance to a world approaching 1984, it was a natural product of the 1920s and 1930s and included for instance the earlier and lesser work of Virginia Woolf. The 'literary' novel can also make pleasant writing, as so many unpublished writers know, but decreasing sales show that it is not really needed by enough people, obviously because it is an unrealistic product of current society. Plenty of readers can maintain that they do not 'want' Doris Lessing, for they only read for entertainment and escape. Many people can close eyes and ears to news they do not like, whether it concerns Africa, Marxism, techniques of psychiatry, the sex war, the women's movement (to use convenient but unsatisfactory phrases). The same or other readers could complain that they cannot cope with so many long books, so many 'interior monologues', so many fantasies; they feel too they are being battered over the head and made to listen.

Perhaps Doris Lessing is pessimistic or merely realistic as she looks ahead and who, as the late twentieth century proceeds bumpily down a road so full of land mines, could ever think that was strange? As for the sex-war, integrated as it is with other wars, violence, tyranny and break-up, it is not surprising that one of the most meaningful contributions to the campaigns on all sides comes from a woman, for women, despite recent legislation in Western countries, have still a long haul in front of them before the phrase 'second-class citizen' can disappear from their own thoughts. The contribution had to come from a woman of international experience and outlook, for the average English-born, English-educated woman novelist is still far too coy and insular about the subject. A vital piece of terrain will have been won if a man like the male character in the now famous story *One off the Short List* (In *A Man and Two Women*) were to read it, read, mark and learn. He would learn that many women simply find work more interesting than sex without love, and when he considers the long-term implications of this state of affairs he will have a nasty shock. Women know the situation, they have gone ahead fast, and it is obvious that far too many men are merely standing still.

Doris Lessing never wasted a moment standing still. It was strangely reminiscent of Olive Schreiner that she arrived in Britain from Africa with an unpublished manuscript, and if *The Grass is Singing* could not be another *Story of an African Farm*, *The Golden Notebook*, in fact the whole body of this work, surely has classic status, and her forecasting has not yet come to an end.

7

Devolving (1)

꙾꙾꙾

When administrative devolution is mentioned in Britain people look bored and go away: in 1979 a referendum on Scottish devolution bored the Scots to death and led to the death of the Labour government. But in my prejudiced way I find nothing boring about that intense if unconscious expression of devolution: the regional novel. The category 'regional novel' is not neglected, in Britain at least, and the late Phyllis Bentley, among her many novels both 'regional' and general, wrote a useful introduction to the subject in 1941, although she limited herself to England, assuming this small, crowded territory offered novels enough which needed some explanation for the non-local and especially for the overseas reader.

Yet in its turn the label 'regional novel' may well frighten off whole categories of readers who feel it must be too restrictive to interest them – unless one knows the region concerned in detail, they think the 'atmosphere' will be meaningless, to say nothing of the way the characters talk. Readers from Cornwall, let alone from Los Angeles or Melbourne, may feel that the Shropshire of Mary Webb, the Cumbria of Constance Holme or the Yorkshire of Phyllis Bentley and Winifred Holtby are alien to them, especially since several decades have passed since these writers produced their best-remembered books. Scotland, Wales and Ireland, the latter including both Ulster and Eire, the average non-Celtic person thinks, are in any case different and foreign countries, where by some accident most natives at least speak a language related to English but all the same a language which is too often a joke. If not a joke it is accepted in a prepacked form and expected to be strange – either dour, melodramatic or merely fey.

In the early part of this century women who wanted to write could hardly help writing novels of local interest, because if they were not rich domesticity kept them at home. The Brontës after all had written about Yorkshire and London-born Elizabeth Gaskell in *North and South* was a regional novelist doubled (unconsciously) with a sociological novelist writing about the impact of the industrial revolution. Women had less chance of travelling than men, and women with money and time tended to prefer grand expeditions to Europe and even further, they were not much concerned with local life. But many of those who could not travel became so attached to the places where they lived that they travelled as it were more deeply into them simply by remaining there and absorbing their history in fact and legend until an attachment to local life became an absorbing passion. During the early part of this century a generation of women realized they were not limited to writing books set in London, a sophisticated capital city abroad, a spa or a country house. Women who had walked every day over their favourite fields or hills began to watch with passionate concern the gradual change in village or farm life, and they began to write about it, sometimes noting the changes, sometimes trying to convince themselves that they had not really happened. These women transformed the silence of their predecessors into an articulate and memorable group of voices.

Two of the regional novelists who concern the twentieth-century historian have such a particular appeal to me that I am the first to accuse myself of special pleading. I was born in Shropshire, the county inseparably identified with the novels of Mary Webb, and brought up in Cumbria, the setting for the group of novels written by Constance Holme and so successful that they were included by Oxford University Press in the World's Classics series during her lifetime.

The story of Mary Webb is not so much sad as ironically tragic, for very few people were on her side as woman or novelist until it was too late, and she herself was often her own worst enemy. Much of the story was of course known locally but Gladys Mary Coles' biographical study *The Flower of Light* (1978) revealed Mary Webb as a figure of much more than local interest. She was born Gladys

Mary Meredith in 1881, daughter of an Oxford-educated Protestant churchman and teacher of Welsh descent whose family had
been in Shropshire for three generations. Shropshire is one of the
English counties bordering on Wales, and until it was touched by
the tentacles of the industrial Midlands it remained longer than
many other areas agricultural, isolated and old-fashioned. The
villages and small towns of Shropshire, the open country with its
curious hills and rocks like the Wrekin and the Devil's Chair, were
so important to Mary Webb, as she became in 1912, that she
literally could not live away from them. Her husband, born in
Shropshire and Cambridge educated, soon took care to accept
teaching posts only in their native county.

Her early life sounds like a page from an only-too-familiar case-
history: the sort that produces writers, especially women writers: a
dour mother of Scottish origin who believed in discipline rather
than love, an intelligent understanding father and this daughter
who immersed herself in nature and soon began to write near-
mystical poetry. Her devotion to animals turned her into a
vegetarian, she soon became anaemic and also began to suffer from
Graves' disease, which eventually killed her. When she was 31 she
married Henry Bertram Law Webb, five years younger than herself,
who had nursed her when she was ill and showed no surprise at her
choice of wedding guests – seventy inmates from an old people's
home. Despite a brief exile in Somerset, where he was temporarily
working as a teacher, the couple knew several years of near-total
happiness devoted to poetry, philosophy and mysticism.

It was during the exile that Mary Webb began to write something
more sustained than poems and *The Golden Arrow* (1916), the first
of her six completed novels, grew out of homesickness for her native
county, memories of her dead father and an intensely emotional,
near-pantheistic love of nature. In the book is the equally intense
emotion of a woman whose love for her chosen man is total, proud
and yet forgiving. There is also the contrasted pair of women who
occur in most of Mary Webb's fiction, almost as though she were
identifying two sides of her own nature with two types of women
she had found in this 'lost' county: Deborah, who seems an
idealized figure belonging to an age even older than the late

Victorian period in which the book is set, and Lily, the kind of cynical sophisticate who appears in all English villages but nowadays at least soon makes plans to leave. The most memorable 'character' in this novel is the countryside itself and when the book was published by Constable in the dark days of 1916 this was noticed, along with the intensity which has so often marked writers of Celtic origin and is now regarded as 'hysterical', fit only for 'romance'. The novel was reviewed by a few journals but it was no seller. The same was true of *Gone to Earth* which came out the following year, for Mary Webb, who had not begun to write fiction until she was thirty-five, was now writing at frantic speed as though to make up for lost time.

Gone to Earth may well be the best of Mary Webb's novels because it is very much a Shropshire book and at the same time its theme has a universal relevance. It is ostensibly about the half-Welsh Hazel Woodus (her mother was a Welsh gypsy), a natural victim of society and especially of men, but its concern is deeper, its concern is for every victim of society, not only human victims but animals. Hazel dies while trying to save her beloved fox-cub from the hunt and if these last few pages of the book are melodramatic who is going to complain about that while so-called civilized people still find it exciting to attack animals with much noisy ceremony while riding about the countryside in expensive fancy-dress. This is no place to discuss the ethics and practicality of fox-hunting although, if foxes are pests, there are surely other ways of coping with them today. Mary Webb's protest in *Gone to Earth* is a sign that opinion was changing and after all a woman novelist is often the first person to start a revolution: Harriet Beecher Stowe and Radclyffe Hall are just two of the names that come to mind here. There is a good deal of unfairness in the current attitude towards Mary Webb, who is too often dismissed as a humourless writer of overwrought sentimental prose interested only in Shropshire folk-lore and just about as faded as the old sunbonnet she was so fond of.

Early in the First World War she and her husband attempted that way of life that became so popular in the 1960s and after, in Britain at least. He gave up teaching, they lived in a rented cottage nine miles or so from Shrewsbury, used the grand piano as a writing table (Henry's essays, *The Silences of the Moon*, had been published in 1911) and Mary Webb walked all the way to Shrewsbury where she sold flowers and vegetables in the market. She apparently did all this more for the avoidance of waste than for profit, of which there was very little. But she missed no detail of life in the market and recreated it in her novels.

The most famous of her novels was the last, *Precious Bane*, although some fragments of the uncompleted *Armour wherein he Trusted* were published later. *Precious Bane* has been published and studied all over the world and at the time of writing is probably less read by the literate in Britain than it ever has been, for many people may be keen on learning how to spin but they apparently do not want imaginative descriptions of a love-spinning and even less do they want to hear about sin-eating: most of them do not acknowledge the existence of sin. Mary Webb's sin, according to many critics, is her attempt to revive by artificial literary means the way that people thought and spoke (and wrote) in Old Shropshire:

> Mother winnocked a bit, to hear I was off to Plash, for she was low and melancholy from abiding under the shadow of death. She'd been so used to humouring a tempersome man that she felt as restless as you do when you've just cast off the second stocking-toe of a pair. She'd sit quiet a bit in the chimney corner, and you'd hear the wheel spinning softly, like a little lych-fowl. Then suddenly she'd give over spinning, and wring her hands, that always made me think of a mole's little hands, lifted up to God when it be trapped. . . .

The reader may get restless too, pretty quickly, but the secret is simple: the reader must be not merely someone whose eyes scan the page, he must be a listener, as with Scott or Hardy, for speech makes a person, whatever brand of language he or she utters. There is no perfect way of translating it on to paper and if Mary Webb had not had a good ear her attempt might have failed. As it is, the language of Prudence Sarn with its local words and special cadences – always the cadences of a woman's voice – makes her a living person and not a mere figure of fun.

Fun was something Mary Webb probably lost with her father's death and lost sight of totally as she continued to write but failed to sell, despite the Femina Vie Heureuse Prize for *Precious Bane* in 1924–5. According to her biographer she had a good sense of humour but from the novels we remember only ironic flashes, especially perhaps in *The House in Dormer Forest* (1920). The Webbs came to live in London, Mary missing Shropshire incessantly but aware that she needed more publishing contacts and the stimulus of meeting other writers. She found both, and for a time was a regular reviewer in *The Bookman* and *The Spectator*, but she did not find much happiness, even in her attractive Hampstead cottage. There was obviously a *farouche* quality about Mary Webb, acccentuated by her poor health and by what can only be described as a kind of mental illness, the desperate over-generosity of the insecure which led her to give away more than she earned to people who had nothing at all, or at least said they had not. Constable, Dent and Hutchinson had published her, *Precious Bane* went to Cape and it was the Cape directors whom she would pester in an undignified, embarrassing fashion for money she only used to give away.

Even the devoted Harry Webb became less devoted and fell in love with one of his students. It is hard to say who has the harder time, writers' wives or writers' husbands: I would say the latter, but fortunately the professionalism of women writers has increased so far that they are no longer financially dependent on anyone, while a temporary husband, lover or casual man is adequate if the writer decides she wants children, the only reason usually for relying on a male partner.

Until her mid-thirties Mary Webb needed nothing beyond Shropshire and its hills, woods and fields. When she had transmuted all this into books she wanted recognition and help as much as a child needs love, for she remained a child in many ways. So many women writers have had more publicity than their work deserved, but Mary Webb inspired nobody in the publishing world to do much for her. The books drained her, she was left with nothing to give except the extraneous things – hats or food or, at least once, a piano – that she bestowed on her 'poor'. She needed something in return, and an occasional book review was not enough. Rebecca West stated that she was 'a genius', while Edwin Pugh, the critic, whose name means very little now, continually praised her, once at a meeting of literati at which she was present.

One January day in 1927 however she received a letter from Stanley Baldwin, then British Prime Minister. It has often been quoted, but cannot be quoted too often: 'My people lived in Shropshire for centuries before they migrated to Worcestershire, and I spent my earliest years in Bewdley which is on the border. In your book I seem to hear again the speech and turns of phrase which surrounded me in the nursery. I think it is a really first-class piece of work and I have not enjoyed a book so much for years.' This was higher praise than she had ever hoped to hear, it was potentially the start of a new life for her, but it had come too late: ten months later she was dead.

The six completed novels were later published with illustrations by Rowland Hilder and the prefaces were written by Stanley Baldwin, John Buchan, G.K. Chesterton, Robert Lynd, H.R.L. Sheppard. This 'collected edition' is still collected, even if it is not rare, but intellectuals do not take Mary Webb seriously (mainly because they have not read her) and it has been assumed that if she died in 1927 she expired a second time when Stella Gibbons published *Cold Comfort Farm* in 1932. Like *Precious Bane*, it won the Femina Vie Heureuse prize. It has always been too easily assumed that this parody was aimed only at Mary Webb but Gladys Mary Coles has recorded Stella Gibbons' denial: the cold comfort was to be found in many authors, including Sheila Kaye-Smith and the Powys brothers. The situation now is that *Cold Comfort Farm* is a set book for English literature examinations in Britain and students have to work back to Mary Webb and the other writers to find out what it is all about.

Mary Webb's novels are crowded, overcrowded perhaps, with old legends from Shropshire and from over the border in Wales. Her life story is a legend which any writer of any sex or type would surely try to avoid, especially since it proves that in some unlucky cases anyone can make money out of a book except the author. She had died at 46 in 1927 but only a year later *Precious Bane* and the earlier books were selling so well that Henry Webb was able to retire into a gentlemanly literary life. He married the student with whom he had fallen in love and had two children. He died from a fall while climbing Scafell in Cumbria, his widow remarried. Her second husband was no less than Jonathan Cape himself and how wise he was to buy the Mary Webb copyrights from her. She died at 46, as Mary Webb herself had done. No sooner had the copyrights expired in 1978 than at least two cheap editions of the work appeared in Britain.

The modern reader obviously finds her books over-emotional, like those of some inspired amateur, and a female amateur too, but forgets that this emotionalism was one of the ways used by some writers of the early 1920s to approach a new outspokenness. Apart from D.H. Lawrence and a few others there was still a tight-lipped quality about so much of British writing, and *Lady Chatterley's Lover* was after all not written until 1928. Since the Second World War English-language novelists have been so preoccupied with the physical aspects of sexual relationships that they have not had time to write about the emotional side, the side which happened to interest Mary Webb. Outside fiction only Richard Jefferies had conveyed the kind of pantheism which she tried to express. It is irrelevant on the whole to compare her with Hardy, whose preoccupations were much more complex, but how flat and feeble are the books of Sheila Kaye-Smith in comparison. Mary Webb seems to have been born in order to express the spirit of Shropshire, for in some ways she was as old-fashioned as this county, so awkwardly placed between Wales and the industrial north and Midlands. Only someone of Celtic origin could have seen layers of surviving older worlds and realized how Shropshire and its people resisted any takeover bid from both Wales and England. They remained secret and separate, moving between the closed worlds of the cottage and the 'big house', looking out from small kitchen windows, as Hazel Woodus did, on to the brooding Shropshire landscape, watching its changing moods and changing with them through patterns of sun and shadow. Modern books on the history and topography of Shropshire have found they can no longer describe the county – they have to quote from Mary Webb. This is what Edmund Vale decided when he wrote about it in 1949 (The

County Book Series) and he chose to include her description of The Devil's Chair from *The Golden Arrow*:

'On the highest point in the bare, opposite ridge, now curtained in driving storm-cloud, towered in gigantic aloofness a mass of quartzite, blackened and hardened by uncountable ages. In the plain this pile of rock and the rise on which it stood above the rest of the hill-tops would have constituted a hill in itself. . . . Dawn quickened over it in pearl and emerald; summer sent the armies of heather to its very foot; snow rested there as doves nest in cliffs. It remained inviolable, taciturn, evil. It glowered darkly on the dawn; it came through the snow like jagged bones through flesh; before its hardness even the venturesome cranberries were discouraged. For miles around . . . it was feared. It drew the thunder, people said. Storms broke round it suddenly out of a clear sky; it seemed almost as if it created storm. No one cared to cross the range near it after dark – when the black grouse laughed sardonically and the cry of a passing curlew shivered like broken glass. The sheep that inhabited these hills would, so the shepherds said, cluster suddenly and stampede for no reason, if they had grazed too near it in the night. . . . It was understood that only when vacant could the throne be seen. Whenever rain or driving sleet or mist made a grey shechinah there people said, 'There's harm brewing.' 'He is in his chair.' Not that they talked of it much; they simply felt it, as sheep feel the coming of snow.'

Mary Webb did not speak Welsh fluently but in the west of Shropshire at least every native is aware of a different country not so many miles away and she of course introduced Welsh and half-Welsh characters into some of her novels. But she rarely used fiction to make direct comparisons between the English and Welsh nature, as a much younger border writer did in the 1930s and '40s.

'Margiad Evans' was in fact born Peggy Whistler in Middlesex in 1909. Her father was half Welsh, her mother had Irish, Scottish and Yorkshire ancestors. She came to Herefordshire as a young schoolgirl and soon realized that both the English and Welsh sides of this border county were her real home. She began to publish stories in the 1930s and would certainly have become and remained better known had the Second World War not interrupted British publishing generally and had she not died tragically in 1958, aged only 49. All her fiction, in which restless sexuality, a kind of pantheism and a lively country-style humour are oddly mixed, was partly autobiographical, while her *Autobiography*, originally published in 1943, and the first title to be republished (1978) in the current Margiad Evans revival, is non-factual. It is the story of how an imaginative, sensitive person acquires a creative spirituality in solitude, that particular solitude known only to a few people who are immersed in the life of nature yet not the nature-lovers of today, who merely take their sociability and their sandwiches out of crowded houses into the open air. If Richard Jefferies and *The Story of my Heart* are often invoked in connection with Mary Webb they are even more relevant in the case of Margiad Evans who had the rare gift of communicating extreme depth of feeling without the emotionalism which so many contemporary readers of Mary Webb find repellent. She could also express her own telling sense of humour in her fiction, notably perhaps in her short stories, a sense which Mary Webb possessed but could not introduce into her novels with the same cheerful ease.

Country Dance (1932) is a very short novel, illustrated with Margiad Evans' own watercolours, which could in fact be set and costume designs for a theatrical ballet. It was the first of her novels to be republished (1978) and was the same year made into a successful television drama. Ninety out of its ninety-three pages consist of 'Ann's Book', the journal kept by Ann Goodman, the daughter of an English shepherd and a Welsh mother, living on the Welsh border. She thought she would marry the Englishman Gabriel Ford, but her Welsh blood drew her inexorably to her father's master, Evan ap Evans, whom she thought she hated. Of those ninety or so pages few are without violence, some of it frightening, all of it due to the clash of Welsh and English tradition. Ann was going to marry the Welshman but she was strangely and horribly killed – probably by Gabriel, but Evans ap Evans could possibly have committed the crime himself. Margiad Evans was 23 when she wrote this, and the whole of borderland farming life is in the story, with no detailed descriptions, no lyricism as in the Mary Webb novels, a sentence here and there describes the changing seasons or domestic events, for this tale is told by a young woman who is naturally busy all day, milking, gardening, keeping an eye on other people's children, lighting the copper fire to do a fortnight's washing and doing what country people certainly used to do, to the dismay of today's nostalgic townswomen: 'Today we bake bread pies and tarts that we may go a week without cooking.' Out in the fields there is lambing, sheep scab, flooding, ruined hay. In the village there is both a church and a chapel, there is social life of a sort, a dance where Ann refuses to dance with the Welshman who loves her; there are fights, an accident with a scythe and of course a funeral, that of Ann's mother.

In the three unemotional pages of fact and comment which end the book after the violence recorded in the diary is all over, the author sums up the whole deeply emotional story which Ann, her father and her would-be lovers had lived out: '. . . there may be those who will discern the subtler underlying narrative that bound the days together, the record of a mind rather than of actions, a mind which though clear in itself was never conscious of the two nations at war within it. Here is represented the entire history of the Border, just as the living Ann must have represented it herself – that history which belongs to all border lands and tells of incessant warfare.

'Wales against England – and the victory goes to Wales; like Evan ap Evans, the awakened Celt cries: "Cymru am byth!" with every word she writes.'

No Welsh writer could have written this book, because they could not have known what it is like to be English. Such writing belongs truly to the border and as such appeals possibly to more readers than the strictly Welsh stories of, say, Kate Roberts, although they have wide and continuing success in the States. In 1940 H.E. Bates, introducing the *British Short Stories* of that year, noticed that one third of them were Welsh; possibly this was because the Welsh, like the Irish, are a nation of poets, and the short story is so often an extended poem because it can never escape the limitations of at least one aspect of form, namely, brevity.

Country Dance was followed a year later by *The Wooden Doctor*, an odd book which was successful because it was so different from the average novel published in the early Thirties. Yet many young women, especially in the English provinces, would find scope for self-identification, for it is about a girl who finds no affection at home, falls in love with the local doctor, who is not interested in making any response but means so much to her that she cannot take an interest in anyone else. She goes to Wales, writes a book. *The Wooden Doctor* itself is full of unhappiness and pain, including an extraordinary description of the pains of cystitis, which ought to be popular among the militant female sufferers of today, but the whole book ends with laconic acceptance of reality:

All this took place some time ago.
My book was published.
Oliver sends me red tulips on my birthday.
And the Irishman (the doctor) married a young girl a few months after my return.
And that's the end.

At this period Margiad Evans never stopped writing, *Turf or Stone* followed in 1934 and the extraordinary *Creed* in 1936. Its emotional depth is hard to describe – irresistible sexuality, violent reactions to orthodox Christianity and to what the central character comes to see as true Christianity; suicidal tendencies, alcoholism, mother-daughter hatred, death. The story and the treatment of it could surely only have happened in or near Wales, but its implications are anything but local. No author, woman or man, ever wrote a book like it. If new readers find it strange or old-fashioned then they should realize they have lapsed into a citified, armchair way of life and they had better get out of it before total desiccation sets in.

Apart from many short stories, all with their own brand of violence, humour and fantasy Margiad Evans completed no more fiction. Her last book, *Ray of Darkness*, published in 1952, knew enormous success even in the days when interest in illness and how to cope with it was less ghoulish than it is today, for it is another, more factual autobiography, telling how a woman in her early forties came to know she was an epileptic and realized, as she had done in *The Wooden Doctor*, that again she must come to terms with a situation whose end she knew. She died in 1958 of a tumour on the brain. Her poetry is yet to be rediscovered but her prose, some of the most individual writing of the 'Thirties and 'Forties is now fortunately alive again. Its vigour is such that it could not be forgotten for long.

Outside Cumbria in the north-west of Britain there are few people nowadays who know the work of Constance Holme well. Those who recognize the titles best, even if they have not read the novels themselves, are the people dealing in secondhand books, for there is a small but steady demand for these out-of-print titles. How few authors in their lifetime have seen eight books, consisting here of seven novels and one volume of stories, published in the neatly handsome dark blue format of the World's Classics? Sir Humphrey Milford, for a long time Publisher at the Oxford Press, found these books and their author very much to his liking.

Why did he choose the work of an undemonstrative woman from Cumbria for inclusion in the prestigious World's Classics list? Nothing she wrote about took place outside that small area between Milnthorpe (where she was born and where she died) and Morecambe Bay, where the rivers Kent and Leven join the Irish Sea. If my own home had not been in the same region for over twenty years I too would probably have never read these novels and wanted to share them with other people, those unlucky enough never to have been north or west of Arnside. The air has always been full of legends. The Holme family inherited their part of them for they shared the Viking inheritance so often found in the area and gradually became farmers and land agents. They also traded with Spain. Constance Holme's mother was a Cartmel (the name of a well known Priory and village). 'The Cartmels', wrote Alan L. Brown in *The Serif* (April 1964) 'had a tradition that a castaway from an Armada Galleon wrecked in the Bay, had been adopted into their family, giving it a recurring exotic element very different from the normal strain.' Spanish sheep were also said to have swum ashore and continued to live and breed on the local fells.

When we remember the old Welsh and Shropshire legends that

Mary Webb used in her novels it would be hard to find a greater contrast than Constance Holme's handling of the family legend in *The Old Road from Spain* (1916). It is the story of how Luis felt too close to Spain yet not close enough, and was finally drowned on the shores of Morecambe Bay where his Spanish ancestor had met the same fate several hundred years before. It also tells the strange story of the 'sheep-doom' which in her 1932 preface to the World's Classics edition the author described as 'my own fabrication, but to those who understand sheep it is not as far-fetched as it may seem. Sheep are queer creatures – lonely and fated and mysterious since the days of the Bible, which so often used them in its imagery. Strange tales are told of their amazing race-memory, going right back through the ages. . . . Their conservatism . . . amounts to a passion almost terrifying in its intensity.' Few readers today might decide to read a novel with such strange and apparently disparate elements, but there is an unhurried air about Constance Holme's books which manages to make the oddest events seem unsurprising and meaningful, local and yet universal.

Reading *The Trumpet in the Dust* (1921), about the problems and sufferings of a charlady, one suddenly realizes why Constance Holme's novels are not likely to have an easy, wide appeal now to the general reader: too many of her characters are old. There is in fact nothing young about Constance Holme's work. She herself was the youngest of fourteen children, she married at 35 and had no children of her own. But she wrote exceptionally well about old people, especially in those two short books which are included among her so-called 'Greek' novels, *Beautiful End* (1918) and *The Things which Belong* (1925). The 'Greek' quality came from a passionate devotion to the unities: the day in the former novel when an old man decides to leave a nagging daughter in law for a kind one, but finds himself compelled to go back to the nagging without even spending a single night in the house (once his own) where his room had been so carefully prepared. In the second of these two novels an elderly gardener thinks he will retire and go to Canada: but within twenty-four hours he and his wife have decided to make no change in their life. They will stay where they are.

It is no good looking to this author for highly wrought

descriptions of any favourite fells or tarns in Cumbria, which now of course incorporates the old Westmorland and North Lancashire. She is as reticent as Mary Webb was lyrical. In *The Old Road from Spain* there is a three-line description of market-day in the small town of Witham: 'The old town was full of farmers and their wives and dogs, 'quality' gossiping and shopping, and makers of other men's welfare hurrying to their wordy council-halls.' Nothing could be further from the Lullingford market-day in *Precious Bane*. Reticence was Constance Holme's personal manner in fiction and it is the manner of most Cumbrian people, despite their passion for wrestling and beagling. She allows herself a line of colour here and there: 'stripped woods against an opal sky, deer moving through the hollows of a park, some silhouette upon an edge of hill' – but action, when it happens, such as the flood disaster in *The Splendid Fairing*, seems inevitable and is always described with great control.

Constance Holme never produced any 'yokel colour', to borrow the useful term invented by Elizabeth Drew in *The Modern Novel* (1926), all her dialogue is comprehensible even if it is the talk of farmers, gardeners and country people generally. Sir Humphrey Milford was perhaps wiser than he knew to include this author in the World's Classics, her work *is* classical, and the small scale of it is deceptive. The voices and the background are Cumbrian, the deeper inference applies to the whole of humanity. As the daughter and wife of land-agents Constance Holme wrote about land, property and families, but fortunately not from a financial point of view; she wrote no line or word that was not essential and described no mood or emotion unless it were essential too.

She admitted to a phase when she was influenced by Tagore but knew she must cling to her 'down-to-earth' style. She observed her characters from the middle distance and liked to keep the editorial staff of the Oxford University Press at the same distance too, as her letters to them show. Only Sir Humphrey Milford could do no wrong and after his retirement she made it clear that she had been accustomed to corresponding with the Publisher and did not wish to receive letters from more than one person at the Press. In life she no doubt encountered autocratic behaviour among the 'quality' and their land agents, but in her books this attitude is translated into respect for private opinions and decisions, especially among older people. There is compassion, but no tears fell on the manuscript, of that one can be sure. Constance Holme is the least emotional of novelists writing about country life in the corners of Britain. Painters know how difficult it is to paint mountains, Furness fells are not so daunting, and this is why Constance Holme's books will be the things-that-belong for the north-west corner of England. Hugh Walpole, in his 1939 Foreword to *The Herries Chronicle*, had to admit he was a foreigner, although he felt the people of Cumberland and Westmorland had accepted him. How totally foreign he remained can only be judged when one has read or re-read the handful of novels written by Constance Holme between 1913 and 1925.

Constance Holme belonged to the north-west, one of the few women writers associated with the area. Dorothy Wordsworth wrote refreshingly well about the countryside but was even less interested in story-telling than her brother. Mrs Gaskell wrote about industrial change in south Lancashire, Frances Hodgson Burnett was born in Manchester and much later Beryl Bainbridge was to write about Liverpool. But in the meantime some of the most impressive writers from the north of England came from Yorkshire, which is to the east. When Vera Brittain began to write *Testament of Friendship*, about her friend Winifred Holtby, she may not have realized that when she mentioned Yorkshire writers, and only those of her own generation, she named only one man:

'A hundred years hence, literary tourists will find in Yorkshire the opportunity for many pious pilgrimages to places hallowed by association with celebrated writers of this generation.

'Perhaps they will visit first the stocky pugnacious statue of J.B. Priestley, which may then stand before the Alhambra Theatre in Bradford, where the dramatised version of *The Good Companions* celebrated its first night, and Phyllis Bentley, eagerly arriving too soon, waited on the steps for twenty minutes in the bitter wind. From Bradford, the metropolis of the West Riding, it is only a short journey to Halifax and the old-fashioned villa where Phyllis Bentley herself lived with her mother, screened from intruders by a tree-darkened by-road. Crossing the county diagonally to the North

Riding with its wild forbidding cliffs, the pilgrims of the twenty-first century will certainly explore the little sea-coast house where Storm Jameson was born at Whitby. And then, because of Winifred Holtby – younger than the others, yet dead before them – they will turn southward to the wold village of Rudston, in the East Riding.'

Phyllis Bentley was born in 1894, the same year as Priestley. Her novels and longer sagas knew great success over the years and she has been continually respected. She wrote with total understanding of life in Yorkshire, especially family life, for her own was bound up with the traditional Yorkshire industry of cloth weaving, the occupation of her Halifax forbears. Her work has the same traditional Yorkshire quality and if you like good tweed you would probably have enjoyed her novels a generation ago. At the moment, when solid virtue is out of fashion and family life has cracked, I cannot see that most of the novels could appeal to young people, but her work is an excellent example of how one woman, through her detailed local knowledge and patient study of technique can express the life of important social groups in a big geographical area. Her work proves one thing that ought to be obvious but is still easily forgotten: a good regional novelist, like a good historical novelist, must be a good novelist *tout court*, and not let the local landscape, whether town or country, physical or social, predominate, or their work will remain local. If the landscape is the mere word-equivalent of a photograph, it will have no value as part of the novel and the said novel will inevitably remain local.

Phyllis Bentley could move out of Yorkshire and write a historical novel about Julius Caesar, *Freedom, Farewell!* (1936), reflecting the rise of Nazi Germany, but essentially of course she was preoccupied with the rise and fall of industrialism. Her sagas were well planned and readable to the addict, but her work in general lacks that spark which gave brilliance to another Yorkshire writer who never forgot her county yet travelled so far in more ways than one. Winifred Holtby, a farmer's daughter, was born in 1898 and interrupted her degree course at Oxford to do active war work in 1918. Most of her story has been told by her close friend Vera Brittain in *Testament of Friendship* and forty years later both feminists and non-feminists should know more about her. It was she who wrote, in the early 1920s, in a *Yorkshire Post* article: 'I am a feminist because I dislike everything that feminism implies. I desire an end of the whole business, the demands for equality, the suggestion of sex warfare, the very name of feminist. I want to be about the work in which my real interests lie, the study of inter-race relationships, the writing of novels and so forth. But while the inequality exists, while injustice is done and opportunity denied to the great majority of women, I shall have to be a feminist with the motto Equality First.' Her attitude was not militant, but essentially reasonable. She wanted 'a society in which sex-differentiation concerns those things alone which by the physical laws of nature it must govern, a society in which men and women work together for the good of all mankind, a society in which there is no respect of persons, either male or female, but a supreme regard for the importance of the human being.' She saw her feminism as a temporary necessity only. 'And when that dream is a reality they will say farewell to feminism, as to a disbanded but victorious army, with honour for its heroes, gratitude for its sacrifice, and profound relief that the hour for its necessity has passed.' Her attitude was a long way from the militancy that exploded in the United States in the 1960s and spread patchily to Britain.

The Yorkshire where she was brought up gave Winifred Holtby an invincible feeling of security and she never wavered in her attempts to publicize and even solve the problems that concerned her most. Her first attempts to do so in fiction were not successful and no one would call *The Crowded Street* (1924) a well-written or persuasive novel. Its principal theme – the difficulties of a middle-class girl in the West Riding of Yorkshire in finding a huband – would have been much more convincingly handled by May Sinclair, and the heroine is not interesting enough to hold our attention. However the setting, especially when the First World War came, 'right in the middle of the tennis tournament', may fill in some historical details for younger readers.

Winifred Holtby had such energetic brilliance in her socio-orientated journalism that it is almost touching to see how she struggled to become a novelist. Ever since the posthumous *South Riding* became a bestseller after 1936 all Winifred Holtby's work has acquired, and still possesses, a strong historical interest. The militant feminists will find her practical moderate attitudes unexciting but those who are as moderate as she was will find it worthwhile to read the book on *Women and a Changing Civilization* which she was commissioned to write in 1934. She would have been delighted to see how much progress has been made by 1980.

It was Winifred Holtby's visit to South Africa in 1926 which had deepened her vision and automatically broadened the range of her writing. The novel which grew out of this trip, *Mandoa! Mandoa!* (1933) did not have the attention it deserved (although it sold well), because its publication came too close to that of Evelyn Waugh's *Black Mischief*, also about an African state.

It was in Africa that Winifred Holtby noticed something below the surface of life that nobody had meant her to notice. It did not take her long, between lectures and social occasions, to see the three superficial worlds of South African society – the cultured upper crust, the leisured women, the business men and then what she called the Fourth City, the twilit, segregated city of the useful but difficult 'natives' whom, the denizens of the other worlds believed, it was dangerous to educate.

This discovery, and the platitudes uttered by the average whites she met, meant a great deal to her, as Vera Brittain has recounted: 'Sometimes, as Winifred meditated on these statements, they seemed to have a familiar ring. Suddenly, one day in Pretoria, she realised why. In her mind she began to substitute the noun "women" for the noun "natives", and found that these fiercely held, passionately declared sentiments of white South Africa coincided almost word for word with the old arguments in England against women's enfranchisement, women's higher education, and women's entry into skilled employment.' The parallel was extraordinary. 'She even perceived – as Olive Schreiner had perceived before her – a close relationship between the two forms of subjection, for she knew that every year since 1907 the Union Parliament of South Africa had considered and rejected a bill for the enfranchisement of women, though it was lost by one vote only in 1923.'

This perception of second-class citizenry was an early mention of something that British, American and French women began to notice as the decades passed after the Second World War. Superficially they had achieved more freedom but for years, until the appropriate legislation was passed, every woman taking a job knew she would be paid less than the man at the next desk or the next machine. In South Africa Winifred Holtby had seen women acting as good hostesses, some doing a little social work, but not too much, she had met two successful writers, Sarah Gertrude Millin and Ethelreda Lewis, but she had not seen much active crusading by anyone on behalf of the submerged fourth African world. In London later, working hard in journalism, and becoming a director of Lady Rhondda's weekly magazine, *Time and Tide*, she kept in touch with such kindred spirits as she had met and never forgot what she had observed in the South African cities and in society generally.

In the early 1930s Winifred Holtby was intermittently very ill with what was then described as Bright's disease. Nowadays we would call it chronic nephritis and there is no miracle cure for it. She had had an idea for a novel, and wrote to Phyllis Bentley that it had come to her unexpectedly 'after a rather depressing evening spent with my-young-man-who-never-will-be-more-than-my-young-man.' This was the man she had known all her life and if neither gave the other up neither seemed able to take the relationship further. Slowly she began to write the book, interrupted by her own illness, by family problems, journalism and the many demands people made on her, for her reputation was growing. She reluctantly accepted the fact that writing this novel would be a race against death; she won, but only just, leaving a completed but un-edited manuscript. She put her whole being into *South Riding*, the title being her own invention, since Yorkshire has (or had) only a North, East and West Riding, or 'third'. Her fiction technique was greatly improved now, and her experience of journalism had taught her how to speak out against any form of oppression and suffering. She had never lost her Yorkshire practicality or her interest in women or her sense of humour.

But the externals of the book do not make it look an 'easy read': 589 pages, eight 'books' each named after a department of County

Council administration, and a five-page character list, which
includes real people such as the 'broadcast entertainers' Elsie and
Doris Waters; Ellen Wilkinson, Socialist MP; and Commander
Stephen King-Hall as a broadcaster for the Silver Jubilee celebrations of 1935. The stories and the imaginary people in these 'books'
are interlocked, they may sometimes be over-simplified, leading the
novel towards the fatal description 'best seller', but if you feel
strongly that all families deserve a house and not just an old railway
carriage, that even daughters of poor families deserve the chance of
a good education and decide to put all this and much more into a
novel, then you do not think of Virginia Woolf as a model, you are
more likely to remember pamphleteers, journalists and classical
novels written by, say, Dickens, Mrs Gaskell and even Charlotte
Brontë, for surely Councillor Robert Carne's mentally ill wife
contains a reminiscence of Mrs Rochester. Unlike Phyllis Bentley,
Winifred Holtby seems to prefer a heroine as her central character,
and although one feels vaguely sorry for Carne it is Sarah Burton,
the unorthodox headmistress, who keeps the story together.

The range of the book superficially is local, but its implications,
which are never stressed, very far-reaching. It is less concerned
with the industrial scene than the work of Phyllis Bentley and if
Winifred Holtby had in one way returned home one can sense that
she had seen too much of London and travelled too far in other ways
to consider herself now as having returned for good. Still, she was
concerned with the intermingling of town and country life, life in
large houses and small pubs. Admirers of Charles Edward Booth,
that underrated novelist of the East Riding, may find Winifred
Holtby ladylike and middle-class, but it is impossible to compare
these two writers here. There will never be much mention of
Winifred Holtby the novelist in critical histories of English
literature because she did not let intellectual concepts dominate her
writing. She was most closely concerned with the practical issues
round which she had constructed her story. But so many of the
problems it poses are still unsolved and that is why so many women
writers find themselves today prolonging Winifred Holtby's
reluctant but inevitable feminism.

Looking now suddenly southwards one thinks of Barsetshire and Wessex and realizes that no writer of the twentieth century can rival Trollope or Hardy in the regions they have established as their own, even if Angela Thirkell was able to take over the ready-made Barsetshire. One writer who obviously learnt from Hardy and sometimes stayed too close to him without contributing enough of her own was of course Sheila Kaye-Smith. Born in Hastings, Sussex, in 1887, she published her first novel in 1908 and continued to write for another forty years or so. The titles of some are very well known, especially perhaps *Sussex Gorse*, *Green Apple Harvest*, *Joanna Godden*, and addicts enjoy the Sussex edition, with of course a Sussex map across the end-papers, leather binding and a signature in gold. Despite this fine dress these novels today seem disappointingly pedestrian, with the ghost of Hardy so often leaning over the farmyard gate. Joanna Godden, who took over her father's farm, inevitably recalls Bathsheba Everdene in *Far from the Madding Crowd* while Moneypenny in *Tamarisk Town* makes us think somehow of the Mayor of Casterbridge. The characters and the events are either ordinary or melodramatic but it is only fair to list the compensations – 'Tamarisk Town' is Hastings-St Leonards, and the Romney Marsh area is well and unsentimentally described in *Joanna Godden* and other books. Perhaps the first novel, published when the author was only nineteen, is the most interesting today. This is *The Tramping Methodist* (1908) which is an historical and a geographical novel in one. The narrator is less intriguing for his crises of faith than for the places he tramps through. Readers from East Sussex and West Kent will forgive practically anything as the hero goes through every village they know, especially their own. They will even forgive, for the sake of local topography, the sentimental conversation on the next to the last page:

'"But how will you know when we are in Sussex? We are nowhere near the Rother."

"But the Kent Ditch, dear. We shall cross the Kent Ditch – and then I shall kiss you." '

A novel like *Sussex Gorse* was surely one of those in Stella Gibbons' mind when she wrote *Cold Comfort Farm* and I wonder if this author, in search of yet more material, in addition to the only too vulnerable Mary Webb and T.F. Powys, ever looked at *Wrastalls* (1918) or any other of the Cornish novels by Mrs Dawson-Scott, remembered mostly now for her foundation of the P.E.N. Club in 1921. One look at one page could be enough to find more than anyone could need of that 'yokel colour' so cheerfully described by Elizabeth Drew. Yet she found Sheila Kaye-Smith a 'virile' writer, an epithet intended to be a compliment. Perhaps this is the quality which makes her more readable than the mass of second-rate women novelists writing about country life but if her name is something of a household word in the south-east of England there seems no depth in her work and nothing to admire beyond her devastating industry.

So much then for a few novelists – or at least those of them who are remembered without too much effort today – who wrote about a particular locality in England. But what about Scotland, readers will ask hastily, and Ireland including both Ulster and Eire? The written language at least, excluding Gaelic and Irish, is more easily understandable than the spoken variety.

Three older women writers with a Scottish background deserve special mention, even if they have not produced a whole row of books about the country. Surely no one could resist the appeal of Catherine Carswell's book *Open the Door*! which in 1920 won a prize offered by a Glasgow newspaper for a first novel. It is clearly autobiographical; it is also universal – how to escape from one's family, however much one loves them, how to escape from the stifling existence of a provincial town, Glasgow in the author's case. Catherine Carswell was already 50 when the novel was published, but there is a total freshness about it, an atmosphere that comes from a clear-eyed look at life and an ability to write about personal experience, a woman's insistence on following a career of her own and living with the man she loves without marrying him. There is a positive, optimistic quality about this book that makes it a pleasure to read. I imagine that any woman born in the English provinces, and more particularly in the north, before 1945, will identify very closely with Catherine Carswell's heroine.

Outside this novel the author is remembered most for her long championship of D.H. Lawrence when he was a far from popular figure. Her biography *The Savage Pilgrimage*, published in 1932, deserves to be reprinted as much as the novel.

Over the centuries Scotland has produced some fine women poets, and the nineteenth century gave us the entertaining Susan Ferrier and the hardworking Mrs Margaret Oliphant. The latter, who died in 1897, wrote novels in order that she and her children could survive, using all her memories of her home country which unfortunately she left when very young. The social climate has still not yet helped many women to be articulate as writers of fiction in the twentieth century and still identify with Scotland. Dame Rebecca West, born Cicely Isabel Fairfield in Eire, was at school in Edinburgh but no one would attempt to link her work with any one place, although London predominates in her fiction, with Paris a close second.

The Scots are infinitely less talkative than the Welsh or the Irish – it is as though Sir Walter Scott covered so many pages that no one, man or woman, has since felt equal to the challenge as far as fiction is concerned. During the clearances thousands of Scots were forced out of their own country and nowadays many of them are pleased to be out of it by choice, provided they can go back briefly from time to time. One younger writer from Scotland, Elspeth Davie, deserves special mention, particularly for her short stories. She and her still younger colleagues have proved that they have escaped from the stifling atmosphere caused by the gloomy heritage of the Presbyterian church and decades of poverty and unemployment. Someone who nearly did not escape was Ishbel, heroine of *The Upas Tree*, which the Scottish-born Eva Hanagan published in 1979. This brilliant novel 'fixes' the attitudes of the last two or three generations in Scotland for ever.

The Irish writers on the other hand seem always to be part of it, and they sound, in contrast to the Scots, perpetually over-articulate and never stop talking. Amongst the Irish writers of the twentieth century there are now more and more women, who seem to survive in a specially Irish way the terrible guilt they at least pretend to feel on avoiding surplus children. The influential writers of earlier times belonged of course to the ascendancy and were not troubled by these problems. Maria Edgeworth was envied by Scott while Somerville and Ross created some of the funniest writing ever produced by women: if they were in fact women, but that problem does not concern us here. Lady Gregory wrote no prose fiction: Elizabeth Bowen may have come from Ireland but her work would hardly have developed without her life in London. Kate O'Brien wrote many excellent historical novels, achieving a high standard of professionalism and avoiding the main faults of the genre. One of her successors among the Eire-born, Edna O'Brien, made a good start with *The Country Girls* in 1960 and surely no one could fail to find it funny, but after a few more titles what a falling-off was there. It is no good being a quarter Irish or so if you want to appreciate this kind of writing, I imagine you have to be totally Irish or else a total non-Irish foreigner. Otherwise it does not seem any more credible or stimulating than the usual contributions to women's magazines, although these latter have amended their rules slightly to fit in with the so-called permissive society.

There are many other excellent Irish women novelists, Jennifer Johnston for example, and they deserve to be better known in Britain at least. Mary Lavin, although born in the United States (in 1912) is a first-class writer of short stories and *The House in Clewe Street* is a classic of Irish life but much more than a 'local' novel. And surely the most exciting and controversial of all Irish novelists – she still regards herself as one – is Iris Murdoch. She seems to me such a rich and rewarding writer that I have tried to write something about her in the last chapter of this book. Only Ireland, it seems to me, could have produced such a person.

The British Isles are so small, so industrialized and so heavily populated that the survival of regional novelists today, apart from the obvious romantics, might have seemed unlikely. And yet, against a background of would-be or reluctant nationalism never was local history more closely studied, local radio more talkative. The old-fashioned regional novel belonged mainly to the countryside, whereas now it has moved into the towns. The British women novelists of today cannot be identified with a vast country area, as Eudora Welty and Flannery O'Connor have been identified with the South in the United States, there can never be another Mary Webb, and readers must be content with Mary Lavin's Castlerampart or Beryl Bainbridge's Liverpool. Some kind of regional novel will survive, because after all, life is local, even in a pedestrian precinct, but only if the local is somehow the universal, as with the few novelists I have mentioned here. The picturesque is not much use in the novel today, the human landscape is what matters, and high-rise flats are seen more often by more people than is the Devil's Chair. I hope all the same that the 'regional novels' I have mentioned will remain as something more than part of the nostalgia cult.

8

Devolving (2)

The novelists of Australia, New Zealand, Canada, South Africa and the West Indies are by extension regional novelists also and like those of England itself they have the special value of a local appeal doubled by a universal one. The appeal remains local only if the author wants it that way and prefers not to cross into the next valley. The novelists of the truly devolved Commonwealth, women no less than men, are making a more than worthwhile contribution to English fiction at present, and it is ironic to think that Doris Lessing wrote so cogently about the former Rhodesia that she was once forbidden to return there.

For most modern historians the first twentieth-century woman writer from Australia was Henry Handel Richardson, who was born there, in Melbourne, in 1870 and given the names of Ethel Florence. To the confusion of the historians she left the country when quite young to study music in Germany. But without her years at school there, and without her father's career there as a doctor – a sad career, for despite his brilliance he suffered a mental decline – she would never have written *The Fortunes of Richard Mahoney*. It consists of three novels, published between 1917 and 1929, and is surprisingly readable. It has a clear Australian flavour, it gives the feel of the landscape, the way people lived, the sound of the language in an effortless way. But it is a waste of time trying to read it in a hurry. One can only assume that the tempo of life in Australia was like this and it has been said more than once that Henry Handel Richardson was the precursor of Patrick White, the novelist whose name symbolizes Australian writing today. A sentence quoted at random from the start of *Australia Felix*, the first of the *Mahoney* trilogy, seems reminiscent now of Sidney

Nolan too: 'Here went no one but himself. He and the mare were the sole living creatures in what, for its stillness, might have been a painted landscape. Not a breath of air stirred the weeping grey-green foliage of the gums; nor was there any bird-life to rustle the leaves, or peck, or chirrup. Did he draw rein, the silence was so intense that he could almost hear it.'

There are many new women writers in Australia today, including notably Susannah Pritchard and most library readers at least will know the name of Ruth Park, whose first novel *The Harp in the South* won a newspaper prize in 1948. It is full of Irish immigrants, tears and suffering and grit, a novel of poor people in Sydney which may be a kind of reportage with something of Edna O'Brien about it, but again it gives the flavour of a particular way of life. The author has gone on writing with success and is now published in Britain.

Anyone who wants to know what younger women novelists have made of Australia today must read Helen Hodgman, an English-born much travelled member of that extraordinary group published by Duckworth in Britain. To be a member, as I have indicated elsewhere, you should preferably be female and write short realistic novels which are easy to read, diverting on the surface and reflective of social problems in a non-didactic way; some of the problems have already been explored, some not, and none can be forgotten after a Duckworth novelist has written about them with her corrosive ink. Even Auberon Waugh learnt something: he read *Blue Skies* by Helen Hodgman (1977, set in Tasmania) and had what he called his 'first real glimpse of the mind-boggling horror involved in being a housewife'.

Henry Handel Richardson may be for the historians of Australian writing but Helen Hodgman is for now. How pale seem the feeble housewives of Margaret Drabble in comparison, and I cannot think of any contemporary English novel in the same context as *Jack and Jill*, winner of a Somerset Maugham award in 1979, the year after its publication. Horrible, from page 7, the start, to page 111, the finish, this is the story of Jill, the Australian country girl whose mother died when she was five, who survived her father's upbringing and eventually married Jack, the man who came to help him around the small-holding farm. But she did not marry him until he had been crippled in the Second World War and she had become a successful writer for children by writing about a fantasy-child she would never have. But Jack had the child, with Raelene, a drop-out girl who dropped in, Jill delivered it and at the end, with Raelene on her grateful way to San Francisco, she is all set to love her husband and bring up this useful if accidental child. The book has that terse 1979 flavour plus a sardonic gritty note that must be Australian, without any obvious attempt at down-under 'yokel colour'. It deals with a very small group of people and the non-Australian reader is not distracted by attempts to describe Australia through any type of wide-screen technique.

The most important Australian-born writer of the century is probably Christina Stead, but she belongs to another group of novelists: those who had to make a second appearance, due to complicated circumstances, before they were fully appreciated. This group is dealt with in Chapter 10.

Apart from Katherine Mansfield, who is discussed briefly in Chapter 1, New Zealand has produced two unusually interesting women writers, Sylvia Ashton-Warner and Janet Frame. The former published her autobiographical novel *Spinster* in 1958 and re-used her experience in the non-fiction *Teacher* five years later. No other writer perhaps has used pioneering educational work (among Maori children in this case) to such effect in fiction. There have been many thousand spinster teachers in the world and their image has been the reverse of glamorous. After *Spinster* and the film which followed, the teacher-figure came into her own and if Sylvia Ashton-Warner has so far published only one novel it is an unforgettable one, teeming with impossible schoolroom situations that the heroine actually enjoys, and how positive, how unquenchable she is: 'The thing about teaching is that while you are doing it no yesterday has a chance.' She discovers and communicates more about teaching than any training college lecturer ever dreamt of: 'They ask ten thousand questions in the morning and eleven thousand in the afternoon. . . . And the more I withdraw as a teacher and sit and talk as a person, the more I join in with the stream of their energy, the direction of their inclinations,

the rhythms of their emotions, and the forces of their communi-
cations, the more I feel my thinking travelling towards this; this
something that is the answer to it all; this . . . *key*.'

Her later compatriot is Janet Frame, who was born near Dunedin
in 1924. Apart from some short stories, her first novel, *Faces in the
Water* (1962) was written during hospital treatment for a mental
breakdown and made all the stranger because she herself had
worked as a nurse for some time, after a university education.

She came to Britain and found a cooperative publisher (W.H.
Allen) who installed her in an apartment and thereby encouraged
her to go on writing. Ten or so novels to date proved the investment
worthwhile. It is no good expecting the novels to be straightforward, they are not, and the strange aura of death that surrounds, for
example, *Daughter Buffalo* (1973), set in the United States, is not
for the squeamish. The early novels are set in New Zealand but in
the case of Janet Frame it could be said that New Zealand is an
accident: she and her novels could have happened anywhere, she is
an example of what is meant by the alienation of the individual, but
an example which demonstrates how the individual can break out of
the casebook and through the release of writing escape from that
particular illness. Whether the writer is cured is another matter – it
would be wiser to say that she/he is comforted, the writing is the
life, a heightened, sometimes terrifying form of life, but not the
twilit existence of mental illness or neurasthenia.

Four hundred and fifty paperback pages described as 'rich,
powerful, fascinating – the novel of an independent woman and her
urgent need for love.' This is *The Diviners* by Margaret Laurence,
her fourth novel, 'the no. 1 Canadian Best-seller', as Bantam Books
took care to add in 1975, a year after the book had been first
published by Knopf in the United States. It sounds daunting to the
English reader, whose horizons are so miserably narrow, and in any
case the blurb could convince us that we have read it all before: 'For
Morag Gunn, growing up in a small Canadian prairie town is a
toughening process – putting distance between herself and a world
that wanted no part of her. But in time the aloneness that had once
been forced upon her becomes a precious right – relinquished only

in her overwhelming need for love. Again and again, Morag tests her strength against the world, learning to live and love exactly the way she wants to.' A small girl, living in a Manitoba small town, loses both parents (polio), is brought up by a childless couple who like her own family can never forget their distant Celtic origins and the Highland clearances which sent them to Canada. Morag meets Jules Tonnerre, half Indian, half French Canadian, who lives on his wits and fascinates women.

The intelligent heroine makes so good that she marries a Professor of English, he refuses to have a child, she writes a novel. She meets Tonnerre again, leaves her husband, has her much-wanted child with Tonnerre, who vanishes at once, and then she becomes a successful novelist. Her daughter is her pride, joy and worry. The father re-appears briefly, dies of cancer of the throat, the daughter drifts away from home and her mother, and the novel-writing Morag is essentially alone. The novel-writing Margaret Laurence obviously has remarkable stamina, the book would have been better if shorter and the would-be interesting technical devices, such as 'Memorybank movies' are not interesting at all. The various themes are plaited together into a design that is well-planned but thank goodness not over-neat. Canadian writers understandably have been preoccupied in the past with Canadian themes to such an extent that a good deal of their best, most deeply felt work could not easily reach a world-wide public, even if the themes in question – especially the relationship between the French- and English-speaking provinces – were not without parallels somewhere outside North America. Jules Tonnerre and his daughter Pique are especially interesting because obviously they are figures in a Canadian landscape but could be translated to other countries with problems of minority and mixed races – and in fact there are few without them. The European reader may have liked to see a little more of Tonnerre but is not allowed to: the author evidently wanted him to remain mysterious and remote but was perhaps more interested in the heroine. Morag is presented as very brave because she had the child she wanted, by the man she had chosen, alone, with no support from society. The situation is the reverse of the one in Rosamond Lehmann's *The Weather in the*

Streets, where Olivia chose in the end not to have Rollo's child. Paradoxically though Morag is less brave than she thought because it is clear she preferred being alone. As a writer she preferred to substitute readers for family and friends, she preferred to build a career dependent on solitude while knowing she could break out into the world from time to time when she chose to. If writing is a risky business it at least allows the average author to act out that remark about 'God preserve me from my friends'.

Margaret Laurence was born in Manitoba in 1926. If the writing by which she is best known rarely leaves Canada in theme this is not true of Margaret Laurence herself, who with her engineer husband spent a few years in what was Somaliland, translated Somali legends which so far had only been known orally and wrote about the country in *The Prophet's Camel Bell* (1963, Toronto). A time in the Gold Coast, now Ghana, followed, she later lived in Britain for some years but at the time of writing is again domiciled in Canada. Perhaps her best known novel is *The Stone Angel* of 1964, on the theme that has been used by such different women novelists as May Sarton and Yvonne Mitchell: an old woman looks back at her life. Hagar is 90, she has a lot to remember, about the last generation of pioneer life that has now vanished for ever, about the problems of husbands and sons, which never vanish and probably account for the novel's popularity. Women novelists seem to enjoy the recollections and imaginings of women on the way to dying: perhaps they are preparing themselves for a similar end or at least for the task of looking after their elderly mothers and mothers in law. *The Stone Angel* is written with skill but I for one cannot read it with pleasure. All the same, Margaret Laurence has shown herself an energetic writer, especially interested in her women heroines and their problems. Reading her is like walking along a rocky, gritty road, but it's good for the muscles.

A very different writer is Mavis Gallant, more of a city writer perhaps, and different in at least two major ways: she is well known internationally for her stories in the *New Yorker* while at the same time she prefers to live in Europe, Paris in fact, rather than in her native Canada. Women, she once told me, have a much better time in France, and it's a good place to be a writer in. She is less concerned with the obviously large-scale, one suspects a view across the prairies holds no emotional excitement for her. She is clearly fascinated by the comic oddness of people and if for example you find both the Canadians and the French (those of Paris, France) odd and funny and sometimes alarming, then the ideal novel is *A Fairly Good Time* (1970) which will give you an excellent time. No writer I can think of in any country has been quite so merciless about the French, for too many Britishers, writers included, are inexplicably over-romantic about them, even in the post-Beauvoir, post-Sagan era. Mavis Gallant has published several novels to date, they form a classic contrast to those of Margaret Laurence and they travel well, brilliantly in fact, and in their measured, ironic way seem much easier to read and enjoy than many novels from the United States, where the language, like the culture, is so far from that of Britain.

The natural landscape of Canada takes one's breath away and the towns seem to breed an unexpected emotional intensity in their inhabitants. An outsider wondering in an amateur way why this is so concludes that it may be due to several factors – the enormous gulf between country and city life, which must cause a grave shock to the system, and the noisy presence of the United States along the continent-wide border, a situation in which no other predominantly English-speaking country finds itself. No wonder perhaps so many Canadians seem to have had difficulty in finding their identity. This is the theme, or part-theme of Margaret Atwood's novel *Surfacing* (1972) in which the heroine goes back to the island where she grew up. In theory she intends to discover why and how her father has disappeared, in fact she discovers herself and all she might have been, still could be. Margaret Atwood, who was born in 1939, is well known in Canada for her poems as well as her stories and novels. *The Edible Woman* (1969) may sometimes be a little diffuse, but it is brilliantly funny, its humour often based on psychological problems: who could forget the young man who always needed ironing to do, the only way he could work through his obsessions and see the crooked made straight?

One of the best known women novelists of Canada has written in French: Gabrielle Roy, who has achieved classic status, writing moving stories of individuals in the French Canadian scene and using the straightforward technique of the classic French novel. The English-Canadian women writers, whose ready-made market is obviously much bigger, are quite different, but like Gabrielle Roy and her younger compatriot Marie-Claire Blais, equally preoccupied with their heroines. Alice Munro's *Lives of Girls and Women* has in fact become a classic. The male novelists of Canada are not household names outside the country, and the women seem to travel more easily. Anyone who ever became addicted to one of the senior writers, the ironic, sophisticated Ethel Wilson, for example, can only wish she had written much more. The heroine who gave her name to *Mrs Golightly* (1961) is the classic North American wife innocently struggling with the more idiotic aspects of the business-convention world. Although Ethel Wilson was born in South Africa, she is identified with Canada, where she spent most of her life.

At the mid-century and after there has been no shortage of writers from South Africa – Alan Paton, Laurens van der Post, Daphne Rooke, but by 1980 one name, that of Nadine Gordimer, was the most talked of and read. The name evokes a clear set of facts: here is a writer who has written novels from inside the explosive socio-racial situation in South Africa, novels which are as far from average propaganda writing as possible, work of distinction by any standards, and unmistakably written by a woman. Inevitably one is drawn into comparing her work and her situation generally with those of Doris Lessing. Born near Johannesburg in 1923 she has been writing regularly since the age of 30, producing stories and novels which make up a closely integrated body of work. The reader can pick up any title at random and realize that its author is a highly skilled artist who presents a closely observed human situation and at the same time conveys a political and social problem, usually one without any obvious solution. That might be, the reader will say, a straightforward description of Doris Lessing's work: but there are obvious differences, for Doris Lessing often writes with a hard steel pen on a piece of slate, and when particularly concerned to bring home a message she can, to change the metaphor, beat a drum very loudly, while in her less compelling work the characters are not so much people as the voices of propaganda.

Nadine Gordimer has never written in this way and as a result readers do not take fright, not even men readers. Doris Lessing seems to identify more closely with those of her heroines who somehow fail rather too often to make satisfactory relationships with other people, and a heroine of this type appears, with slight variations, in a great number of books – Anna Wulf, Martha Quest. They are not notable for their feminine qualities. The Nadine Gordimer heroine is essentially feminine and although not always lucky in love she has a greater potential for happiness both within herself and with men, for she dramatises herself less often and shows more genuine concern for other people. Elizabeth Van Den Sandt in *The Late Bourgeois World* (1966) is a case in point: she did not know whether her ex-husband Max loved her but she loved him enough to accept all his revolutionary ideas and difficult friends. There is a warmth about her which comes through in the way she describes the people she sees: 'For more than a mile I was stuck behind a huge truck carrying bags of coal and the usual gang of delivery men, made blacker by gleaming coal-dust, braced against the speed of the truck round a gleaming brazier. They always look like some cheerful scene out of hell, and don't seem to care tuppence about the proximity of the petrol tank. There was a young man with a golfer's cap pulled down over his eyes who held on by one hand while he used the other to poke obscene gestures at the black girls. They laughed back or ignored him; no one seemed outraged.' She would have appreciated some warmth or response: 'But when he caught my smile he looked right through me as though I wasn't there at all.' Sometimes she did get a response: 'When I drew up before the raised glove of the traffic policeman. . . . I realized that he was smiling back at the female behind glass in the manner of one responding to the unexpected, but never unwelcome overture.'

Throughout the whole book the heroine is aware, and makes us aware of her femininity while she sees clearly how the old conventional role of women cannot operate any longer in a country where social life was apparently on the point of violent change. Sexuality is an ever-present element in this short novel, and obviously the book succeeds because people, even revolutionaries, their wives and their friends have an inescapable sexual life. Max, the heroine's ex-husband, a radical activist, brought his revolutionary violence into his physical relationship with his wife: 'Max was wonderful in bed because there was destruction in him. Passion of a kind, demonic sex; I've had it with others, since. With every orgasm I used to come back to the thought: I could die like that. And of course that was exactly what it was, the annihilation, every time, of the silences and sulks, the disorder and frustration of the days.' And when one of his former colleagues in revolution comes to see Elizabeth in the hope of borrowing money she is aware that he too is conscious of her sex.

Nadine Gordimer is not interested in creating characters who are cardboard expressions of a tense political and social situation, just sufficiently alive to hold conversations and persuade the reader he is reading fiction. She is concerned with real people, and as anyone who has ever been involved with underground or even overground politics knows, the slogan-painters, the bomb-makers, the canvassers and the pamphlet writers are always human, nearly always inefficient and in many ways unsure of themselves. This is why *The Late Bourgeois World* is essentially fiction for today, for its uncertain end is the uncertainty of the society it depicts. A novelist of less subtlety could never have been so unobtrusively convincing.

She began as a good story writer and developed into an excellent novelist without ever passing through a journalistic phase. Those who think of her as a small-scale, 'feminine' writer should read her later work in order to judge how she learnt, apparently without effort, the secret of handling a large cast in multi-racial scenery, as in *The Conservationist* (1974). It is narrated in the graphic present, somehow conveying the sound of a South African voice with its individual intonation and especially conveying the physical varied splendour of the country, so easily forgotten by those concerned only with political issues. Five years later *Burger's Daughter* earned some enviable praise, in Britain at least, and the author, who is obviously so interested in her heroines, has skilfully kept this daughter both in the centre of the picture and on the edge of it. This last novel has brought her problems. Two of her earlier titles were banned for several years in South Africa, and in July 1979 *Burger's Daughter* was withdrawn from sale there two weeks after publication. The Publications Control Board was to assess its 'desirability'. It concerns a communist leader in South Africa, where two such real life leaders have been sentenced to life imprisonment. It is well worth quoting what the London *Guardian* reporter in Johannesburg reported on 5th July 1979: . . . 'Ms Gordimer described her novel as a "work of pure fiction".

'She said: "I write what I see in my society. If some judgement comes out of that, then it is implicit. In that way, my writing is political and committed. If it is a political novel, then that is the nature of the society". . . .

'Stressing her opposition to Stalinist ideology, she said of South Africa's Communists: "Their contribution to the black struggle for a human life has been tremendous . . . I don't think you have to be a Communist to acknowledge that. You have to grant it if you have any sense of proportion and truth". . . .

'She cited the fate of a short story presented at the University of Iowa, by the black writer Miriam Thlali. Although the story was not published in the formal sense, it was listed as a banned publication.'

Nadine Gordimer's sense of proportion and truth allows her to continue living in South Africa and to say at least most of what she feels about its present, past, and, by implication, its future, in her fiction. Her political attitudes and her artistry seem inseparable, and she has not yet been exiled or forced to surrender her passport. She is never aggressive, she is notably, constantly writing as a woman, with the courage and sensitivity such creatures seem to possess by natural law, and with all the interpretive mastery that is granted to some of them when they are sufficiently gifted and single-minded.

Of all former British dominions none have been less encouraging to potential women writers than India and Pakistan, for social conditions generally have not favoured women in any case. A few remarkable Indians have earned extra attention because they are women – Indira Gandhi, for example, but who are the women writers of the Indian continent, before and after the Indian Independence Act of 1947, writers that is who are known outside their own countries? The sad and understandable fact is that the ordinary reader cannot easily think of many names. One novelist I enjoy is Kamala Markandaya, whose voice sounds as I would expect a woman's voice to sound when speaking from an Indian village, as in *The Two Virgins* (1974), one of her many novels. She married a Britisher, came to live in London, and several of the books have been set there. Another individual voice is that of the half-Indian Anita Desai, whose skilfully understated evocations of Indian life are unforgettably vivid, full of movement, colour and subtle patterning. By 1980 her name was on the Booker Prize short list and her public is increasing at high speed. The latest known name among Pakistani women writers is that of Bapsi Sidhwa, whose sense of humour in *The Crow Eaters* (1980) is particularly compelling.

Ruth Prawer Jhabvala's experience of India has been of a very special kind. The non-Indian can still look at photographs of her and assume that she was at least half-Indian, but she is only so through environmental influences. She was born not in India but in Germany, although her parents were Polish. The family came to Britain in 1939, where she read English at London University. Soon afterwards she married an Indian architect and went to live in India, where she began to write stories and novels.

Perhaps *The Householder* is the best known, because of the film, but one of the most impressive of the novels is surely *A New Dominion* of 1972, because that is what India has been, administratively speaking, for many years now, while revealing nothing 'new' in any other sense. The adjective as used here is best interpreted as ironic, for the only newness is in the way India has influenced the outside world during the last half century or so, mainly because that non-Indian world was waiting for some ray of light to penetrate its self-created darkness. The export of gurus was obviously such a contradiction in terms that little good came of it, and even less came of the import of guru-seekers as described in this novel. The novel is immensely rich and complex, yet it has none of that sprawl which has made so much fiction from and about India as hard to take as India itself. The book is carefully planned in three sections and there is a short cast list of Indian and Western characters. The Indian characters represent all those aspects of Indian life which the foreigner can hope to understand without actually visiting the country; they represent the contrasts between the material and spiritual, between the aspirations and achievements of various groups of people.

In *A New Dominion* the author presents Indian and Western characters whose relationships, complex and continually changing, both between themselves and with the other group, illustrate the past, present and possible future of the continent, or at least the Hindu part of it. Like any outstanding novel included, through reasons of geography, in the genre 'regional' writing, it cannot limit itself to local events. Obviously many Indian writers have written many books without any reference to the years of the British Raj, but it is a historical fact, whether the Indians, or the British, like it or not. Although one school of thought maintains that India never changes, the British 'domination' obviously affected the aspirations at least of some Indians and the situation now is that there is a different kind of minority problem in India: a few Britishers 'stayed on', Miss Charlotte, in this novel, was one of them and after thirty years in the country she could hardly do anything else. Superficially some of the other characters might seem 'stock' and people who begin the novel by reading the blurb could be put off when they hear that there is an ageing Indian princess, and young men who have formed 'a delicate friendship' together. After mentioning the guru-seekers the blurb-writer does however make one good point: 'It is not clear whether their emotions for the guru are entirely spiritual – but then, this is a country where it is difficult to make very clear distinctions.'

Ruth Prawer Jhabvala achieves her extraordinary effects precisely because she can indicate this fact and come as close as humanly possible to making the said distinctions. Only someone who had lived for a long time in the country could have done this, and her observation was never superficial, because as she has said, surprisingly perhaps for someone who has worked so much in films, the visual presentation of life does not interest her much. The verbiage that clouds some novels of Paul Scott could never settle over Jhabvala's work, her perception and interpretation are too rapid and, no doubt because she is a woman, never destructive. The women characters in the book are not destructive either, while the men are either feeble or violent: no wonder the phrase 'Mother India' is still current (Katherine Mayo's book was published in 1927), for 'Father India' would be wrong from all points of view.

It is piquant that this telling picture of a new dominion should come not from a British-born writer but from someone who had come to Britain from Europe for refuge and education. Irrespective of her life in India and her preoccupation with the country, this author is one of the few people who have taken the novel in English right away from its tea-party in Barsetshire atmosphere without being in any way avant-garde or becoming unreadable to those who prefer novels to tell a story. The plot of *Heat and Dust* (1975), which won the Booker Prize for that year, is for instance quite simple: we know that Olivia, the heroine, is going to leave her husband and go off with the Nawab of Satipur, for this is stated in the first sentence, but we read every page with rapid concentration to find out precisely how it is going to happen. *Why* it is going to happen is only too obvious – the bored young wife of a civil servant has nothing to do except listen to the other boring wives of boring civil servants. In the second sentence of the book we learn that this happened in 1923, when such events – apart from the boredom – were probably rare. The author uses the device of a story within a story, which sounds as boring as the British Raj, but in her hands it is not, for she uses it to add to the suspense and to make the reader aware of the actual presence of India, the real, unpicturesque, 'independent' India in which the narrator is living. And all the time one is reminded of what the author once said about her non-visual approach: not once is there a single sentence describing the Nawab or what he looked like. We know he had a large Rolls Royce, but otherwise we have to feel, through the mind of Olivia, something of his personality. We may decide that it was not the Nawab, but India itself, which broke up Olivia's marriage, and of course we also learn that love-in-elopement did not last. It would have been surprising, given the Nawab's character, if it had.

Ruth Prawer Jhabvala found that life in India affected her health and she is now more closely identified with the United States, where she has observed what the 'success ethos' does to people. She has also observed that US culture has much in common with that of India and believes that European cultures have survived in these two countries in a 'purer' form than in their own lands. If she publishes no more novels she is still one of the few important novelists of the century.

The last writer of Commonwealth origin whom I would like to mention belongs, like Christina Stead, to Chapter 10, *Resurrecting*. This is Jean Rhys, born in Dominica in 1894. Her father was Welsh, her mother Creole, but she left the West Indies for Europe when she was an adolescent and never went back – except in some of her writing.

The writers of the Commonwealth and former Commonwealth countries have been immensely important to Britain during the last three quarters of the century and it is no female chauvinism to say that when it comes to big names the women tend to outnumber the men. They have made a significant contribution to pioneering achievement, for they have worked conscientiously, and with artistic success, in the stony fields of socio-politics. The countries in which they lived offered splendid material to writers like Jack London, preoccupied with man against nature in wide open spaces. Women may have felt somewhat agoraphobic about all this, especially after too much of life had been spent in kitchens, or trying to cook without a kitchen. The women writers have never under-appreciated landscape, but they have determinedly kept it in its place. The English-language novel, as written in England, has been described by Eva Figes, quite correctly, as 'parochial'. The Commonwealth writers mercifully have broader horizons, not only because they live in bigger countries but they and their characters tend to enjoy more positive action and move about the world. As a result, even when they seem caught up in 'local' events they are perpetually aware of their universal implications.

[9]

Learning and Teaching

❦❦❦

If one divided all books published into a few broad categories most would fit into the two obvious ones – entertainment and education. The entertainment novel has often been disparaged in Britain, probably due to some aspect of Protestant guilt, and Jane Austen in *Northanger Abbey* used more than one character to scorn it (although she herself did not) as 'full of nonsense and stuff'. Yet readers still actively demand 'novelty' and that is why many people read novels and a few people buy them. Perhaps most of these readers think they want pure entertainment but it is surprising how many of them enjoy a little instruction on the way, learning from Virginia Woolf's *The Years* how middle-class women carried out charitable work in London, or about the details of campanology from *The Nine Tailors* by Dorothy L. Sayers.

Perhaps most people do not realize how much they owe to those part-time women teachers who instruct us through novels. These novelists do not think of themselves nowadays as teachers, their educational work is not always obvious, and fortunately is much less so than it used to be. These teacher-writers – apart from the writers for children, who are outside our province here – are of course the historical novelists, and their ancestors number at least three women who deserve to be better known outside the reference books. The earliest, Clara Reeve, who lived from 1729 to 1807, is the least known of them all but she made no claim to be an innovator – she acknowledged in the third (1780) edition of *The Old English Baron* (originally *The Champion of Virtue, A Gothic Tale*, 1777) that her book was 'the literary offspring' of *The Castle of Otranto*, which Horace Walpole had published in 1765. She claimed modestly that *The Old English Baron* was romance, not history, because it idealized both fact and behaviour. Mrs Ann Radcliffe (1764–1823) was less concerned with history than with Gothic horror, and it was her *Mysteries of Udolpho* (1794) that so bewitched Catherine Morland and her friends in *Northanger Abbey*. These books use 'history', or perhaps merely 'the past', the shadow of history, to create a strange atmosphere in which mysterious, 'frightful' things were liable to happen and thousands of readers, like the spectators of today who enjoy horror films, demanded to be frightened. '. . . are they all horrid?' Catherine Morland asked Isabella Thorpe, who was giving her a list of books, 'are you sure they are all horrid?' Mrs Radcliffe was indeed successfully 'horrid', although not so interesting as Clara Reeve to that most successful of all historical novelists, Walter Scott. He even defended Reeve's historical inaccuracy because he knew that readers could not grasp a totally alien atmosphere. He also admired the third woman writer who at least attempted to give a historical background to some of her books, as well as a regional one, Maria Edgeworth, who lived mainly in Ireland but also lived and travelled in Britain and France.

Scott's success with the historical novel, after 'horrid' tales had become less fashionable, was of course prodigious and international. As the nineteenth century progressed into industralization there was, by reaction, an understandable interest in the history of remote and unmechanized times, which explains the success of Harrison Ainsworth, Edward Bulwer-Lytton and Charles Kingsley, none of them remarkable historians. At this period few women seem to have produced historical novels of lasting interest; the exception was George Eliot, who was unfortunately tempted through the current fashion for history to write *Romola* (1863), set in the fifteenth-century Florence of Savonarola, and the one almost boring book she ever produced.

Totally boring now, but highly successful in their time were the 150 or so books written by Charlotte Yonge, who lived from 1823 to 1901 and is occasionally admired by those who enjoy 'improving' sentimentality. Charlotte Yonge wished desperately to improve everyone's mind, especially the child-mind, but tended to treat children and adults in the same way. She was of course writing as a Christian, as were most of her contemporaries. Men writers, even if they did share her enthusiasm for the High Anglican Church, assumed that their readers, of any age, were British and Christian enough to become nationalistic empire-builders; women writers assumed their readers were Christian enough to become good wives and mothers, or if they failed to find a husband, good teachers in their turn. Charlotte Yonge was 'good' and believed in the subjection of women.

The women writers who followed her were less reactionary, less exclusively 'good'. They did not attempt to be adventurous but they enjoyed a foray into remote history. They are still in their way concerned with morality because one result of using history for your story is that you can prove the results of good and bad behaviour. In 1906 Marjorie Bowen published *The Viper of Milan* with unparalleled success, and part of that success was surely due to the last-moment triumph of good over evil. In the last chapter, entitled 'An Instrument of God', the wicked Visconti is stabbed to death, and the readers who demanded eight reprints in five months were surely glad to see such a triumph of good, after enjoying an action-packed display of evil, a new type of 'horrid' novel, which would have been inconceivable in a contemporary setting. The dialogue moves fast, and there is the right amount of background description. This latter is especially interesting to women, for the author obviously enjoyed describing the clothes worn by all her characters, but never listing detail for its own sake. Splendid stuff, within its limits, more readable for addicts than many later novels by more literary figures. No wonder that Marjorie Bowen, who lived to a great age and wrote a vast number of books under a variety of names (including *General Crack*, by 'George Preedy', 1928), has earned the admiration of Graham Greene, a writer who enjoys active storytelling and has been so often deeply concerned with moral values.

Marjorie Bowen has had no shortage of successors and they have never lost their preoccupation with morality, even if it is no longer easy, in a secularized society, to prove that good must triumph over evil: for what is 'good'? Unless one is convinced that historical biography is likely to reach the truth more closely – and there is no guarantee of this, for a biographer needs insight just as a novelist does, even if its quality is different – there seems every reason for writing historical novels. They appeal to readers of all ages who want imagination, adventure, something more than escape. The readers want to identify with the characters of a historical novel: the young can look forward to taking part in some vast impossible event, a battle, an exploration, a royal marriage. They may unwillingly have learnt and half-understood something of history, while now, with a good novelist, history can come alive for them. Even a not-so-good novelist can help, for if the Hungarian-born Baroness Orczy had not created Sir Percy Blakeney, the Scarlet Pimpernel, a whole generation early in the century would have known little about the French Revolution. Her hero carried out daring rescues in the best Hollywood manner, snatching people from the shadow of the guillotine. The Baroness did not write well but she created a type, otherwise her 'Pimpernel' would not have been quoted in so many different contexts concerned with rescue, and there would not have been titles such as *The Tartan Pimpernel* by Donald C. Caskie in 1957.

Young people cannot argue about historical 'facts' or interpretation – that is the pleasure of the middle-aged readers, who can indulge in slight nostalgia, remembering when they were young enough to imagine all these adventures possible. Older readers of course, depending on their personality, with relatively little of interest in their own present or future, can now start living again, and more deeply than if they were reading a contemporary novel, for they have learnt to relate the past, and their own past, to the present, if only in limited fashion. They have also seen history repeat itself, they have seen twentieth-century tyrants behaving in ways that invite comparison with Julius Caesar, Bonaparte or Bismarck.

It is a help if historical novels can deal with famous or infamous people of whom the reader has at least heard. These readers, like newspaper readers of varying types, are consumed with curiosity about the lives of the rich and famous, and sometimes even of the poor and unknown. Journalists tell them these details, usually about living people, historical novelists teach them, with more persuasive conviction. These teachers can indicate, in a way journalists have no space to do, the lessons of history and the lessons of life. They can show how the great or even the obscure figures of history – Rupert of the Rhine, the Young Pretender, Lady Hamilton – actually lived, and how the private lives of unknown people were affected by the public lives and deeds of kings, queens, religious, political and military leaders.

During the nineteenth century women writers seem to have been content to learn from their male colleagues, but in the twentieth so many novels on historical themes have been written by women that it is only possible to mention some of the most outstanding by any criterion, including some which have survived, some which should have done and some which continue to be successful even if the minority critic finds them unenjoyable.

In 1923 the Edinburgh-born writer whom we know as Naomi Mitchison was 26. She was a daughter of J.S. Haldane, an internationally famous professor of physiology, and she married a barrister whose career in politics led her to be an active left-winger for the rest of her life. In 1979, when she was 82, the appearance of her autobiography earned her wide publicity but not too much reference to the first novel she published, in that year 1923, a historical novel entitled *The Conquered*. It is the story of Mcromic, one of the 'conquered', one of many thousands, in Gaul during the time of Julius Caesar, and it is immensely sad, as a novel on such a subject could hardly fail to be. When it was published the Great War in Europe had only been over five years and there were as we have already noted two kinds of novelists at work, the entertainers and the reminders – Arlen's *The Green Hat* and R.H. Mottram's great novel *The Spanish Farm* both came out in 1924. When Naomi Mitchison chose an historical subject she decided to look a long way back in order to focus on the present and the future, and her novel of conquest, occupation, treason, nationalism and death has an extraordinary lasting power. It seems to prove an aspect of women's particular success when they write on historical themes, their capacity to convey compassion without sentimentality. There is no need to mention the scores of writers who never move beyond the sentimental, and they keep their readers immensely happy. When male novelists write on historical themes they have tended to be much more concerned with the aggressive aspects of their story – fighting, torture, punishment. It is surely not because they lack compassion, it simply occupies them less because its expression has not entered so much into their daily lives. Women, of course, tend to find this expression natural, while men have had to learn it.

In this novel Naomi Mitchison obviously thought herself with full understanding into Meromic's states of mind, and she found no reason to idealize him. She accepts and explains, indirectly, all his actions and can see the motivation behind them. When a writer of vision uses history as a theme the result is anything but escapism, and this story is no exception. Ernest Barker noted in his preface three aspects of the book which are relevant to the historical novel in general. He preferred imagination to accuracy and he wanted understandable dialogue: 'An historical novel may be true in art, and true even in history, without exactitude of historical detail. The Iliad is written round a fact (for there was a siege of Troy); but it is not composed of facts. An historical novel is also written round a fact; but if it is to be a work of art, there must be a free weaving of imagination round the fact. . . . If the novelist of classical times were to make speech, dress, and other appurtenances true to the text of a classical dictionary, he would hardly make his puppets live or his action move.' His next sentence seems a crucial text for anyone who wants to write an historical novel. 'These ancient figures must break into modern speech if they are to touch us.' Naomi Mitchison had obviously come to this decision without any difficulty, and how one wishes more historical novelists, including Thomas Hardy, had done the same thing. Ernest Barker claimed that he was not worried by the inaccuracies which had probably been 'consciously' introduced by the author, for he was concerned with more important things. 'I let the swing of the story sweep me forward: I let the characters impress themselves on me as realities: I let the sketch of the Gauls . . . stamp itself on my mind as perennially true.'

Any historical novel which allows 'exactitude of historical detail' to be more important than 'the swing of the story' is likely to be a failure, as Flaubert's *Salammbô* was, but the critical standards of the late twentieth century demand almost the impossible of the historical novelist: this teacher-writer must somehow convey the atmosphere of a period and place without tempting the reader to examine details for possible inaccuracy. Even more important than the question of exactitude and realism is the way in which a good historical novel can illuminate contemporary events and the human situation generally. That is why Ernest Barker, in his preface, related the Gallic wars to the history of the Celts and the state of Ireland at the time the book was published.

During the 'Twenties and 'Thirties, that era of living and partly living, when a great number of women were busily turning out detective stories and romances, earning good money for themselves and good entertainment for their readers, many writers were seriously at work researching and writing historical novels. The name of Margaret Irwin reminds the older reader of many attractive books, unfortunately neglected ever since the so-called 'Swinging Sixties'. She was brought up and educated by relatives who were scholars and teachers. Like all the best-educated people however she did a great deal for herself, mainly through a steady reading of Walter Scott's novels, from the age of ten onwards. Her first published novel came in 1924, *Still She Wished for Company*, set in the 18th century. Although this title is by no means forgotten by her admirers, the best of her historical novels came later: *Royal Flush* (1932), the story of 'Minette', Charles I's daughter Henrietta Maria, who was married to Louis XIV's brother; *The Proud Servant* (1934), the life of the great Scottish leader Montrose; *The Stranger Prince* (1937), about Rupert of the Rhine; and a trilogy of novels about Queen Elizabeth I, starting, in *Young Bess*, with her life as a girl. The reader of 1980 may find these titles too picturesque, but there is a dignified quality about these books, the author has read and absorbed her history carefully, but never lets it overwhelm her.

She did not regard herself as an academic and her approach might now be attacked as 'amateur', but one forgives her a great deal because she had not only grace but a sense of humour. The introduction to *The Stranger Prince* for instance is entitled 'Without Whom'. Nothing could be less academic than the opening sentence: 'A bibliography has always filled me with awe. Many of the most illuminating "sources" of one's work come accidentally in casual, desultory reading, not for any set purpose'. The author then gives us an intriguing description of her general method:

'What, for instance, was that crumbling-edged book that I pulled out of an upper shelf in the old library of a country house in County Waterford, in which was a verbatim report of witnesses of the Ulster rising in 1641? There, on the very page I opened, was somebody reporting that he had seen Alasdair Macdonald walking down the streets of Belfast with his arm tied up in a string (not sling), because he had tired his wrist with killing 50 Scots and 40 Englishmen in one day. (Alasdair was the chief abettor of my *Proud Servant*, but it was too late to mention this characteristic touch in that, so I have put it into *The Stranger Prince* instead.) But I saw no more of that book, for the luncheon gong clanged and the afternoon was devoted to live-stock, a cause as lost as that of the Stuarts.' No historical novelist of the 1980s would dare write that now, even if catering for a popular readership.

Yet the non-academic approach has many compensations, for the author appears to us as a person in her own right, researching happily in houses rather than in museums: 'And that collection of King Charles' letters to his wife, printed immediately after Naseby by his enemies as propaganda, which I came on in another house, together with many of the original pamphlets of the Civil Wars. I have quoted extensively from them, but I can't give a list of them, as I could if I had got them out, properly tabulated, in a well-regulated fashion in the British Museum.'

Anyone who enjoys this kind of research can only envy Margaret Irwin. Women readers of the succeeding generation should not regard her as outdated, for her imaginative approach led not only to a compelling series of interpretations, she was obviously deeply concerned about the way people lived, especially young people, and especially women. Her royal figures are human beings and do not spend their entire time being 'royal'. Here for instance is the exiled Elizabeth of Bohemia, the remarkable 'Winter Queen', becoming aware of the generation gap:

'"What has happened to you all?"' she asks two of her daughters, Elizabeth and Louise . . . '"You are not of my race and being. You all study and argue and give yourselves airs as artists or philosophers or scientists or God knows what" ' . . . ' "you've no feeling, no heart, no impulse, and no conscience – and yet you're so conscientious . . . you'd experiment with anything in the cause of your art or science . . . Lord, how drab it all is, this learning and arguing – my father (he was James I of England) always said, 'Give learning to a hundred women and you spoil ninety-nine'. Eliza and Monsieur Descartes, you and Mynheer Honthorst – you are young, you are beautiful, you are *my* daughters, and that is all you can do to amuse yourselves, flirting or arguing, it's all the same, with two middle-aged middle-class ugly foreigners who have to think or paint for a living." '

Her daughter Louise had a ready answer.

' "But, Maman, *I* have to paint for a living. I sold a picture only this week, or we should have had no meat from the butcher."

' "You did not sign it?"

' "No. Gerard Honthorst did. With his name it fetched a much better price." '

Her mother thought that one of her children should command better prices than a 'mere' professional painter but at least it was more dignified for Louise *not* to be a painter. She did not care for the painting business. ' "Why must you be untidy because you paint pictures? You don't do your hair with your paint brushes do you, though indeed it has that appearance? . . ." '

Margaret Irwin did not claim to be a scholar, but it is curious to compare what she wrote with a few lines from John Buchan's *Montrose*, published in 1928. He referred to the Princess Elizabeth as a 'handsome bluestocking and friend of Leibniz', but he mentioned the wrong philosopher. He described Louise as 'charming, kind, ill-dressed, artistic' and dismissed as an 'idle tale' the story of a 'projected marriage' between her and Montrose. Keith Feiling, the historian, wrote an introduction and was apparently not troubled by such oddities as the reference to Leibniz. Readers who want to know what Margaret Irwin made of the 'idle tale' should read *The Proud Servant*, after noting the way in which Louise refers to Montrose near the end of *The Stranger Prince*, which was published later.

The author remains readable because she carried out Ernest

Barker's indications in his introduction to *The Conquered*. Her people speak the same language as her readers, and she is interested in humanity, not in morality. She wrote of men and women with equal insight but, aware of her own limitations, she preferred to write of human relationships rather than of great deeds on the battlefields, she was much more than a fancy-dress novelist, and in her gentle way she was a realist, telling, us, through her essentially attractive people, something, if not all, of what happened in history.

In 1933 a woman academic writer suddenly produced one of the best historical novels ever written by any standard: Helen Waddell published *Peter Abelard*, a novel based on the well-known story of the fourteenth-century lovers in France, a book still read and admired nearly fifty years later, and one which on its own would justify the existence of that much-questioned genre, the historical novel.

Part of this novel's success is due surely to the fact Helen Waddell not only possessed immense erudition but to the grace and skill she used in keeping it in its place. There is Latin and Old French in the text, but it never obstructs the progress of the story and the reader is never made to feel ignorant because the sense is always quietly conveyed in some way or other. Despite the highly emotional story there is always reticence. In two sentences Helen Waddell describes the kind of life led by Heloise just before the birth of her son:

'And in the long September nights, before he left for Paris, she would sit and help Hugh the Stranger with his tallies, as she used to help Godric at Argenteuil: the two baskets of crab-apples that Helvis paid for her cottage, the cartload of turf that Hucbald owed for his cutting in the bogland where the Sanguèze rose, the four perches of Autumn ploughing that Nicholas was to be forgiven, because of the lameness of his mare. He [Abelard] had left Paris to come back to her on the Vigil of St Thomas the Apostle: when he reached her on Christmas Eve, his son was already three days old.'

Heloise's life is shown as temporarily at least bound up with the life of the peasants, and we know that details of *their* lives would have been only facts in old documents to anyone who could not introduce them into a 'live' situation. One remarkable thing about the novel is that Helen Waddell made it harder for herself by choosing to call her story after Abelard and although the book is not written in the first person the author makes us conscious throughout that he is at the centre of the story. Although obviously she is equally concerned with Heloise she never identifies with her or encourages the reader to do so. The author describes Heloise as a highly intelligent member of the church who never ceases to love God, who loves Abelard but says that she would feel demeaned by marriage: as a bond between them she wanted 'no bond but your love only. I am not ashamed to be called your harlot. I would be ashamed to be called your wife.' Historians know that Héloïse did in fact write words to this effect and the woman reader of today enjoys the feeling that this distant romantic heroine was only romantic through legend, not through reality. Helen Waddell shows in the book that she cares for people and suffering animals even more than she cares for historical research and interpretation, but it is the realism of her vision, blended with a reticent poetry, that has made this book a classic. Twelve years earlier, in 1921, the experienced if romantic novelist George Moore had published his version, *Héloïse and Abelard*, full of colourful detail, as far from Helen Waddell's treatment as possible, somehow false, and with no message for the late twentieth-century reader who enjoys a deeply emotional story but demands realism rather than romance.

Otherwise one of the best novels with a mediaeval setting that the twentieth century has produced is surely *The Corner that Held Them* which Sylvia Townsend-Warner published much later in 1948. No one has evoked convent life with such brilliant realism and related it to the world outside with so much humour and such an array of convincing characters.

To return briefly to the 1930s, there came in 1937 an unexpected novel by someone who has always been regarded as a poet rather than as a writer of fiction. This was *I Live under a Black Sun* by Edith Sitwell, and in her foreword the author makes her position clear: 'This novel is founded upon the story of Jonathan Swift, Stella and Vanessa. But not only the details of that story, but also the framework, have been changed. I have drawn copiously upon the works and letters of Jonathan Swift; in some cases the language of the latter has been modernised.' This unique book cannot strictly be described as an historical novel and reads as a contemporary one with an undefinable thread of poetry woven into every page. The 'history' is literary history, and the well-educated reader must play the game with the teacher-writer who apparently has no other purpose than to immortalize, as a fictional character, the remarkable, puzzling and somehow underestimated Swift.

Naomi Mitchison, Margaret Irwin and Helen Waddell succeeded in making history live, even when dealing with remote eras. So did D.K. Broster, who wrote a great number of historical novels during the 'Twenties and 'Thirties, the best known being the trilogy *The Flight of the Heron*, *The Gleam in the North* and *The Dark Mile*, all from the second half of the 'Twenties dealing with the ill-fated Jacobite rebellion in Scotland in 1745 and its aftermath.

Teenage readers of Broster during the late 'Twenties and 'Thirties do not forget her. It will be interesting to see what happens to the devotees of Winifred Elliman, who took her professional name of Bryher from the name of a small wild island in the Scillies group, off the Cornish coast. Bryher has been dismissed by Avrom Fleishman, author of *The English Historical Novel* (1971) as 'slight', but this does not seem to me accurate. He no doubt used the word partly because her novels are usually short, the action limited and the characters few. She gives no long and detailed descriptions, even when writing of events at Paestum in Italy during the fourth century B.C. This was her novel *Gate to the Sea* (1959), and the historical situation might have tempted a writer to build up a complicated world because there was every scope to embroider on the scant evidence available. But this book is only 123 pages long, an extended short story, some might say (until they had read it) and the plot itself is simple: it tells the story of 'Harmonia, the priestess and guardian of the Poseidonian relics, as she faces the increasing power of the Lucanian conquerors and the disintegration of her people'. The Lucanians had dominated Paestum after Alexander's death in 326 B.C. and the ancient Poseidonian culture had been nearly extinguished. Eventually the small group of people at the centre of the story are able to save the symbol of their presiding goddess Hera and escape in the hope of founding a new colony elsewhere. I give these details to show how obscure the subject might appear and how quickly, without any indication from Bryher herself, one begins to think of world history since 1945, with the endless movements of refugees in more than one continent, attempting to keep their culture alive by fleeing to unknown countries.

When writing of historical novelists a great number of commentators have quoted those lines by Wordsworth:

'Old unhappy far-off things
And battles long ago'

which seems to identify the subject matter. Bryher, fortunately, and perhaps because she is a woman, has not spent much time describing battles, although she can evoke terror with great intensity, and she is never interested in descriptions of violence for its own sake. The last pages of *Gate to the Sea* are full of a desperate dash for safety, but the violence of the pursuers is indicated very briefly: the thud of chariot wheels and the dust, literally the dust of battle, at the Gate to Paestum itself. Bryher took the not very usual step in this novel of including several photographs of the ruins at Paestum, as they are today, with no captions and no signs of the contemporary world about them. The sight of a ruined city can often be the first indication to many people, and not only young people, that history actually happened and goes on happening. Bryher's achievement in this novel was to fill those buildings with the people who had once lived there, people as she imagined them and people who are not too far from us. About Bryher's writing there is always a poetic, dream-like quality and as the reader reaches the end of the story he/she does not wake too quickly, for that dream, which is never falsely lyrical, does not fade at once, it has been imagined and conveyed with too much sureness, it is never flimsy and most of all never weighed down with overpainted backdrops or a concentration on physical details. Bryher is almost alone among British historical novelists of the later twentieth century in preferring to describe love and religious devotion rather than the physiological violence of war and sex. Which explains no doubt why she is temporarily out of fashion and why at the same time she will never be totally forgotten.

Another novelist who sees historical themes in a similar way is Patricia Ledward, who at the time of writing has published one historical novel, *Root of Grace*, in 1969. It is the story of Elizabeth Gaunt, the last woman to be burnt at the stake, nearly three hundred years earlier, in 1685. It would be hard to find a more moving and less sentimental novel, mercifully using twentieth-century speech, and the problems it raises, again without any insistence on the author's part, are endless, they are the basic problems concerned with loyalty and justice. Elizabeth Gaunt spent a great part of her life helping the poor, for how would they have survived without the help of individuals, in that troubled period of British history between the death of Oliver Cromwell, the restoration of Charles II and the Monmouth rebellion in 1685. The novel demonstrates how women writers in the historical field are on the whole much more interested in a single figure, heroine or hero, sometimes surrounded with a family, rather than in a vast group. Patricia Ledward shows us, through her few main characters, all that was happening at the time. Her heroine married one of the Levellers, about whom not much has been written in fiction, she was a non-violent revolutionary and fanatic, and aware all her life of that remarkably English problem: class-consciousness. It would be hard to find a historical novel with less obvious colour, less glitter, with fewer attempts to please the reader who wants entertainment. It is a sad story in a grim world and without any obvious attempts to convey a lesson it inspires the reader with admiration for the type of moral courage that has always been unfashionable, the only type of courage that can lead to perpetual regeneration.

But fashions in the historical novel, as with other types of novel, obviously follow the fashion of the times, and readers are not particularly interested in quiet, deeply emotional fiction with an underlying message of austere morality. Younger readers in particular want a romantic ingredient, and this is easy to find at any level, while many of the same readers obviously demand information to be brought to them in fictional form, especially after they have rejected orthodox but inevitably boring methods in the classroom. This explains the immense success of Rosemary Sutcliff, whose novels published over the last twenty years have covered many different periods of history in the ancient and more modern world. Her industry and stamina have been nothing short of miraculous, but some of the novels can be daunting, the people and the relationships seem too easily lost among the external details.

Yet an exception must be made for that extraordinary book *Sword at Sunset* (1963), in which the author's achievement is more imaginative than usual, and not merely informational. Imaginative writers of all kinds, from Tennyson to Jean Cocteau, John Steinbeck and Peter Vansittart, not counting historians and critics, have felt compelled to write in some way about Arthur of Britain, but it might seem strange that these writers have all been men. Women have re-told the legends for children, and after all the *Mabinogion*, that ancient collection of Celtic tales, was translated by Lady Charlotte Guest in 1877, whether we approve her editorial work or not. Perhaps women writers of orthodox beliefs have felt that Guinevere's infidelity to Arthur was too shocking, that she had let the side down and there was no excuse for her. On the whole too, as we know, women writers have not been too much drawn to descriptions of fighting, even if the issues fought over were deeper than the conquest of a material kingdom. If Tennyson and the Pre-Raphaelites had romanticized Arthur and his peers nobody, except Peter Vansittart, in *Lancelot* (1971), has demolished the romance more completely than Rosemary Sutcliff, not for the sake of destruction but for the sake of realism, for she believed that if Arthur ('Artos', she called him), had lived, this is the man he would have been, created by his background and the world around him.

If one has grown up to the sound of Tennyson's lines

> So all day long the noise of battle roll'd
> Among the mountains by the winter sea . . .

and the sight of Tintagel castle through the mists of painting or music, it may be hard to take *Sword at Sunset*, but if the whole Arthurian legend is to mean anything today then its 'matter' must have some realism in it before there can be any superstructure of symbolism and the search for the ideal. And if anyone is tempted to think of Rosemary Sutcliff as a romantic novelist they could read the description of Artos's wedding night: Guenhumara (Guinevere to those with the Tennysonian background) cooks some honey cakes, her husband realizes that he should have carried her to bed, but he had been out to look at his horse, and neither partner enjoyed the nuptials. I suspect many readers may find the scene good for a laugh, but when they have read the 480 pages of the book they would not dare laugh at the author's achievement, especially the sustained narration by Artos himself all the way through. The novel may be too long, the tempo insufficiently varied, but in its isolated way it justifies the twentieth-century continuation of that odd genre, the inevitably educational historical novel.

By the mid-twentieth century the historical novel in Britain had established itself as a serious genre, clearly separated from the historical romance, although writers of the latter, succeeding Marjorie Bowen and Baroness Orczy, earned vast quantities of readers and money. The romances were, indeed are, mainly read, one assumes by women and teenage girls, while men and teenage boys relished A.E.W. Mason and then much later moved on to C.S. Forester. Comparatively few male novelists of literary ambition have applied themselves seriously this century to historical fiction: could it be that they believed it more suitable for women, both as writers and readers? Yet no one would question the achievement of Robert Graves, and Jack Lindsay also. There is the prolific Alfred Duggan, the brilliant J.G. Farrell and a great number of writers in the United States, including isolated titles such as Gore Vidal's *Julian* (1964).

There have been 'isolated titles' in Britain, too, in various circumstances, among women writers, and *Peter Abelard* was such a one. Rose Macaulay for instance wrote *They Were Defeated* in 1932, a story set in Cambridge in the seventeenth century, introducing various contemporary writers, and thought it some of her best work. In 1948 the Canadian-born Hope Muntz wrote a highly successful novel *The Golden Warrior* which was introduced by the historian G.M. Trevelyan. It told the story of Harold and William, in other words it told how the Normans conquered Britain in the eleventh century and in his foreword G.M. Trevelyan made some interesting points. 'It is not an ordinary historical novel,' he maintained, 'for the historical novel usually avoids the great personages and the famous scenes, and fills its canvas with imaginary characters. . . . The atmosphere is that of a heroic drama sustained throughout.' He then continued by showing why the novel succeeded: 'The impression is undisturbed by irrelevant archaeological description, or by modern speculations on the results of the Norman conquest. So the book has a real aesthetic unity. It is purely human in its appeal, leading to a tragic climax, after which silence falls on the field of battle.' It is the humanity that gives the novel its readability, as with Margaret Irwin, and as G.M. Trevelyan adds, 'modern ideas and questions' do not intrude, but 'they are latent and implicit'.

'Human appeal' is no doubt the secret of women's success in the historical novel, for they are not inclined to write novels without it. It is when they overdo it of course that all critics cry 'sentimental', and sales are immense. These successful 'isolated' novels are particularly interesting when written by someone with experience in other types of fiction. It seems strange to list Iris Murdoch's *The Red and the Green* (1965) as an historical novel, but it is a novel of recent history, not strictly a contemporary novel. It required intellectual and imaginative effort, for it describes events taking place before the author was born. Admirers of Iris Murdoch were surprised by its appearance. Yet it proved that an imaginative novelist is likely to write a first-class historical novel when she really cares about the subject, when she introduces all that 'human appeal' that G.M. Trevelyan wrote about and quickly makes her readers devoted to Millie Kinnard, amusingly over-described by the publisher's blurb writer as 'fast, feminist, and only just respectable'.

However, the most successful historical novelist of the mid-century among women writers has surely been Mary Renault, who again had written several novels on contemporary themes before she produced a series of titles which made her name inseparable from the legends of Theseus, the history of Minoan Crete and the early life of Alexander the Great. Her literary career might have been academic, her doctor-father saw that she went to Oxford and she thinks her parents might have expected her to be a teacher. Indirectly, of course, she became one, through writing. She began to write early and confesses to a bad and fortunately unpublished novel set in the Middle Ages. Several others, non-historical, were published: including *Purposes of Love*, *The Friendly Young Ladies*, and *North Face*, while she worked as a nurse. Another novel won a major prize from Metro-Goldwyn-Mayer, who did not make a film of it but gave the author a generous amount of money allowing her to become a full-time writer. She had nursed during the Second World War and her novel *The Charioteer* (1953) was set in military hospitals soon after the Dunkirk rescue operation of 1940, telling a story of homosexual love.

Then came a new life, starting with emigration to South Africa, and a new kind of writing, with the successful publication of *The Last of the Wine* (in 1956). It has a fictional hero, Alexias, who is reaching manhood at the end of the Peloponnesian War which had already lasted some twenty-five years. The author produces a panorama of social history, including family life, friendship, or *amitié amoureuse* between Alexias and his friend Lysis, and most interesting of all, perhaps, the different and fascinating life led by the philosopher Sokrates and the members of his circle. The publisher's blurb writer, afraid lest potential readers would be put off by the remoteness in time of the book's setting, tried to relate past and present: 'It was a time in some respects not unlike our own, when men born into a heritage of security and power felt the structure of their lives being undermined by forces which they but dimly understood.' Men: that is what Mary Renault's novels are about, for in ancient and even modern Greece women have made only brief, mainly decorative appearances. Strangely enough they counted much more as goddesses and heroines of legend, the latter including particularly figures such as Phaedra, Hippolyta and of course those unforgettable members of the Atrides.

Since Mary Renault is concerned mainly not with Greece but with the still mysterious civilisations of Crete, her novels might well have been hard to follow for the average reader, for as she was writing *The King Must Die* (1958) and its sequel *The Bull from the*

Sea (1962) the discoveries in Knossos, which seemed destined to convert legend into history, were not fully known to or understood by many non-scholars. Mary Renault seems to have earned her readership because she has linked some known aspects of the ancient world to similar ones in modern civilisation, especially the cult of violence for its own sake, and usually exercised by men. She describes it in a straightforward way, a way colourful enough not to frighten away women readers, who no doubt feel that all these ferocious scenes are comfortably far away in time at least. There is plenty of fighting, sometimes described apparently for its own sake, in a way reminiscent of so many films, especially from the United States where the editors never seem to work on the battle scenes. It is obvious that Mary Renault is evoking a society based on violence but one that was sophisticated on the surface and of course uninhibited by any Christian taboos. There is fighting between men and men, between men and animals and often, when it comes to sex, between men and women. Love, in the modern Christian sense, does not exist and would have been anachronistic. When the young Theseus, in *The King Must Die*, finds the door bolted to the sacred Queen's apartments he decides to enter by jumping from the battlements to the terrace. There follows a remarkable scene.

'She tried to bite me. . . . As we swayed struggling, we tripped on the bath, and overturned it as we fell. There we lay in a wet welter on the checkered floor, among scents of spilled oils and unguents and broken jars from the bath-stool. . . . "For once in this room", I thought, "it shall be a man who says when." In that same moment, I felt a pain in my shoulder like a bee-sting. She had caught up the dropped paring-knife. It was not very long, but long enough, I think, to have touched the heart, only I moved and spoilt her aim.' Naturally blood begins to flow, he had nearly choked her, and 'Then I picked her up out of the mess and water, and carried her to bed.' Later the Queen wanted the room cleaned up and Theseus admitted that 'it looked as if conquering troops had sacked it.' Nearly a quarter of a century has passed since Mary Renault wrote this scene and perhaps this is why it seems little more than funny now, although that was surely the last thing she intended.

Then, in *The Bull from the Sea*, there is the fight between

Hippolyta and Theseus which unfortunately does not reach the level of the classical epics, where resonant language is so well matched with reticent expression.

The novels are very well stage-managed, full of colour and movement, from the swell of the sea to the Bull-dance in Crete. The author likes to describe physical things, especially men's bodies and clothes: 'the soldiers polished their black limbs with oil; and the Captain sat combing his long dark love-locks, stripped to his codpiece, while the boy burnished his gilded loin-guard and his helmet chased with lily-flowers.' This from *The King Must Die*. Sometimes women merit a brief description: 'Women with parasols leaned together heads crimped and bound with gems; slim men half-bare, with gilded belts and jewelled necklaces and flowers behind their ears, led spotted hounds as languid and proud as they.' The author relishes this kind of description, so obviously do her readers, but the price paid is the absence of any deep personal relationship. I cannot say 'human' relationship, for these figures are not human, they have emerged from legend into historical fiction but they remain two-dimensional, as though on a sculptured frieze, although this is a kind of moving sculpture. The author is fascinated by men and adolescent boys, women do not concern her or her heroes very much. It is only fair to add that comparatively little is known about the lives and thoughts of women in these remote civilizations. Their obvious role was that of mothers to heroes, otherwise they were goddesses or priestesses or sacrificial victims. If Greece produced a handful of women poets, we have not yet discovered the existence of a similar group in Minoan Crete.

In 1979 Sue MacGregor of London's BBC asked Mary Renault, reminding her of the homosexual relationships she had introduced into her earlier books, if she regarded herself as a pioneer writer on this theme in fiction. The author replied that she wrote about individuals. The relationship between Alexander the Great and 'the Persian boy' is developed in great detail in the novel with that title in 1972 but again somehow there is not the depth which one senses in the characters depicted by Bryher, although she never enters into great detail. There is every kind of richness in these novels, and *The Praise Singer* of 1979 showed a welcome turning away from violence, the reader learns a great deal about the ancient world, what the people did and how they lived, but somehow not how they felt. The author obviously decided that she could not presume to invent these feelings, just as Marguerite Yourcenar decided she could not include dialogue in the *Memoirs of Hadrian*. Mary Renault is a highly efficient author in the lineage of historical novelists, one reads her for information and entertainment, as one reads the work of Peter Green and Henry Treece, but never for that extraordinary combination of scholarship and emotional insight that one finds in *Peter Abelard*.

It is a curious fact that among the eighteenth-century ancestors of the historical novel women seem to have slightly outnumbered men and to have used history more for its 'horror' than for its fact, fiction or even romance. During the nineteenth century a preoccupation with Christian morality led to a fading of 'horrid' fiction until Sheridan Le Fanu developed the ghost story so brilliantly and Bram Stoker began to exploit Dracula. Women writers, from 'Vernon Lee' (Violet Paget) to May Sinclair and Elizabeth Bowen have proved themselves excellent writers of ghost stories, or at least short stories with evocative non-realistic themes. This type of story-telling has continued alongside the historical novel, and the historical element has faded from it.

During the twentieth century hundreds of women writers have devoted themselves to historical fiction, sometimes continuing, if unconsciously, the moral instructive line of the nineteenth century, almost always interpreting history in human terms and at the same time unobtrusively educating their readers. The fact that violence has played such a large part in Mary Renault's historical novels is partly a reflection of public taste, the desire for a physical thrill which echoes the early desire for 'horror', the actual enjoyment of feeling one's hair stand on end. When the horror is embodied in legend or remote history it is somehow less disturbing than in scenes more closely related to our own way of life. But I would say that most readers are no more disturbed by violence in the historical novel than in the old- or new-fashioned detective story or thriller. The much talked about 'body in the library' is just a theatrical prop and nobody imagines it is real. If violence in the historical novel worries any reader there are plenty of such novels without it, especially those written by women.

Unlike Mary Renault, who has produced an impressive number of novels requiring great stamina in research and writing, Helen Waddell limited herself to one story. On the whole though historical novelists seem to be as energetic as their ancestor Sir Walter Scott, and this energy is not limited to those writing at the costume-ball level. Women writers in this latter group have been incredibly prolific, often using two or even three names and keeping thousands, if not millions of readers, mainly women, comfortably happy, offering no new historical interpretations, avoiding uncomfortable realism – this is usually left to the men – keeping characters at the level of magazine fiction and allowing readers to identify with them. The moral lessons of history remain in a shadowy fashion, especially where the novels deal with actual historical characters, but nobody must be upset and history provides good reading when it is familiar and cosy. Women characters offer a particular interest to twentieth-century women readers in this genre because in some sections of society they were protected in a way that seems enviable to some nowadays, while certain among them could wield great power through dynastic marriages or liaisons, and a woman who showed independence of spirit was of course breaking all rules.

In fact women novelists have shown 'independence of spirit' often enough by writing just one or two historical novels in a long career of fiction-writing because they felt compelled to write a particular story. Mary Webb left an unfinished one and that too-soon-forgotten novelist F. Tennyson-Jesse wrote *The Lacquer Lady* in 1929, probably her masterpiece. The heroine, Fanny, is 'daughter of an Italian father, and a mother half English, half Burman', and the novel tells how her love-affair actually led to the annexation of Upper Burma by India, which took place in 1886. This is no far-fetched romance but a true story, which the author learnt from an expert in Burmese law – a Britisher – and was able to tell in detail because she twice visited Burma, heard all the details from him and from a few surviving people who were actual witnesses to life in the famous Golden Palace of Mandalay. It would be hard to think of any story more potentially romantic, but the author has avoided all the obvious pitfalls, she has even described life in Burma without any garish local colour. There is description, fortunately, and plenty of it, but the keynote is realism. This is a rare example of a historical novelist taking over the historian's task, for if the average reader wanted to find out exactly what happened in this Far Eastern corner in 1886 he would have to look out historical works which would give obviously some of the facts known to official chroniclers, but not the truth of *la petite histoire* which has in the long run as much value as history itself, for it supplies details of motives and behaviour which can influence events far more than the people concerned could ever imagine themselves.

Another brilliant example of a single historical novel is *The Birds Fall Down* which Rebecca West published in 1966. It deals with an imagined incident from Russian history in the early part of the century and the central figure, as in *The Lacquer Lady*, is a young girl. Because the heroine and the events which overtake her are not romantic but 'real', the novel reads more as though it were living history than mere fiction.

It is odd to think that both Sir Arthur Conan Doyle and Ford Madox Ford wrote historical romances when embarking on their careers, books which did not earn them great reputations but are studied now because they show how the writers were influenced by current taste. In 1980, by a curious turn of events, several men novelists have rediscovered the historical novel as a vehicle for serious writing, while at the top literary level women seem to be deserting it, as though they relished the heat of the day and did not want to be thought of, however unfairly, as escapist. Yet the historical genre suits them, and if some women are now writing about the future the majority, if they retain their capacity as teachers, will probably continue to prefer the past. And oddly enough the wheel has come full circle in another way: the Gothic, 'horrid' novel came back some time ago, written mainly by women. In a snobbish way I confess I prefer the older sort, because I think even the authors half-believed in the horror, whereas now even the readers believe only what the dust-wrapper tells them.

10

Resurrecting

❦❦❦

Since the Second World War endless reputations in all the arts have been made and lost, and by a coincidence three women writers, two of them born at about the same time thousands of miles from Britain, had to make a second appearance before their reputations were finally established, if, that is, a reputation can ever be final. One of the women was re-discovered writing again after a gap of twenty years or so, the brilliance of another was under-appreciated at first and yet another moved temporarily out of sight for a long time for little reason other than the short-sighted judgement of her publishers.

One would like to think that Jean Rhys herself found more happiness in life than the recurring women – almost always the same woman, who does not grow up beyond a certain point – in her books. From the surface it seems unlikely. She was born in Dominica in the West Indies in 1894, one of a large family of children born to a Welsh doctor and an English creole wife. She was more solitary-minded than the other children and when she was sixteen came to Britain with an aunt for further education. She in fact went to RADA after a short time at school but could only stay there one term for her father died and there was no more money for fees – the first of many tough situations Jean Rhys had to face as a young girl. The prospects of finding work were slight and so she joined a theatrical touring company which went round Britain's provinces with that popular but totally uninteresting show *The Count of Luxembourg*. Her part in the chorus could hardly have been interesting either. It must have a strange experience in the days just before 1914 but this is what she chose rather than a return to Dominica. One thinks of Colette who went on similar tours, playing in mime and music-hall, between her first and second marriages.

But when Jean Rhys was twenty-four her life changed in some ways upon her marriage to Jean M. Langlet, a poet and song-writer, half-French, half-Dutch. It was still an unsettled life, and the couple moved about the Continent, living mainly in Paris or Vienna. After four or five years of marriage and financial bad luck her husband was imprisoned for theft and she divorced him. Some good luck was to be hers, nevertheless, for the stories she had begun to write were shown by a friend to the British novelist Ford Madox Ford; he liked them enough to include some of her work in the last number of his *Transatlantic Review* in December 1924. Ford also liked the author and for a few years she joined the quasi-married household in Paris where Ford lived with the Australian painter Stella Bowen.

In 1927 there was a mysterious end to her relationship with Ford, but he wrote a preface to her collection of stories *The Left Bank* published by Cape in London that year. She came to London, remarried, and in 1928 Chatto published her first novel *Postures*, known in the United States as *Quartet*. This was the first book in a group of four, the last of which appeared in 1939, published by Constable, *Good Morning, Midnight*. It did not appear in the United States until nearly 20 years later. Her second husband died in the 1940s and she later married his second cousin, who predeceased her. As far as writing was concerned there was a long silence until *Wide Sargasso Sea* was successfully published in 1966, to be followed over the next thirteen years (she died in 1979, aged 84) by intermittent but glowing praise, varying from critical articles to endless published photographs showing, continental-style, an elderly face almost buried beneath its heavy make-up. There were attempts by television producers to explain and demonstrate the mystery of her interrupted career and the peculiar nature of the 'Jean Rhys woman.'

It was part of the author's bad luck that the last of her four early novels appeared in 1939, the year when many good books obviously failed to reach the readers who at any other time would have been only too glad to read them. We re-read any book by Jean Rhys now with positive excitement in some ways, sadness in others.

The excitement is due to the technique which appears to be no technique and to the way in which the stories have not dated in most essentials, for they seem in fact to have anticipated a whole school of writing. At first glance there seems to be 'no technique' because one has the impression of a woman talking and probably using her own experience without much inventive addition. The author returns constantly to the figure of a woman who is lonely, deserted, unhappy, waiting for her regular allowance from some vague departed lover or benefactor in order to survive. In the first novel the heroine is an orphan from the West Indies, a fact which reinforces the impression of a strong autobiographical element, while in *Good Morning, Midnight* the heroine Sasha might be the author remembering her existence as the wife of a struggling poet. Yet the reader is not too much tempted to probe these possible 'facts' or precisely how the author transmuted them into fiction because the psychological development in the book, however slight, is utterly absorbing.

The first interesting point is the way in which the heroine develops from a figure not unlike that of Colette's Renée Néré in *La Vagabonde* and *L'Entrave*, so conscious of her departed lover and her own loneliness, into someone who after much suffering and complaint learns to tolerate her situation, even if positive happiness will never be hers. No one reading these novels today, and certainly no woman reader, could fail to notice one thing: if the Rhys heroine could have earned her living she would not have been at the mercy of men and dependent on some miserable allowance. Of course she could be a prostitute, or nearly so, and oddly enough it was this work, undertaken in an amateur spirit, that gave her enough self-respect and strength (again in *Good Morning, Midnight*), to refuse one man and accept another. The psychological twist here is characteristic of French fiction, not English. Perhaps it was too sophisticated for the novel-readers of 1939, they would have needed to work their way first through several generations of French authors from the later Colette to de Beauvoir and even Sagan before they could see the extraordinary modernity of this treatment.

The average woman reader of Jean Rhys today may be angry with these apparently helpless creatures who accepted to live this way, but they must realise that historically there were plenty of women like this, that from a psychological point of view there will always be some of them. Are they a group of lazy masochists, those women who cannot escape this situation? Do they search it out? And did Jean Rhys in her way accept the situation as an author whom nobody, for three decades, wanted to read?

She had come to Europe from the comfort and warmth of the West Indies, as Colette had left her happy provincial childhood for Paris. Jean Rhys has been compared to Katherine Mansfield, who also came from a comfortable home far from Europe, but I believe Mansfield came with some aggressive ambition, and an allowance from her family, whereas Jean Rhys had neither. She was a much more feminine woman, and she waited, as women do, to see what would happen. Men are inclined to say that silence from a woman writer means personal happiness – for women, they maintain, usually start writing when they are unhappy – and after her return to Britain Jean Rhys, one assumes, knew a life more satisfactory than penniless wanderings and a *ménage à trois*.

It was due to BBC television that she was traced in the mid-1950s, living in a cottage near Exeter in the south-west of the country. The British critic Francis Wyndham had read her and written about her as though she were long dead, but now came the possibility of a true resurrection, for she had not given up writing, she was actually, she said, at work on a novel. The resurrection was not instant, but after seven years *Wide Sargasso Sea* was completed and published with great and deserved success. It must surely have taken a long period of isolation for a writer to choose such a subject – the pre-history of Mr Rochester's first wife in *Jane Eyre* – and to handle it with such imaginative brilliance. The writing was different in some ways now: Jean Rhys felt obviously that she could write more freely about the background to her own childhood, heightening the whole story with the atmosphere that must have existed a century or so earlier. The relationship between this book and her own earlier writing, the admixture of the Charlotte Brontë elements, and the reasons which led her to write this brief but extraordinarily moving book the way she did would occupy an academic critic for a long time.

Critics, men critics as it happened, helped to resuscitate Jean Rhys but it was obviously her own development as a novelist that led to the success of *Wide Sargasso Sea*. Women readers in particular now find they can read her as a new and up to date author, for they are so much more aware of the reasons that drive women into the wretched situations she portrays. The Left Bank and the seedy Bloomsbury settings that she used are all the more effective now because she described them not as something 'picturesque' and external, but as something that was a natural part of her heroines' world. Although we realize she probably saw them herself at uncomfortably close quarters she always had the skill to keep the heroines and not herself at the centre of the fictional situation.

If women want to be independent they must have the chance to work, as they all know. Jean Rhys suffered bitterly from the economic situation when men spelt money, and while she and her heroines knew they still liked and loved men for their own sake, she herself had been vulnerable from the start, for had her father not let her down, unconsciously of course, by dying, and therefore removing her money supply? Money problems killed her first marriage. Ford Madox Ford liked her and her work but he was perfectly willing to sign two translations she made from the French, under his influence, although he acknowledged later that she had done the work – he would not have been capable of it, he said, but translators in any case were not given much credit at that period, especially if they were translating contemporary authors. Jean Rhys was probably at this moment too interested in Ford for his own sake to object if his well-known name was to appear with those of the writers: in this case one of them was Francis Carco, who had been a lover of Katherine Mansfield – the novel was *Perversité* – and the other was *Sous les verrous*, written by Jean Rhys' first husband under his pen-name of Edouard de Nève. Both Ford and Jean Rhys have since cleared up this mystery.

She was obviously vulnerable, but she escaped oblivion through her innate artistry and the self-confidence it gave her. It is a strange fact that women writers become 'lost' more often than men and can suffer from too much publicity when they are 'found' again. But a genuine artist like Jean Rhys can even survive those painful photographs of an aged, over-maquillé face, because no make-up, fortunately, can change the expression of those perceptive, compassionate eyes.

Christina Stead was born in Australia only fourteen years later than Katherine Mansfield, she has been publishing novels since the middle 1930s without anyone except a few critics and a small number of initiate readers appreciating them or in fact knowing much about them at all. Britain's Virago Press began a courageous effort to resurrect her in 1978, she received serious critical attention and her readership is now gradually expanding.

The women writers who have sometimes been forgotten for too long are the non-aggressive ones, or those whose appeal is superficially at least small and special. Second-raters as we know move in and out of fashion simply because they are second-raters and their appeal has little to do with purely 'literary' values, they are usually an aspect of social history or minor cult figures like Firbank or E.F. Benson. Christina Stead is a first-rate writer who has been neglected, but for once it is comparatively easy to see why, and the neglect has nothing whatever to do with being a woman. The best, or the best known of the novels, say, *For Love Alone* (1945), *Letty Fox: Her Luck* (1946), or *Cotter's England* (1967), are not easy to read. They are long, full of people and incident and talk, they need hours of careful, concentrated reading and this is why they will probably never be high-selling novels. They are individual but not experimental, they are full of energy, physical and intellectual, full of humour too, but the difficulty one has in reading them comes I think from a kind of fragmentation. The light appears to fall on one or two characters briefly, in one setting, then it shifts, as in a well-known type of stage production, high-lighting others. In *For Love Alone* for instance Jonathan Crow's lecture and discussion group about 'the love cult' forces students of all ages (and readers) to hear some strange things: 'It was a disordered, impertinent paper; but no one seemed to notice that and to himself it seemed the pure fluid of thought; it was reason arraigning hypocrisy. He had a collection of ideas . . . injected with eccentric legal, eugenic, and medical fancies with a few facts about the sexual act (still unknown to at least some members of his audience) and which was constructed on the plan of those wild religious books of visionaries and sectaries which have a crumb of everything and appeal to one great need.'

Earlier we had been told about 'Mr Jonathan Crow Who Coached in Latin', and about the Tutorial College, 'a dingy, penurious private school, run by an old high-school teacher on the sixth floor of an old office building, near the Central Railway Station. . . . Poor teachers, and poor students, and graduates without jobs coached there and were of all ages, but all were men. The teachers were mostly thin, tense, fretful and with tired eyes behind spectacles.' Crow was the poor boy who toiled for academic success and remained a poor young man, despite agonising economies. He at least pretended to admire the 'grit' of his student Teresa, the heroine who thought she loved Crow, but Crow did not believe in love.

When faced with the dense, but never dull nature of the writing one tends at first to pick out paragraphs here and there, about Australia, about London, about young people, using any method except the orthodox one of working from beginning to end. Out of the 41 chapters, set roughly half in Australia and half in London, one selects a particularly intriguing title: 'The Countless Flaming Eyes of the Flesh', 'There are Many Abandoned Orchards in the Valley', 'Love is Feared: It Dissolves Society', – some of these reproduce the first sentence of the chapter itself. Then one glances at it, becomes intrigued, moves a chapter back, a chapter forward, and realizes that all chapters are intriguing, whatever their title. There is a richness about it all as though something is held in check, as though the whole air is humming with ideas and stray thoughts waiting to be absorbed by the reader.

You pick out fragments which happen to interest you in some irresistible fashion and think 'that's exactly right', like certain sentences in Jonathan Crow's letters from London: 'The English have been revolting since Wat Tyler but the People of Property are still in the saddle'. Or that other Australian reaction: 'I have begun to see the web of their social system. It is built up on precedent and the "by accident" or "muddling through", which is true enough, is only the outside. Inside, they're tough; the muddle is not so muddled that an outsider can stumble inside.'

Further, women readers will be fascinated by the character of Teresa, so full of 'grit', she was told, working, studying, loving the unlovable Jonathan Crow, and the said Crow makes a short speech towards the end of the book (most of Christina Stead's characters make speeches) which will make women boil with indignation but they will admire the rhetoric: 'I have never met a single woman who could think a thing through'. . . . 'They reason by fits and starts and always behind it is some ulterior motive, of which, perhaps, they are not always, in fact not generally aware. They are not self-knowers. They accept all the shibboleths, all the old wives' tales – don't you sometimes wonder how two nations can exist side by side in the same house, for twenty years, in the same bed? One is brought up on myths and one bringing to fruit scientific research, operational problems! Of any couple, compare the man and the woman, what do you find? Always the patent superiority of the male, even where a brilliant woman, so-called, appears to have married her inferior. Women talking about babies, frills, maids, cooking, men talking about politics and the latest inventions – or, at any rate . . . football, baseball, but something outdoors, external, something to do with the real world.'

Perhaps both men and women will find it old-fashioned now. In 1945, when the novel was first published, the air was not full of this sort of talk, and too few people have realized how often Christina Stead was in the van of circumstance. And in 1946 few people were ready for Letty Fox and her extraordinary life in New York, described by Hilary Spurling after its reissue in 1978 as 'something like a combination of *What Maisie Knew* with Edith Wharton's *The House of Mirth*'. But Letty's success proves the French dictum that virtue is never rewarded. This is a tough book, its heroine a tough child and an even tougher young woman out for all she can get and to hell with everyone else. Letty is a product of North American society, I feel, and not too often found anywhere else. But the Jonathan Crows of this world could never have imagined that the book was written by a woman. He could never say 'everything's ruined by her womanism', as he said of Teresa Hawkins, for Christina Stead has never suffered from such a weakness.

No writer of today has been more internationally-minded. She seems to have left Australia for good in 1928, travelling and living in Europe as well as in the United States. Some critics have thought *The Man who Loved Children* (1940) her best novel, but it is hard to choose. As readers develop enough stamina to come within sight of hers (they will never catch up) she will become better known. The new atmosphere of the women's movement, which must surely concentrate now on achievement, is right for her. Everything about her is large-scale, positive; she is realistic, but in a way not found in any other writer. There is never any 'arrangement' of dialogue or incident to make things easier for the reader. The 'speeches' which are such an integral part of her work are the one 'unreality' she allows herself. Perhaps it is not unreal, perhaps it is an Australian, a New World quality, but it is an enviable one.

Most talk about Christina Stead seems inadequate, most recent reviews have been full of hyperbole. She has been described as 'The most extraordinary woman novelist produced by the English-speaking race since Virginia Woolf', there have been quotable mentions of her 'prodigal display of imaginative power', 'her jewelled vocabulary, her analytical psychology'. One of the reactions I have enjoyed most, and one already quoted in 1945, was that of someone from a vanished generation, Sir John Squire: 'Her verbosity is that of passion and of genius. . . . To me it resembles the wild eloquence of *Wuthering Heights*.' Maybe that is how Emily Brontë's masterpiece may have struck a contemporary. In a page so full of quotations there is no harm in adding yet one more: 'Her neglect by critics,' wrote Martin Seymour-Smith in his *Who's Who in Twentieth Century Literature* (1976) '(she is missing from, patronized or perfunctorily dismissed in all but one of the standard reference books in English) is a strong reason to feel dismay about the practice of letters in our times.'

The answer is not so much laziness, perhaps, as surprise, which is less easily acceptable than shock. It is easier to accept someone like William Burroughs or Erica Jong or Monique Wittig because one has not encountered anything like them before. On the surface Christina Stead appears to be 'like' other novelists but she is not, she is only herself. She is not 'just' Australian, but I wish I knew Australia in order to enjoy her more. Obviously that busy, lively continent where she was born – a third generation Australian – had a lot to do with what one can only call her genius. She remains a continent to be discovered.

Back in Britain, 'The Rediscovery of Barbara Pym' could almost be the title of a novel, and it provided one of the best stories of the 1970s in the gossipy little world of publishing. She had been first published in 1950 after working hard at a novel, following advice from her eventual publishers Jonathan Cape. After moderate success for eleven years or so and appreciation from a small but devoted group of readers she was suddenly informed that taste had changed and her books were no longer interesting, or so the Cape directors believed. For fifteen years or so the author was forced to accept the situation but she made no attempt to write differently in order to keep up with the changing taste that her publishers claimed to have noticed. She went on writing mainly for herself, but she did so for a long time. Then came the kind of 'break' that does not happen often to authors: when in 1977 the *Times Literary Supplement* asked a group of critics to name the writers they considered the most under-valued the results were fortunately less predictable than the tedious lists of favourites issued every Christmas.

The biographer and critic Lord David Cecil and the poet Philip Larkin both mentioned Barbara Pym, whereupon the uninitiated rushed to the libraries in an attempt to cover up their ignorance. With luck they might have found a Library Association reprint of *No Fond Return of Love* (1974), but Pym books do not stand idly on the shelves. Three years later Barbara Pym was photographed and written about in the major British newspapers just before the appearance of a novel which owed its publication to the remarks by the two critics. One is reminded how, fairly early in her publishing career, Ivy Compton-Burnett's novel *Brothers and Sisters* had been rejected by the Woolfs for publication by the Hogarth Press despite a report from an eminent architect that it was 'a work of genius'. Leonard Woolf thought the author 'couldn't even write'.

But what is it about the novels of Barbara Pym which brought about the resurrection situation, so entertaining to everyone, with the possible exception of the allegedly red-faced publishers? It can fairly be said at the outset that these novels, like those of Jane Austen, could only have been written by a woman, they are greatly occupied with the small practical externals which women do not seem able to avoid, and if the Pym heroines sometimes share houses or apartments and sometimes, we assume, from the last page of *No Fond Return of Love*, may even get married, they are essentially solitary women who do minor or part-time jobs and do not worry about money. On the whole they are not merely resigned to their spinsterish life, they make the most of it, enjoy much of it while secretly hoping sometimes that it may not be spinsterish for ever. The heroine is always kindhearted and charitable in the best sense of that word but as she is human there are people for whom she does not entirely care. She watches, listens and records, missing no detail in a way reminiscent of Ivy Compton-Burnett but totally different in the end because the smiles and laughter she provokes are never sardonic or destructive in their criticism. There is always hope for her characters because if they have never spent any time in philosophical speculation they are quietly happy in the shadow of the Church, provided that it is Anglo-Catholic or some respectable shade of the non-Roman English church.

Dozens of women, including Margaret Drabble, have been writing novels in Britain with heroines who are solitary and hate the idea. These heroines are painfully at work trying to find themselves and it is good of publishers to allow them to do so in public. Barbara Pym's heroines have faith in God and even, shyly enough, in themselves, they are not given to complaining for very long at a time, and if there is sometimes a feeling of autumn in the books there is no unrelieved pessimism, surely one of the reasons for her success. Barbara Pym's work has many of the advantages of light fiction without any of its defects. Her novels are intensely readable for the story alone and the quiet humour of the dialogue; for those whose eyes and ears are trained in the artistry of fiction there is a kind of technical pleasure to be found in every paragraph, and so much of the material is immensely comforting, especially to older readers, one imagines, because it is familiar, even if we are not expected to take it all at face value. The portrait of a lady representing 'Prosperity' has 'a nice expression', 'Like the wife of a

Conservative MP about to open a bazaar, don't you think?' Who could forget the more than horrifying English cooking of the originally Austrian Mrs Sedge, who of course could not cook but soon learnt what she was expected to do with cabbage and cauliflower. There was also the clergyman who ate cold brussels sprouts in the middle of the night, only one of the many odd clerics who keep the books going in one way or another. As for the main lines of the plot, the detective-story aspect, or how Dulcie, the archetypal Pym heroine, tracked down the brother of an erring North London priest by way of the Eagle House Private Hotel in the West Country, it is infinitely more inventive than the average mystery because the real people and the caricature people, such as the remarkable Mrs Forbes, mingle in such extraordinary and high-comedy fashion that one cannot put the book down. There is no hope of the reader solving the mystery, whereas the end of the average thriller is usually so obvious and/or so unconvincing, the people are hardly ever real, the humour is stock and the philosophy nil.

Has Barbara Pym a philosophy and would her fascination with the Church put off the secular reader? It is impossible to read her books without concluding that there is an inherited spirit of goodness about them – however ridiculous her vicars and curates, however ghastly the jumble sales for the organ fund, the principles of Christianity are in the background. How else could those near-resigned heroines enjoy their cretonne-covered lives as much as they do, how could they uncomplainingly eat the semolina pudding unless they had been brought up in total Englishness and the shadow of the Church? The novels would hardly exist without Church and church, the institution and the local building. The other comforting thing for the non-Christian or non-churchgoer is that the author is not attempting to propagate the gospel. One feels sorry of course that such unfortunate people must miss a good part of the fun, but Barbara Pym's determination not to convert anyone is such a strong point in her favour that she might even succeed in doing so. She makes the author of *The Towers of Trebizond* seem positively aggressive in comparison, while Graham Greene is a hot gospeller, out to convert everyone.

In 1977 Barbara Pym, re-discovered thanks to the two influential literary critics, was the centre of enough publicity to satisfy any novelist at any stage of her career, and the TV film that was made about her might have come out of her novels. In this remarkable work she, her sister and Lord David Cecil pretended to have tea in the garden of her house in Oxfordshire. No garden could have been more inconvenient to a television producer and perhaps out of sheer despair someone had already had a go at the cake. When they were not moving chairs about everyone said a great number of predictable things and one could only hope that viewers so far unconverted were not put off for life.

Few novelists could have weathered those years of relegation so cheerfully and in her later book, *Quartet in Autumn* (1977) there is no bitterness, and a mature, serious attitude. Once, in an earlier novel, she had seemed to anticipate something of her own relegation, for in a brief list of novels demoted to the bathroom she included one of her own, out of print at the time. This is *Some Tame Gazelle* (1950, reprinted 1978) an infinitely consoling work for middle-aged spinsters and for women who have somehow failed to develop a career despite good qualifications. One sister yearns for a despicably lazy and selfish Archdeacon, whose wife has a first-class degree but cannot knit socks, while the other is forced to lavish her affection on a succession of curates. One might almost see the sadness creeping in, but Barbara Pym knows just how funny to be and never becomes bitter. She loves her women characters and understands that they need to love someone or something. And the men? Well, they are likely to manage without much trouble, for there are so many loving women waiting in the wings, but perhaps they might be allowed to consider that the Thomas Haynes Bayly epigraph to the book may not be irrelevant as far as they are concerned:

> Some tame gazelle, or some gentle dove:
> Something to love, oh, something to love!

Maybe it sounds cosy, 1930ish, for everyone has servants, but even if men find it all 'twee' or more reminiscent of E.F. Benson in the Lucia books than of Jane Austen, the usual name mentioned in comparison, they will learn a good deal about good and even excellent women. What any writer can learn about technique is infinite. Sadly, Barbara Pym died in 1980.

Jean Rhys, Christina Stead, Barbara Pym: it would be hard to find three more contrasted writers, all of them outstanding and 'different', all of them particularly interested in their women characters and all of them, in the end, restored to their rightful place high up on the reading lists. Most men writers move from relegation to retirement. Not so women, they do not give up easily and, fortunately for their readers, they are prepared to wait.

11

Experimenting (2)

✥✥✥

Reading the work of Anna Kavan and trying to find out more about her is a change from the novels of Dorothy L. Sayers, Agatha Christie and their younger successors for here is a real life mystery with few clues and no solution. Instead of a boringly neat ending, a tidily completed crossword puzzle, here is the ending with which most detective stories begin – unexplained death. And the clues are not so much facts as novels and stories covering 30 years.

The question 'What's in a name?' is not rhetorical here, and it is worth noting how 'Anna Kavan' found hers. Back in the 1930s a woman called, or at least calling herself Helen Ferguson published several books described by her friend and executor the late Rhys Davies as 'typical home counties novels', and in fact they are neither interesting nor well written: with the exception of one, entitled *Let me Alone* (1930) with a heroine called Anna. After an unusual upbringing by an eccentric father, followed by a failed lesbian love affair, she marries, for escape purposes, a man who is obviously incompatible. His name is Edward Kavan. Although she hates him she goes to Burma with him, eventually runs away during a great rainstorm but somehow survives this attempted suicide. She had learnt only one thing, from reading a life of Martin Luther: 'How easy and simple to face life from the single basis of her own indeniable individuality. She was what she was: herself. No need for compromise or apology or modification or defence.' A platitude, of course, today, and the average novelist would hardly trouble to make a character say or think anything so obvious.

But the invention of 'Anna Kavan', in the 1930s, meant a great deal to Helen Ferguson, realizing that she needed a room of her own. She had been born in Cannes in 1901, and not in 1903 as she preferred everyone to believe: for she was vain, and wanted to stay young. Most of her early life was spent travelling with her rich parents – of whom little is known – in Europe, South Africa, the Far East and in California. She was an only child and looked back on childhood with a shudder. Later she described it at its worst, and no doubt heightened by the feelings of alienation that soon possessed her, in *World of Heroes*, a piece included in the posthumous collection *Julia and the Bazooka* (1970):

> I was slow in starting to live at all. It wasn't my fault. If there had ever been any kindness I would not have suffered from a delayed maturity. If so much apprehension had not been instilled into me, I shouldn't have been terrified to leave my solitary unwanted childhood in case something still worse was waiting ahead. However, there was no kindness. The nearest approach to it was being allowed to sit on the back seats of the big cars my mother drove about in with her different admirers. This was in fact no kindness at all. I was taken along to lend an air of respectability. The two in front never looked round or paid the slightest attention to me, and I took no notice of them. I sat for hours and hours and for hundreds of miles inventing endless fantasies at the back of large and expensive cars.

Parallel moments occur in so many of the stories that the reader accepts the degree of isolation with which 'Anna Kavan' grew up, and any readers who were equally unlucky identify only too easily with the central figures of these scenes which the author could obviously never forget.

Superficially 'Helen Ferguson' had some sort of so-called normal life: she married and divorced, but of this first husband nothing is known, not even his name. She apparently had a son who was killed in the Second World War but Rhys Davies has wondered if this was not an adopted son. Anna Kavan's second husband was the painter Stuart Edmonds, and anyone who knows her work well will feel something of a shock on seeing photographs of the apparently conventional, middle-class couple in their Buckinghamshire home with the dogs they bred for pleasure and profit.

Marriages apart, the woman who had earlier been 'Helen Ferguson' began to identify herself with the heroine of *Let me Alone*. In writing the novel she had anticipated, or brought to the level of consciousness, her own emotional and mental attitudes: now she turned herself literally into Anna Kavan. She took the name by deed poll and went on writing. But nobody can so easily will themselves into another person, even if nature so often imitates art. She experienced mental illness and spent at least two periods in American mental hospitals, but the Anna Kavan, the writer we know, came out into the world, her mental and emotional changes expressed, simply enough, in a changed physical appearance. Those who knew her well from the 1930s have described her vanity, her cosmetics and her long varnished fingernails, her preoccupation with her image in the mirror. This was more than the usual feminine concern with appearance, it was a search for security in her new personality. She had created Anna Kavan, she had to keep her alive. There may have been cracks in the personality because Rhys Davies told me of at least three longstanding friendships involving Anna Kavan which all ended in unexplained but final rupture. It looked as though the personality she had adopted was like the cosmetics to which she was so devoted: cosmetics can create a work of art but sooner or later something goes wrong – surfaces crack, skin dries up, the real person can be glimpsed behind the mask. Perhaps these friends were disturbed by the former 'Helen Ferguson' lurking behind the Anna Kavan they thought they knew – the Anna who was a good friend, a good hostess and cook, earning her living from middle life onwards as an interior decorator and artist, working from a chic little house in London's Peel Street near Holland Park. Some of the friends sensed her deeper problems: she would have sudden fits of violent temper, disliked talk about sex, and she was apparently upset by any suggestion of lesbianism in herself or in her entourage, not because she was prudish but because she believed women inverts were social snobs. Their male colleagues, she thought, were different and much more reasonable in their social attitudes. What lay behind *her* attitude? Some frightening experience, obviously, but not one that we shall ever know about. In *World of Heroes* the narrator shows a preference for men, which she knew was due to her upbringing: 'My mother disliked and despised me for being a girl. From her I got the idea that men were a superior breed, the free, the fortunate, the splendid, the strong. My small adolescent adventures and timid experiments with boys who occasionally gave me rides on the backs of their motor-bikes, confirmed this. All heroes were automatically masculine. Men are kinder than women; they could afford to be.' But even men were suspect: 'They were also fierce, unpredictable, dangerous animals; one had to be constantly on guard against them.'

There are in fact very few tangible clues to the way Helen Ferguson, creator of 'Anna Kavan' in *Let me Alone*, became the Anna Kavan who even worked for a time on Cyril Connolly's literary magazine *Horizon* and from 1940 onwards, with some gaps which are unexplained but probably clouded with illness, wrote a series of short, arresting books, some made up of pieces which had appeared in *Horizon* and other magazines interested in avant-garde work. I myself have followed up certain elusive, exterior clues but as with most writers the evidence that matters is usually to be found in their work – the recurring motifs can no more hide the truth than cosmetics.

There are some eight Anna Kavan titles, one published by the Scorpion Press in 1963, the rest by Peter Owen (all this in London), and they include a new edition of *Let me Alone*. Why is it that this work, originally called 'experimental' and published in small circulation literary magazines, has survived and become something of an international cult while so much other writing roughly classifiable as *avant garde* has appeared in the same way with some success and then been forgotten? There seem to be three basic reasons: the first is the integration of theme and style, achieving readability without fragmentation, the second is the vivid presentation of the 'split' personality in which the two parts of the divided self are in some ways interchangeable but like an object and its mirror-image can never coincide. The third is the most controversial and of course the reason for the author's inclusion here: this is the writing of a woman, it is impossible to read a page of it, as in the case of Anaïs Nin, and imagine it could have been written by a man. I write this not because I am a female chauvinist but simply because it strikes me that way. Brian Aldiss, in his introduction to the posthumous French edition of *Ice* (*Neiges*, 1975) said that Anna Kavan probably adopted this surname because it made her feel close to Kafka's 'K' in *The Trial* – a fine theory, but perhaps he did not know about the heroine of *Let me Alone*. It would of course be impossible to talk of a 'female Kafka', or a 'male Anaïs Nin', for the psyche is conditioned by biology, whether we like it or not.

What I see as a feminine quality, and others may see it differently, as homosexual or asexual, perhaps, in many of the stories, is the elusive quality which prevents, against all odds, the development of a destructive atmosphere. Anna Kavan may have tried to destroy Helen Ferguson and in the end she hastened the destruction of her synthetic self– if that is what it was – but in all her evocations of illness, coldness and 'scarcity of love' she showed an artistry of a particularly female kind that never lost the awareness of possible warmth, however desperate her own need of it. It is true that her heroines and occasional heroes – if that is the term for those suffering figures – want love as desperately as a child does, but they can, or at least potentially could give it. This comes through in the way the author gathers these people deeply into herself and through them absorbs and translates so much beauty, so much balance, so much richness. I do not use the phrase 'gathering-in' literally and it is less than obvious, for it is only too easy to see these figures as distant creatures – the patient in *Asylum Piece*, the boy in *New and Splendid* (*A Bright Green Field*, 1958) – standing or lying in unreal rooms or hostile environments: the caring attitude is limited almost entirely to artistry.

Does the author care principally for women, as though they were all facets of herself, and have these creatures any depth? To answer the second question first, the characters are not there to have depth, for they are not 'people' like us, the average readers. They are essences of humanity and usually portrayed in extreme situations, sometimes part of the landscape, sometimes juxtaposed with unrelated objects as in a surrealist painting. Very little in fact means precisely what it says and the 'people' are symbols, even though we do not necessarily know of what, beyond the fact that they are there to express the farthest imaginable extremes of behaviour.

The world of present-day reality seems to have held only a superficial interest for Anna Kavan. If she thought she had broken with her past she was mistaken, for it pursued her relentlessly throughout most of these stories and novels: think for instance of the little girl in *Christmas Story* (*A Bright Green Field*) who found the spectacular room with the Christmas tree and all the brilliance of the season – but it was empty, meaningless, for it was empty of love. This was her past, and with extraordinary artistry, by-passing the present, she took her plots and themes into the future, the *anticipation*, the word used in France to describe science fiction. No wonder that Brian Aldiss thought *Ice* the best science fiction novel of 1967 (the author would have been as surprised as Monsieur Jourdain was on learning that he could speak prose). It has an impressive, uninterrupted poetic quality rarely found among most workers in the genre who are perpetually drowning in a sea of technology and must surely have no sense of humour because they do not see how heavy-footed, how unwittingly comic they are.

One need not search for humour or happiness in Anna Kavan's work, for beyond the artistic satisfactions of handling dangerous extremes one will not find cheerfulness breaking in. There are moments of irony, but the new generations of younger readers may find her later work sentimental. Is *Julia and the Bazooka* just that, a lament over the eternal scarcity of love? It depends on how one sees life in general and one's own life in particular. Anna Kavan had one dimension to her life that was rare enough, especially among women, until the 1960s, and that was her addiction to heroin. Even rarer was her use of it to keep going, even if in an artificial way, and most of all to keep writing, whereas so many addicted writers of various sorts seem to use it only as a subject of literary conversation and soon become exceeding dull. Cocteau's *Opium*, written as far back as 1930, is an uneven work, oddly articulate for drug-takers' writing, but of course it was the 'Journal of a Cure'. As for later writers who have recounted their drug-taking experiences, such as Alex Trocchi and William Burroughs, none of them seem to have learnt that extraordinary concentration which surely produced the unnatural quality in much of Anna Kavan's writing, unnatural but only in the way that her rooms, buildings and landscapes were lit with the light that never was on sea or land. The post-Ferguson books are uneven, but this is hardly surprising in a woman whose life was artificially maintained by heroin. They are also, at their best, the work of a poet, written not from the head but from the heart, however deeply that heart was hidden.

The end of her own story was a melodrama in itself. 'I had known for some time,' wrote Peter Owen in his introduction to *Asylum Piece* in 1972, 'that Anna was unwell but without appreciating the seriousness of her illness. Early in December 1968 my wife and I invited her to a housewarming party, and she said she hoped to come – which rather surprised me, since as a rule she avoided social gatherings of this kind.' She did not appear. 'Shortly after the party the police telephoned me, having found our invitation card in her house, which they had broken into at the request of Rhys Davies. She had died on the evening of our party.' She had died too with her syringe beside her. She had been in hospital, would probably not have lived much longer and possibly died of a heart attack.

Writers who experiment with the structure of fiction or with the structure of the sentence are not going to win a large public quickly, unless they introduce a kind of sensationalism that catches attention at once. It is unfortunately true that writers who break open conventional structures sometimes do so because something within their self is 'broken' too, and it can also happen that their research may lead them into the dark waters of the mind until they lose their way. Anna Kavan may have been saved, for years at least, by drugs, Virginia Woolf was not saved; Gertrude Stein seems to have worked through her problems, but she had the survival power of a steam-roller. Regrettably enough, in Britain, some of the most worthwhile women interested in experimental writing have had a bad time of it, partly of course because of their own nature, and one who did not survive was Ann Quin.

Never was one woman so wretchedly typical of her times. Born in Brighton into an ordinary, unrich family she lost her father when very young and found an unexpected and maybe unsatisfactory father-figure in the ageing writer Henry Williamson, who encouraged her to write while they conducted a love-affair. No such affair, if indeed it included love, was happy for her and all her literary successes brought disaster: a grant from the Arts Council in Britain and a Fulbright Award from the United States led only to wild spending, drug-taking, psychosis in London and Amsterdam. In Sweden she was rescued from near death in a snow drift. In the States she was aggressive towards other writers, in London she was rude, ungrateful, abnormal, and at the age of 36 she ended it all: like an Iris Murdoch heroine she walked out into the sea.

She wrote four books. *Three* (1966) begins and ends with suicide: 'And all that's necessary now is a note. I know nothing will change.' And nothing will change my conviction that they are worth more, in imagative terms, than all those successful, professional, predictable, smooth Book Society or Book Club Choices which one might read on a long train journey if nobody had left any evening papers on the seat. A book like *Three*, on which Ann Quin worked very hard, was destined to appear on the list of a small publisher – John Calder – for a large one would have been frightened by the unconventional technique. Yet the book succeeds because it is never for one moment unintelligible, it tells a story and is therefore a novel, for that is surely the criterion that counts, despite all the academic debate about the genre. The story is in the title: three people, Leonard and Ruth, the couple, and the girl who had already killed herself when the book opens, the girl who was mentally ill and in love with Leonard. A story simple and orthodox and only of importance as a necessary starting point. Dialogue, spoken or not, without inverted commas, is merged into the body of the text, there are passages of prose set out like free verse, achieving the effect of poetry without ever turning into that pseudish (to quote Osbert Lancaster) thing poetic prose. Neither is it merely impressionist, it creates a whole social background and most of all it creates people, the way they think and live.

The book is of particular value in our context because it could only have been written by a woman. Ann Quin chose to express a great deal through a continuous evocation of domestic detail, she builds up the cosiness of Leonard and Ruth's life together, with the radio, the cat, the things that make up a home, even the absence of a child, which they both want. The unnamed heroine, of course, is outside the warmth and the cosiness, she realizes she will never 'belong' in the way she wants. She conveys her feelings of failure and deprivation through memories of utterly commonplace things she has noticed and heard: 'Emotions handled, shifted about, dropped, picked up, but always attached as a child's pair of gloves.' The heroine – there is no satisfactory word for this elusive figure – we know is doomed to deprivation, she notices it in others: 'Jam made in a saucepan. I've never had a proper preserving pan. She said. Carefully writing dates on jars.' This use of flat little facts is all the more remarkable because there is no flatness in the final effect of the book.

There are sexual fantasies recurring throughout the novel, hints of a relationship between the two women which underlines the preoccupation with female sexuality which is all-pervading, just below the surface of the page but inescapable: 'A certain intimacy sprang up between us, that somehow never exists when L is around. So much so that I found myself wishing he would remain away longer. As if R plays a role when he is with us. Except I wonder if it is not a certain role she plays with me, when we are on our own.'

Three is an immensely sad book, full of half-realized, failed relationships, prophetic because the heroine resigns herself to failure and death, but every page is intensely readable because the author was creating a new kind of writing, skilfully concealing any effort. Unfortunately she found it easy in one way to write about deprivation, for, like Anna Kavan, she knew so much about it, but it is her artistry, very different from that of Kavan, which absorbs the reader. There is none of the loud crying we find in Sylvia Plath, everything is muted, as though spoken in an undertone, but there is total communication.

The atmosphere of *Tripticks* (1972) is very different, fierce, destructive, sardonic, funny, and written through the voice of a man. Unpromising as that sounds, it is still readable, and there is not much left of the United States social scene when Ann Quin has done with it. In comparison Erica Jong seems highly uneven and exhausting to the reader. Ann Quin demolishes everything, including the women's movement. 'Are you uneasy,' says her male narrator, at how ' "aggressive and unfeminine" your woman editor is behaving? Or a woman lawyer? Or a Weatherwoman? The electric flashes between women's liberation and male chauvinism are now the consuming revolutionary struggle. The single bathroom is open to both sexes, and on its anonymous walls are penned little dialectical nuggets that would bring a blush to the cheeks of Masters & Johnson and Brunnhilde's warwhoop to any half-baked feminist.' Only Fay Weldon has written later in a similar tone of voice and if she has not written through a male character this is no doubt because she has always been happily convinced of her own femininity. Ann Quin was perhaps less certain, despite the undeniable feminine quality of *Three*, and that lack of certainty is difficult to live with. As time went on she was probably less and less certain of many things, notably of any need to go on living.

No one could have been 'like' Anna Kavan or Ann Quin, but they have both contributed to the history of experimental fiction, and especially to that written by women, through their retention of a feminine emotional element. I do not mean that they wrote about situations that were obviously emotional in themselves: neither were they different because they reacted emotionally. They remain absorbing because of the dramatic immediacy with which they translated their reactions. A capacity for doing this is not unique to women – Dylan Thomas possessed it, to name only one writer – but it may be easier for women because they have not been emotionally castrated by the educational and social system, even in Britain. Several other women writers have made interesting contributions to experimental writing in fiction – Christine Brooke-Rose and Eva Figes, to name only two – but these are *intellectual* contributions, they are often absorbing, puzzling perhaps, more than intelligent, but there is still something conscious and artificial about them which stimulates but does not satisfy. How different for instance is that extraordinary poem-novel, that desperate lament by Elizabeth Smart, *By Grand Central Station I sat Down and Wept* (1945), a book which is unique and therefore to be valued, whatever its faults. A kind of synthesis between the emotional and intellectual type of writing is brilliantly achieved by Fay Weldon whose work, experimental in some ways, is considered in Chapter 12. She too is unique, and men readers may well say, in all sincerity, thank God for that.

Those creative writers who experiment do not do so for fun: they *have* to write that way and find the reluctance of editors and publishers inexplicable. The disruption these writers bring into their work reflects disruption within themselves and maybe in their surrounding society. Anna Kavan and Ann Quin tried to write out their intense unhappiness, Anna Kavan almost succeeded because her mental and physical makeup was tough enough to keep her alive for sixty-seven years. She came of a generation better trained in the suppression and disguise of unhappiness. Ann Quin was hardly capable of silent suffering at all, drugs for her were not a way of staying outwardly normal, they were a way of escape which did not work. Ideally all that the two women wrote should be judged at its face value, the biographical details are secondary, but in a society like ours where sensationalism is considered more entertaining than literature, it is hard to avoid them. All real-life horror stories involving women are considered extra-sensational because the majority of people still consider women are less tough than men, and need more protection. Since women are normally by nature more creative and caring than men it seems doubly sad when they suffer from their own aggressive behaviour. Writing of Anna Kavan's *Let me Alone* a *New Statesman* reviewer in Britain stated that 'Miss Kavan . . . is fast becoming something of a cult figure, one of the saints of Women's Lib and the drug culture', and this remark was found quotable by her publishers in their efforts to sell her later books.

In the midst of life is death, and sickness too. The writing of Anna Kavan and Ann Quin, who were intermittently sick people, is of crucial interest to anyone who hopes that increased awareness of illness, especially mental illness, can only help to prevent it. In the past the social status of women protected them, however unwilling they were to accept protection, against the terrifying isolation that can lead to all kinds of illness. Like Edvard Munch's portrait of a scream the unhappiness of Kavan and Quin is an inevitable part of the twentieth-century scene. As women these successors to

Dorothy Richardson and Virginia Woolf are not 'attractive' in the everyday sense of the word. But they draw attention, they inevitably 'attract' in the Latin sense, as Sylvia Plath and Monique Wittig continue to do, and we cannot, must not escape them.

12

Laughing (2)

❀❀❀

Women, we have decided in the face of alleged male opposition, do possess a sense of humour, but one that is different from that so obviously possessed by men. I say obviously because male humour in the Anglo-Saxon world tends to be extrovert, physical and juvenile. Women have never laughed so easily as men have done, and after all before the twentieth century they may not have had so much to laugh at: they even had to be taught how to laugh, and Mrs Humphry ('Madge' of the magazine *Truth*) in her 1897 social primer *Manners for Women* devoted six whole pages to the necessity and culture of the laugh. She also maintained that humour is cultivable but that 'There are whole days when one does not laugh', which 'amounts to neglecting a privilege'.

A few women writers of all kinds have known how to laugh in fiction, and perhaps Jane Austen was the first and one of the best of them. In the early twentieth century there was the amusing chat of Mrs Alfred Sidgwick, who wrote a great many novels over several decades, including *Cousin Ivo* (1899), there were the very different novels of Ada Leverson, then there was Rose Macaulay. When the lights went out over Europe in 1914 something of the laughter died too, and it is worth remembering again that the idiotic entertainment fiction of the 1920s was almost entirely produced by men, while a new generation has revived it during the 1960s and 70s. Humour grew darker under the steel pen of Ivy Compton-Burnett, during the 1930s in particular, and by the time the Second World War had realized the worst predictions of the European surrealists and the English intellectuals of the 'Thirties – the former laughing in a 'different' way and the latter hardly capable of a smile – a good deal of comedy was turning black. Although the black comedies written for the theatre have always received most publicity in this field the novelists have made a sizeable contribution, particularly, as it happens, the women. Addicts of Muriel Spark relished the macabre element in novels such as *Memento Mori* and *The Ballad of Peckham Rye*, but true connoisseurs of black humour have surely found their real heroines in those novelists of the 1970s, Beryl Bainbridge and Fay Weldon.

It is too early to consider the entire careers of either of them for in 1980 they are far from over. What matters are the conditions in which they grew up. After the lights of Europe had gone out for a second time – and who would have thought it possible? – there may have seemed even less to laugh at, but since the human spirit is apparently incapable of defeat there was one crucial change – if it is difficult to laugh in the old-fashioned way at the old-fashioned jokes then you have a choice of three courses: you don't laugh any more, which is unthinkable, or you laugh at the old jokes in a new way, or you laugh at what are in effect new jokes – things that nobody used to think were funny, at least in fiction. Death, for instance, was funny in music-hall jokes, and murder was funny in a play like *Arsenic and Old Lace*, but more than half the century had gone by before novelists began to use death in this new way – the main incident in a novel that is a funny novel.

The Bottle Factory Outing (1974) is perhaps the funniest novel of the last ten or twenty years, but it was far from a first novel. Several early ones were reprinted after the author became famous: a familiar story. Its immediate predecessor, one year earlier, was of course *The Dressmaker*, a novel full of people who can only be found in the north of England: or so anyone born south of Cheshire thinks. Nellie, the dressmaker, stabs the American soldier with her scissors not so much because he was breaking her niece's heart and going to bed with her dotty sister but because he was damaging Mother's furniture. It is possible to laugh at Nellie and Marge and Rita, but not for long, when you realize that Nellie meant what she said at that crucial moment just after the death: when her sister had said it was wicked. Nellie didn't want any 'talk'.

' "We haven't had much of a life", cried Nellie. "We haven't done much in the way of proving we're alive. I don't see why we should pay for him." ' And she wasn't talking about money.

Beryl Bainbridge has an enviable ear for the sentences that express all aspects of a complicated social context. When she has on occasions put 'real' people and their talk into novels, she once said in a broadcast talk, they did not recognize themselves: she forgot, of course, that they had no ear for the total recall of dialogue and no stage experience, as she had had, to help them notice the drama that can be present in everyday events and curiously absent in events which happen only once in a lifetime. In *The Dressmaker* she was preoccupied (as in *Harriet Said*) with teenage girls and their sexual problems, plus the problems of women who take too much or too little responsibility: Nellie and Marge. Their brother Jack was only good for one thing – he had to drive the dead American soldier (in the shroud Nellie had made out of a curtain) down to the docks and get rid of him. He did it, because he had been told to do it, but it made him vomit.

Nobody felt much, if any, guilt about this death but they knew they had to get rid of the body. In some ways the same set of circumstances occurs again in *The Bottle Factory Outing*, Freda dies, as Ira had died, partly out of clumsiness, and again someone has to dispose of her. There is no point in trying to describe the end of the book, for no one who has not read it would believe it. Beryl Bainbridge in this novel made death and body-disposal funny in a new way, yet death is not dismissed as something unreal and without importance, as it tends to be in the old detective stories and the new thrillers: death is death, and you have to deal with it in whatever way seems practical.

The way it is dealt with, and the way the whole book is organized, would provide material for a detailed analysis of how the particular comic effect is obtained. Half of it comes from close and lively presentation of a social situation that is full of violent contrasts yet unified by the bottle-factory itself. The quasi-tragedy of Freda's whole existence is due to her social situation – she is a déclassée and failed actress. 'All her life she had cherished the hope that one day she would become part of a community, a family. She wanted to be adored and protected, she wanted to be called "little one".' (She was what is called 'a big girl'.) And she was in love with Vittorio the trainee manager at the bottle factory. Brenda, her room mate, was on her own too, having left her drunken husband, who had surely been too far removed from the life for which she had been educated – 'private school and music lessons and summer holidays playing tennis' – but Brenda survives because she is more in touch with reality than Freda, even though Freda appears to be more practical about money; Nellie and Marge were contrasted sisters in *The Dressmaker*, Freda and Brenda seem almost two halves of one split personality. A good deal of the comedy is due to contrasts, particularly the contrast between the English women and the Italian men, with Maria, the one Italian woman included, balanced as it were by Patrick, the Irish van driver. Patrick's achievements in the lavatory-mending scene are so much funnier than the bed-burning incident in *Lucky Jim* that I wonder how long the latter will retain its already wearied reputation.

No mechanism of comedy is missing from *The Bottle Factory Outing*: there is straightforward clowning, so rarely well handled by women, who on the whole do not enjoy it very much; there is variety of speed and timing, which the author manages like an orchestral conductor dealing with Stravinsky, and of course that sense of form which characterizes the best women novelists of the 1970s. One has only to glance a second time at the first two and last two pages to see how carefully worked out is poor Freda's fate, for in her beginning is her end. The entire book is theatrical, every line of dialogue rings true, provided of course you listen to it and do not merely read it, and no woman reader is going to overlook one thing: the women characters who dominate the book may be odd but Freda has her magnificence and her purple cloak while Brenda has her self-depreciation and her curious devotion to her friend. The men? They are selfish and feeble and if Patrick has a certain skill it is perhaps fitting that he only used it for mending a lavatory and he mends *this* lavatory because he hopes to lay Brenda.

The 1975 novel was called after a man: *Sweet William*; he was hardly that but he was irresistible to women and Ann the heroine was just one of the many who could not and did not resist him. Despite her job with the BBC and her room in Hampstead Anne is as unsophisticated in her different way as Brenda but more aware of the social situation of men: 'She had been taught that men were different; she had digested the fact of their inferiority along with her banana sandwiches and her milk. Men were alien. Her mother and Aunt Bea preferred the society of women: all girls together – leave the nasty men alone with their brutish ways and their engorged appendages. Men were there to pay the mortgages and mend the fuses when they blew. Send them out onto the path to clean the car and hose the drains, brush the lupins from the grass.' Yet this apparent simplification did not simplify anything: 'Out of William's arms and beyond his full attention, she was terrified of him, of the power he exercised. She didn't want to love him if it hurt like this; she would be better off despising him.' Ann was not living a lonely life, as Brenda and Freda did, but like them she was adrift from her environment, which was bridge-playing Brighton. She could only tolerate the home atmosphere for a weekend: 'She was there, but she was only visiting. She could bear it for the moment – the torment of being related to her mother and father, the wounding. She was waiting to go back to London, where there were no enemies. . . .' Before the Second World War it was an accepted fact that one left one's provincial home to escape one's parents and Ann's case is a sad commentary on the fact that the flight is still necessary, even if one has to come only from Brighton and not from those unmentionable northern counties.

Most readers, unfortunately, can identify with a heroine who cannot stop herself falling idiotically in love with a man who is a dead loss, but Ann is a heroine particularly appealing to women because she proves there *can* be escape from the appalling earnestness that the Drabble heroines create round themselves. You may not think much of men but you can meet the irresistible one and just do what he says, you can give up your job as soon as he asks if you care about it and he happens to have money. You can have a baby because it is now fashionable to think you want and ought to have one. And when the baby is born it is a relief to find that a woman novelist can make the scene funny for 99 per cent of the time. One is left with that upsetting remark by Ann's mother, who of course was unexpectedly understanding about the baby-crisis: 'You talk about modern life and things being different now. You haven't learnt anything at all. All this permissiveness has led you young girls into slavery.' The sort of remark that could keep young women awake at night because it might even be partly true. Like that other assertion by William himself – 'Who wants a woman with brains?'

What the novel-reading public has obviously wanted and enjoyed for a decade or so as this is written, is a novelist like Beryl Bainbridge, even if *Young Adolf* (1978) defeated many of her fans. *The Bottle Factory Outing* is a classic of humour, convincing too, provided the reader has had some experience of life outside fiction, and if *Sweet William* is less funny in an obvious knockabout way William and Ann are the proof that the war between men and women is not over, and the possibility that women may never win is so frightening that laughter is the only way out; acceptance is not enough, laughter is positive, as the practical woman and the practical woman novelist know.

Readers who do not care for the feminist line in fiction would enjoy Beryl Bainbridge because she is not an obviously feminist writer, until you begin to think about some of the undertones in her books. Only feminists would notice them, say the male-orientated or the 'old-fashioned' women, the sort of women Sweet William liked. It is impossible to think of Beryl Bainbridge without her unique humour, which can be enjoyed for its own sake, but it seems to me more subtle and even funnier when you realize her preoccupation with women and her resigned acceptance of men, those unsatisfactory creatures without whom so many women apparently cannot manage. Some of her heroines have vague if fanciful ideas about achieving happiness – Freda had her dreams, Ann had her love for William but neither had much luck. Brenda seems to think happiness is out of her reach but at least remains alive and unpregnant. One thinks of Ann's future with her baby but without Sweet William and without Gerald, her early and unsatisfactory so-called fiancé whom her baby resembled, and it is probably going to be better that way, in its post-Drabble atmosphere. But fortunately, one feels, she will have learnt something from William that no Drabble heroine ever learnt – she will eventually relax and laugh and feel better, as Mrs Humphry so wisely recommended in 1897.

How different from Beryl Bainbridge and indeed from every other writer is that other woman novelist who cares so much about women, Fay Weldon. *Female Friends* (1975) is a novel about the interlinked lives of three women and their obsessive preoccupation with femininity. Schoolgirl Chloë is so sex-conscious that she takes off her combinations (she was forced to wear them) behind the hedge by the bus-stop and soon loses her virginity in her mother's bed, seduced by a future successful painter whom no one can resist. The two female friends are Grace and Marjorie, their lives, and those of most others close to them, consist, for the purpose of this novel, almost entirely of pregnancy, abortion, miscarriage, birth, dead babies, death in childbirth, not to speak of seduction, rape, adultery, possible incest, group sex and all possible other sexual dramas not so far listed. In this book there is a mention, *en passant*, of lesbianism but this state of mind and body occupies more space in later novels.

The innocent, or at least the unprepared reader might be puzzled by this apparent obsession with the womb and all the problems it can cause. Sometimes the reader may decide that a whole novel is just a fantasy, but *Female Friends* for instance is only partly so: as in the case of Iris Murdoch, where everything can appear ridiculously improbable if one happens to read one of the novels on a day without faith, it is obvious that most women have experienced strange incidents in their lives caused by troubled sexual relationships, incidents they may prefer to forget – but they can't. Those who did not have these unpublishable incidents often wish that they had – for some sort of ghastly life is better than no life at all. Of course there are women who can share some of Chloë's experiences, as she is forced to watch her husband's love-affair with the *au pair* girl, and of course there are women who go back to cast-off lovers, just as murderers return to scenes of crime – somehow these situations are better lived through than avoided. In real life, in the last decades of the twentieth century, fewer women perhaps have babies in Weldonesque situations – one heroine has a baby in her father's bed, another while dying in an air-raid – but freakish situations involving birth happen every day, as every newspaper reader, J.P., and psychiatric social worker knows.

Why does the author deal so exclusively in primitive and apparently destructive behaviour? Her tone is one of tremendous anger, mainly at the way women were still being treated during and after the Second World War; but the anger is directed not so much at men but at the women themselves: they accept this treatment and even condition their daughters to accept it for another generation of life. Chloë's masochistic mother Gwyneth expected to work until she dropped dead, and did so. Does the woman reader finish each book assuming she is meant to hate men, to feel sorry for them in their dimwittedness, or to feel sorry for the women and admire them in their ridiculous capacity for suffering? I think Fay Weldon is committed to love and admiration for women while trying to show them how they go wrong. With the exception of the horrid Helen, Marjoric's cold-hearted mother, they love their children and attempt to understand them, while Marjorie is unhappy because she has none (she miscarried after her husband died and has to make do with a career instead). The author really cares about women, despite the perpetual flash of the knives she handles so deftly and she is clearly not laughing at their expense, she disapproves of what they are doing, still following the bad examples set by their mothers, and wonders if they are bent on self-destruction, for they seem incapable of changing course.

Her message seems to be: snap out of it, think for yourselves and take care that you are not repeating the old pattern. Chloë's *au pair* girl Françoise (who sleeps with Chloë's husband), explains that in 1968, on the Paris barricades, she was beaten as if she were a man and only gave in at the very end because she had to have her university degree, 'for her freedom'. Her employer cunningly asks her, as they wash up together, whether she calls this freedom, and decides that she is 'both ridiculous and humourless', especially when she explains how her fiancé had eloped with her friend the confectioner, who of course earned more money than Françoise earned in the education office and was 'more pretty' although 'so inferior': the situation proving that poor Françoise had not been educated out of class distinction and was still doing the same old feminine chores. The English reader however will be pleased to hear why she prefers to live in England: it is 'the land where the relationship between the sexes is free and decent and honest. Where else in Europe', she adds, 'could we three live thus and be happy?'

'Where indeed,' says Chloë.

Is Fay Weldon's realism too painful? It ought not to be, because it is about something that won't go away, women's suffering and women's silliness, for something in them makes them consider suffering as inevitable. Thanks to the efforts of women over the last hundred years and also to the efforts of scientists of all kinds on their behalf they need not be doormats of such comfortable thick pile unless they positively want to be. But if they do want to be will they please stop complaining that it is all someone else's fault. It is not easy to decide which of Fay Weldon's grim funny books is the grimmest and funniest, but maybe, at the time of writing at least, *Remember Me* (1976) is the winner. It is less physically gynae-cological than *Female Friends* but just as seriously occupied with the inescapable range of women's problems.

In *Remember Me* Helen is a deserted wife, her doctor husband was prised away by the coldly, cruelly ambitious Lily, the type of woman who always gets what she wants. Helen never gets anything, she is the sort of woman from whom is taken away even that which she hath: her successor tries to take her daughter away and after Helen's death in a car-crash (her car was faulty, naturally, and she was on her way to a marriage-bureau assignment) she does inherit her. Lily and Helen are symbols of have and have not, the former is mean because she is well off (she even wants to save Helen's miserable clothes from the jumble sale) and the latter is feckless because she is so poor – or it could be vice-versa in both cases. Among the lesser characters is a woman who has to be melodramati-cally ill in order to attract any attention at all and a lesbian who has found a precarious happiness.

A lesser novelist, with no thought beyond the black and white of the women's movement, might have made Helen all good and Lily all bad: but that would have solved no problems. The men characters are all beneath contempt and those readers, men readers perhaps, who like to have a credible male character about in their current reading may like this book less for this reason. They may prefer the ghastly but infinitely well described Oliver in *Female*

Friends. Could he happen, picking so many quarrels, destroying the unfortunate mother of at least some of his children? Unfortunately, yes, he can and does happen even quite frequently, while the doctor in *Remember Me* is a fairly stock rendering of the frequently met odious man, callous and basically feeble, ready to be manipulated by someone like Lily.

The author obviously cares for teenagers, both girls and boys, and all her novels show clearly how the details of parental lives affect any young people living in the household. The scenes in *Female Friends* where Chloë and Oliver's children appear are like textbook pages brought to life and all mothers should read them. Yet it is the women characters obviously who stay in the mind, even if the reader is torn between a smirk and a shudder as she or he learns of their extraordinary deeds. These women may be unacceptable to women who think they are not like them in any way, but perhaps the author is indicating that all human females *are* potentially like them if we would only admit it, behave and talk as we want to behave and talk. The novels deal with essentials only, and those invisible knives which shape so many pointed remarks have also been used before the books open to slice away everything unnecessary, all those tedious details with which orthodox novelists clutter up their books, those descriptions of country houses or London streets or flats, those analyses of motives. Fay Weldon has removed this time- and space-consuming apparatus and as a result her characters can display their primitive emotions and behaviour without anything to distract them or us.

As for technique, Fay Weldon is much more of an innovator than Beryl Bainbridge, who has been content so far to use traditional form. Fay Weldon's experiments with technique obviously owe a good deal to her work as a radio and TV dramatist; in *Female Friends* for instance there are passages which seem to come from a playscript. Traditionalists, if any such are led to reading this author, may say: Choose between the novel and the drama, do not mix the genres. There seems no reason to object to the mixture, which was in fact used by various nineteenth-century novelists, and the author sees the lows and highs of her book that way, just as life too consists of lows and highs. In *Remember Me* there are other devices, and surely no one can escape a cold thrill when those strange monologuing voices are heard out of the darkness: 'O I am Lily, the doctor's wife . . .'. It is these voices that make the novel particularly memorable, for they echo the grand voices of classical drama, although there is no grandeur in what they have to say.

Praxis of 1979 was one of the six novels shortlisted for the Booker Prize of that year. Sadly, of that six it was the one least likely to win because the whole point of the book would probably have repelled at least half of its potential readers, namely men, despite its inventions, wit and devastating black humour. The point is to make every reader aware yet again of the situation of women, how they allow men to exploit them, how one must have an inconvenient baby at the age of 45 or another out of refusal to accept contraception and abortion: ' "I like sex," said Mary blandly. "And it's much more exciting without contraception." ' Mary has to give up a hospital job because of this accidental baby; for good measure born mongoloid. Praxis decides to suffocate it and goes to gaol.

Never did an author cram so much action, always concerned with sexuality, babies and children, into one book. Without the humour, black and growing blacker, the whole thing would seem absurd. But if the humour is black, there are no black and white attitudes towards any human problem, for the world is not so simple. The author is far too intelligent to have believed that, and describes how Praxis saw her job as editor of a feminist broadsheet: 'She wrote rousing editorials, which she half believed, and half did not, in the same way as she had half believed, half not, her own advertisements for the Electricity Boards. But she felt she was righting some kind of balance. . . .' The author ironically allows Praxis to go through a kind of religious experience:

'She was a convert: she wished to proselytise. . . . Wherever she went she saw women betrayed, exploited and oppressed. She saw that women were the cleaners, the fetchers, the carriers, the humble of the earth, and that they were truly blessed.

'She saw that men's lives were without importance and that only the lives of women were significant. She lost her belief in the man-made myths of history – great civilisations, great art, great empire. The male version of events.'

She saw identification with the women's movement as her salvation, 'But she was wrong. . . . There is no finite point at which we can say, ah, I have arrived: I am saved: I am rich, successful, happy. We wake the next morning and see that we are not.' There can never be a whole answer, not even sisterhood. Fay Weldon does indeed 'right some kind of balance', for if she concentrates on the fate of womb-centred women she can laugh blackly both at them and at the women who seem to deny the existence of the womb. The fact that a woman writer can take these attitudes in a series of intensely readable novels can only help women, for if a man tried to take them he could only write as an observer.

How, say the orthodox, can two such writers as Beryl Bainbridge and Fay Weldon have much to do with laughter, considering their subject matter and their attitudes? Fortunately, a good deal, and principally because we now laugh at things that once were not thought funny. Also, we have to laugh because there is nothing else to do. If we laugh at them we accept them as something that is part of life, and if Fay Weldon seems to exaggerate everything it is because she is determined to make readers not only read and laugh, often out of surprise and shock, but think and act. The non-laughers are unspeakable bores and one can never think of anything to say to them, they are even more boring than schoolboy humour. The atmosphere in Fay Weldon's books is much more tense than in anything written by Beryl Bainbridge, the author will not allow her adult audience much in the way of horseplay comedy, there can be no relaxation from the serious business in hand. The comedy has a searing quality. It does not matter if some incidents seem absurd, and would Praxis Duveen really have suffocated that mongoloid baby? What matters is that she believed her action justified and in carrying it out she is doing what many people, and not only women, think of doing. Only fear of punishment holds them back.

As with that very different novelist Iris Murdoch the fantasy is never as fantastic as it seems. Worse things happen not at sea but in cities and suburbia, and Fay Weldon uses all the persuasiveness that she was able to develop in the advertising world – but obviously possessed in the first place by natural bounty – to make the reader see *how* they happen. Mainly, as we all know, because women may not be able to grow out of their apparently inbuilt masochism. They are not meant to outgrow the life force, but surely they can learn how to train both sons and daughters better. If they do, social life will be more fun for everybody. Despite her violence I suspect Fay Weldon sees some hope for women after a few more generations have gone by, for so many of her characters are positive, while Beryl Bainbridge, despite her knockabout comedy, seems to see women as lonely creatures who have not learnt to laugh at men or even at themselves. Like the Weldon characters however they have decided that men are a poor lot on the whole and there is no point in waiting for them to improve because they won't. I believe these two writers have made black humour the keynote of fiction in a way no male novelists have done. If they appear obsessed with the nationalistic aspects of feminism at least they turn them into highly readable stories. They are not interested in providing escape literature, because they do not believe in it; absolute relaxation is elusive for them, because as women they are too much aware that someone, somewhere is always on the point of making some demands on them. If they do not respond to these demands, even in some small way, they would not be women. The least change in the social scene affects women, because they are vulnerable, caring not so much for themselves as for the young and the old. Women's humour therefore can only be partly concerned with laughter, since laughter for them can only be concerned with part of life.

In 1978 the critic and broadcaster Sheridan Morley looked serious when he told me there was 'a shortage of funny ladies, especially in the arts'. Poor ladies, they are still earnest, and would do better if they remembered how Vera Brittain told their history – they should become women. A reading of Beryl Bainbridge and Fay Weldon would help them, they would learn how to laugh in a new way.

[13]
Observing

❀❀❀

If there is not a great deal of exciting experiment in British fiction at this late stage of the twentieth century, there is at least evidence that more writers, and especially women writers, are paying much more attention to form. At last several of them have successfully adopted that elegant type of fiction which the French and Italians have used during this century as in fact during earlier ones, the *conte*, *récit* or *novella*, more than a short story, which remains anecdotal whatever its length, and less than a novel. Sometimes British publishers have used the word novella, but they seemed apologetic about it. During the 1970s however several novelists wrote successful short novels. For more and more people reading time these days is short, especially of course for women, who are usually doing two jobs at the same time.

Women writers have been outstandingly successful in this genre, notably in France, where *Gigi* by Colette and *Madame de . . .* by Louise de Vilmorin were masterpieces. The genre was able to flourish more happily where publishers or some Maecenas financed literary magazines of high quality which appeared fairly regularly and introduced new writers into the literary market place; however, there are so few of these now – and Britain produced no *Mercure de France* or *Botteghe oscure* – that writers must usually limit themselves to stories of boringly orthodox length in a few anthologies. Not so Caroline Blackwood, fortunately, whose themes and style fit the short novel format perfectly.

The author was born in Northern Ireland and became the second wife of Robert Lowell, the American poet. She was a journalist before she wrote novels and was therefore conditioned to writing a specified number of words and no more. Her fiction was geared to brevity: the themes are based on situations so intensely dramatic that they could not last too long and the reader could not spend too long reading them either. It is a question of who reaches breaking-point first, the characters themselves in their unbearable situations or those of us who wonder if or how they are going to survive them. It is a big part of Caroline Blackwood's talent that she can present as credible a set of circumstances which might not have seemed credible outside court cases and psychiatrists' collections of case histories. Far too many writers attempt to show odd people in even odder circumstances by slowly building up a solid edifice of oddity and forgetting that the reader who traditionally likes the old-fashioned 'good read' (which tends to be a long read) does not care for disturbing content. These readers do not object to a reasonable amount of upset, because they can identify with that state of affairs and wait with enthusiasm for things to improve, but they do not like to see life getting out of hand and disaster on the horizon. Although such readers do not insist on a diet of saccharine they cannot easily stomach long weighty novels on themes which usually reflect the related social problems of today: alienation and loneliness, all due to what Anna Kavan called a 'scarcity of love'.

These readers have probably been underestimated by too many writers. With Caroline Blackwood they now have a chance to learn and understand something of our serious social problems because they can read about them in a novel of suspense that makes one unforgettable point: who indeed could forget *The Stepdaughter* which Caroline Blackwood published in 1976, in which a deserted wife and her ex-husband's daughter live a ghastly isolated life in a ritzy New York apartment. In the same way *Great Granny Webster*, who gives her name to the novel of 1977, exists in isolation, as her dead daughter had done, going mad in a decaying Irish mansion, a place which sounds like a wicked caricature of Bowen's Court. The narrators in both cases are women, pathetically unpleasant if mad in the former book and *sympathique* and young in the latter. Never did Matthew Arnold's words come so often to mind:

> Yea, in the sea of life enisl'd,
> We mortal millions live alone –

The achievement of Caroline Blackwood is to make every reader of her fiction aware, painfully aware, of this, and the work is all the more valuable because the author never writes any instructions on the blackboard, she is in no direct way didactic, thus working without the flaw that spoils some of the world's greatest novels, and since our context is writing by women we have to admit that even George Eliot suffered from this vice of her times.

Later novelists too, such as Fay Weldon for example, enjoy passing on their judgements and instructions, but this latter writer always manages to do so without boring her readers mainly because she is so violent and funny. On the whole Caroline Blackwood keeps violence and comedy to her non-fiction and the melodrama in her novels is always observed from a distance. Her work is the brilliant production of the reporter turned novelist, revealing herself to have been a novelist all the time. It could also be argued that her non-fiction reveals a novelist playing a reporter, but 'playing' what is a deadly game. The critical success enjoyed by Caroline Blackwood's work is due to two reasons which are inseparable. She belongs to the times by content and form, a writer who is successful because she writes in a totally workmanlike professional way and makes no attempt to be 'literary'.

At this stage of the twentieth century however readers demand fact, drama, poetry, and they expect to find all these elements in at least some novels, along with a story of some sort. The readers are no longer sure if they want 'literature' because they are no longer sure what that is. Caroline Blackwood knows very well that in some important respects literature and journalism have the same criteria – they must communicate clearly, they must have a shape of some sort and they must not waste words. This does not mean that a long work cannot have the status of literature, what matters is that length should be balanced by density of content and by the texture of the writing. No one would say for instance that *Pilgrimage* or *Ulysses* is too long, they need their length, just as *Great Granny Webster* needs its brevity. The long mad years of the narrator's grandmother could not be told at length, the book would have become unbalanced and we would forget the long unnatural years of the great-grandmother's life. As the book stands it is possible to read the descriptions of these life spans, while if the book had been one of 350 pages in length the exhausted reader would probably have given up before the end. There would certainly have been dilution, the book would have been different; Caroline Blackwood presumably conceived it like this, it is her way of making her points and let no one think it is necessarily 'easier' to write a short book than to write a long one. The author had to think her way through a great deal of material before deciding in what precise way she was going to leave out any direct reference to it.

So far there has not been much room in her fiction for the black humour to be found in her journalism, even if pieces such as in *For all that I found There* (1973) could be described as on the way to fiction in any case. I personally remember only the horror and pathos of *The Stepdaughter* but the story of Great Granny Webster has at least the light relief of Aunt Lavinia and the 1920s-type incidents, including abortion, proving that great granny's daughter was not the only mad member of the family: Aunt Lavinia's eccentricity turned into depression and she was the only one to think her attempt at suicide was funny. In fact she killed herself in the end without too much trouble. Great-grandmother's cremation at the end of the book, when the ashes cling to the narrator's coat like snowflakes and possibly get in the one good eye of the housekeeper she had so ill-treated might have been grimly comic but funeral and cremation scenes in fiction, almost always at the beginning or the end of a book, are too much the same and rarely convincing enough. This one as it happens is almost too convincing because ashes *do* blow about and *do* get in the so-called mourners' eyes. If one has had this experience the finale here is something of a let-down and if one has not, then one cannot quite believe it.

If in future novels Caroline Blackwood decides to develop the moments of black humour she clearly relishes, she is unlikely to lose her individuality, her faculty for seeing, as a journalist sees, the few telling details that tell so much more than long analyses. Her work as it stands in 1980 shows her as a totally different novelist from Beryl Bainbridge and Fay Weldon, lacking the macabre knockabout farce of the former and the violent, ironic feminism of the latter, working always with a light-meter and therefore recording her subject matter from a suitable distance, in sharp focus and with well balanced areas of shadow, the shadow always of the right depth. Does she, on the strength of her few novels so far, deserve classification specifically as a woman novelist? some will ask. Is a reporter – and she is still a reporter even at the most intense moments of her novels – not outside sex? In the treatment of her themes, yes, perhaps, but in the choice of themes and their expression through character, Caroline Blackwood has chosen to present women characters, women of many types. Men are remarkable by their absence and their feebleness or their failures, the failings which have led to more pragmatic feminism than most people seem to realize. In these novels husbands and fathers are home-deserters, casualties of war or incompetent creatures who could never have been expected to achieve much. It is left to great-granny Webster to commit her daughter to a mental hospital, for the mad woman's husband could not get round to it. The narrator's father, the only man who could tolerate great-granny, is killed early in the First World War. If he had survived he might have developed a relationship with the fierce, straightbacked old lady, and since that would have changed the course of family history – for this short book is a history, not an anecdote – he had to be removed from the scene. There is no hostility to men in these books, but the author uses her strong female characters to remove them, and the men are incapable of fighting back, even if they had dared to try.

In her fiction Caroline Blackwood does not openly criticize men, neither do her female characters, they know instinctively they must manage without them, and the reader is left admiring the author's technique and wondering with slight discomfort how far these women are destroyers of men and whether the short, sharp novel is a sound way of effecting the kill and reporting it at one and the same time. The short novel of the uncomfortable type is like a stimulating injection, its shortness allows one to relish both its form and its message. It would be too easy if all short novels were *ipso facto* books of unforgettable impact, like *The Stepdaughter*, or like the novels of Helen Hodgman, set in Australasia, for if this were the case the whole atmosphere of British publishing would change and life in the book world would probably move at a smarter pace.

That sense of form which brings together such different people as Caroline Blackwood and, say, Beryl Bainbridge, obviously conditions literary juries, or the work of Penelope Fitzgerald would not have been so successful. Her novels *The Bookshop* (1978) and *Offshore* (1979) are interesting because there is no sharpness in the actual writing, no violence as with Helen Hodgman; in the former there is a fascination with all that is most hypocritical but fortunately comical in English middle-class life – awareness of class and the snobbery it entails. The second novel makes it clear that most of us live unsatisfactorily in reach of dry land and are never quite sure if we want security of any sort or not. When some factions complained about the 1979 Booker Prize award to this novelist they forgot no doubt that subtlety is still considered a virtue by others, even if it tends to appear in fiction now only as a kind of afterglow. We might as well enjoy it now in novels written by women, because it is hardly likely to appear in work by men, especially in a world dominated by social pressures and advertising techniques. When everyone demands full-colour frontals there is surely not much future outside poetry for the subtle, the drypoint and the collotype. If there is a turning away in fiction from noise and glamour it will surely be in the work of women.

[14]
Neverending

Between 1954 and 1980 Iris Murdoch has published some twenty novels and there are almost as many ways of looking at her achievement. Some may see it as equivalent to that fabulous firework display described with such zest in *Under the Net*, her second novel published in 1954. Other readers can react very differently, including the novelist Jennifer Dawson, author of *The Ha-Ha*, who described her tartly in a letter to the surgeon-writer David Le Vay as 'the Barbara Cartland of the middle classes'. This apparently unexpected identification could be based on several criteria that do not really matter, such as large output, but it is more amusing to reflect on the more important contrasts. Both writers are apparently concerned with entertainment and morality, they go about their presentation in different ways and presumably the difference in socio-sexual atmosphere expresses the intellectual difference in readership. I like to think of the remark as the ideal examination question – 'explain, discuss and illustrate' – awaiting the British or English literature student who might one day be lucky enough to find an Iris Murdoch novel on the examination syllabus.

Without attempting to answer such an unlikely hypothetical question it seems only fair to point out that the two authors have two totally obvious things in common, they are both women and have enjoyed a great success. By 'success' I mean here only that thousands of readers know their names and read all their books, while critical success is non-existent in one case and hard to analyse in the other. However, since the extent of women novelists' reputations are of great interest in the present publicity-conscious age, it is worth noting that one can know everything about Barbara Cartland, through the publicity machine which she conducts with such efficient enjoyment, without having to read more than one page from any of her books. Her lifestyle is a romance in itself, much more entertaining than those novels which publishers call 'romantic' and another aspect of the theme woman–novelist-as-actress. It also proves, surprisingly, that women who write romantic novels do not possess those 'feminine' qualities of which they make such play in their books. If they were truly 'feminine' they would not have to keep on telling us that they are, and if they really cared for women they would not feed them so much sugar in the form of fictional romance. Everyone knows that it will rot their non-physical teeth.

As far as reputation is concerned the situation of Iris Murdoch could not be more different. Some cheap editions of her novels carry brief biographies, she is known as a professional philosopher with an interest in questions relating to education; some of her work has been adapted for stage television, there is a good deal of gossip about her but in order to assess her as a novelist one has to read the books. Addicts will find that there are none too many and will defend their preferences down to the last veiled reference to some philosophical theory, the last incredible tragi-comic scene, the last sexual fantasy, suicide or murder.

If the flight from reality is one of the most important objections to romantic fiction, can it be said that Iris Murdoch has much to do with the real, the ordinary life that happens all round us? Strangely enough, and this is the most fascinating aspect of her work, she appears preoccupied with unreality and fantasy whereas in fact she *is* concerned with reality – depending of course on what is meant by reality, and no term is harder to define. How Iris Murdoch sees it becomes partly apparent throughout her work, but since it never becomes wholly clear the reader never loses his sense of excitement, a particular type of excitement with an emotional-intellectual mix.

As for reality in the more or less normal sense, the everyday scene that few of us can escape, the approach is indirect, nothing is what it seems to be and yet in the end we accept that Iris Murdoch is constantly dealing with reality, however paradoxical that might appear, and after following the most unlikely methods helps us to see extraordinary truths about ourselves and our society. At the same time she is an entertainer, and enchanter even, and is probably the only Irish/English writer of today who can suddenly produce a 'shock' situation and not be in any way shocking. When we read in *A Severed Head* that the sinister Palmer Anderson and his half-sister are in bed together the shock might have been much more than surprise, we might have found the situation obscene – but we don't. This is due to the speed with which the situation develops and the total absence of physical detail. Some readers may actually laugh, not because the situation is funny in an obvious way but the only method of applauding the novelist's skill is through a kind of thrilled laughter – another example of the 'new' laughter – while at the same time we must surely laugh at ourselves, partly for failing to guess what was coming and partly because we have a brief glimpse of our own surprise. And if anyone asks 'where is the reality?' the answer is that the author, working on what she knew about her own characters in the book and about people in real life, has created reality out of a situation that is *potentially* real. Moreover, every reader knows how often one can meet a Murdoch character in 'ordinary' life.

As we have already accepted, the word 'reality' admits of several definitions and one of the unnerving things about reading Iris Murdoch is that she is obviously capable of using widely differing interpretations simultaneously. This seems to me one of the most intriguing reasons for the unique atmosphere of her novels, and there is of course the interplay between her definitions and those unconsciously adopted by her readers. How could such a situation fail to entertain?

Even within one novel characters can obviously live in different worlds, but usually a balance is achieved because the extreme behaviour of one or more people is countered by the more or less 'normal' conduct of others. *The Nice and the Good* (1968) for example, shows how this can happen. Does anyone believe for a moment that the civil servant Radeechy could exist as he is shown here and carry out celebrations of the Black Mass in the basement of the Home Office, in the middle of London's Whitehall? It is a fine piece of melodrama, but in one sense it is also 'realistic' because, given luck and guile, a minor obsession can easily grow into a major one. Circumstances allow this to happen in *The Nice and the Good* until the day Radeechy, for various reasons, could go no further and shot himself. There was a time when such incidents were known only to psychiatrists and psychologists, who do not often write fiction. When it comes to reading fiction they might find that produced by Iris Murdoch too disturbing, for they would be led, through *déformation professionnelle*, to look at some of it with a clinical eye, and therefore find no relaxation. More and more readers of the ordinary kind nowadays are likely to have had some experience, if only indirect, of personality problems and their treatment. Those readers who have suffered from inadequate psychiatric treatment, usually through their own failure to cooperate, will not enjoy Iris Murdoch, and in an unkind way I would say that served them right, for they had obviously not wished to be cured and therefore have lost the chance to enjoy this absorbing author.

Many other aspects of the novels are a direct reflection of the social scene. There is for instance a fascinating example of that contemporary situation, the extended family, obviously destined, for various reasons, to become more and more prevalent, at least in Britain. Given the divorce rate, the lack of jobs and houses one wonders how many people would live otherwise, even if they do not realise, especially among the middle-classes, exactly what they are doing. In *The Nice and the Good* Paula's husband has left her, so she and her children are living in Dorset with Kate and Octavian. In the same human complex live the widowed Mary Clothier and the alienated, alien Willy, plus several other people of various ages, the kind of group one has now learnt to recognise in 'real' life, as though nature had indeed begun to imitate art. How this group of people, a fairly average 'mix' on the whole, are involved with the unaverage story of Radeechy is well known to all Murdoch addicts but, like most of the novels, can hardly be summarized adequately in a few sentences. The secret of integrating seemingly irreconcilable elements belongs to this author alone. We begin to think of something akin to crossword clues – one set 'real', the other 'unreal', and by some magical fusion of the two the human puzzle is solved. The 'magic' may be written off as 'Irish' by some and praised as super-intelligent by others, while those who prefer academic analysis should read A.S. Byatt's early critical study of the author entitled *Degrees of Freedom* (1965). To explain or even describe successful literary sparkle by the term 'magic' may seem critical failure. A better word is poetry, which always disconcerts novel readers, many of whom profess not to enjoy it. These readers should however note that Iris Murdoch has published poetry of a quality proving she is a poet in her own right, she is not limited to the field of fiction, despite her enormous output.

If Iris Murdoch herself belongs to the family of great artists she is deeply preoccupied with the family situation, whether 'extended' or not. She is not interested in that worthy but tedious type of fiction described as 'family saga', but of course the generation gap concerns her. Unlike so many other novelists of this century she has been less active in describing hate than in describing love, with the result that the members of her families sometimes love each other too much for the orthodox: the result is near-incest, which appears in *A Severed Head*, as already mentioned, and also in *The Time of the Angels* (1966). At the same time other currents are at work among her characters, obviously tending to destroy family life in the old-fashioned sense, for she is quick to deal with one of those situations which preoccupy a large proportion of people today, consciously, unconsciously or professionally. It is not so much a 'situation' but a psychological and social problem: homosexuality. It is extraordinary to realize that, in Britain at least, many novels about homosexuality have been written by men novelists, but they were not actually published at least during the first part of the twentieth century. The classics of the genre belonged to the ancient world or to Germany and France, if one accepts the term 'classic' as suitable for Petronius, the Thomas Mann of *Death in Venice*, the Jean Cocteau of *Le Livre blanc*, Roger Peyrefitte or Jean Genet. The fate of *The Well of Loneliness* is well enough known and such was the power of the law in Britain that books such as E.M. Forster's *Maurice* (1971) were simply not published when they were written. Perhaps it has always been 'safer' to write about lesbianism, even when Radclyffe Hall's book was old history, since homosexual relationships between women have never been illegal in Britain. If

Elizabeth Bowen in the 1930s made a few indirect references to lesbian relationships, and Ivy Compton-Burnett included homosexual themes in one or two of her novels it was in fact Iris Murdoch who was the first to present consistently without any fuss or special pleading what we now accept as 'normal abnormality'; no one novel is concerned exclusively with homosexuals, but the novelist assumes that in English middle-class society there are many homosexual couples who live their own kind of married life, encountering the same kinds of problems as heterosexual couples.

Twenty years after its publication *The Bell* (1958) is ancient history and the over-sophisticated would say now that the discovery of Michael's homosexuality, that unexpected kiss, was intended to shock the reader. As the novels continued it became obvious that among the hundreds of characters Murdoch created several were homosexual and even more only half-realized their own problem. By the time we come to *The Nice and the Good* in 1968 we are frankly bored by the undercurrent of homosexuality, as Duncan nonchalantly places his arm round his chauffeur in the car.

But it is not so much boring as 'normal' and that is why Iris Murdoch has made such a valuable contribution to the fiction preoccupied with this theme. She makes no obvious propaganda, never complains about the law. There is a feeling throughout the books that homosexuality is widespread, among men at least, that it is a natural form of behaviour and nobody should be surprised by it, although they should realize it may lead to unexpected incidents. Iris Murdoch has been criticized for the amount of 'fantasy' she includes in her novels but when she deals with homosexuality she is in her way not a fantasist, but a realist. The reason why a hard core of middle-class readers dislike Iris Murdoch is that they find her deeply disturbing and will not admit the fact. A few generations ago endless people would complain, 'Why must they drag sex into everything?' Sex, of course, had nothing to do with love. Now their complaint is, 'Why must they drag homosexuality into everything?' The answer is that any part of the human psyche deserves attention, whether one believes in Freud, Jung or anyone else. Those who have faced up to the problem in themselves will relish every detail of the way this novelist handles it. Those who are frightened by the disturbance to themselves will obviously not enjoy Iris Murdoch. They will think of reasons for explaining their dislike and indicate that this is not suitable subject matter for fiction. They find it not shocking but too private. Yet the very people who take fright here tend to be those intelligent readers who would oppose the banning of *The Well of Loneliness* or *Lady Chatterley's Lover* because they consider the censorship of the arts to be the greatest immorality of all. In her treatment of homosexuality Iris Murdoch proves most convincingly that her so-called 'fantasy' is much closer to reality than many readers want to admit.

Her preoccupation with homosexuality is probably due to more subtle considerations than a plea for acceptance, it is also a message to women: be more understanding of male homosexuals, yes, but more importantly be ready to deal with homosexuality in its latent state, which leads to uncertainty or violence. Remember also that homosexuality in women, latent or not, needs understanding, so does bisexuality. There is a secondary part to the message: women, even when young, should not attempt to imitate men, for this is destructive. Women could do more, the author seems to suggest, to prevent violence, and they should not forget the caring side of their nature. In that particularly brilliant novel *An Accidental Man* (1971) the author almost intervenes to say 'please, care for people, especially understand and care for Dorinda, nobody is trying to help her'. The gradual alienation of this girl, and her death in a nameless hotel, form one of the most sadly memorable aspects of a rich and thought-provoking book, one that is also a condemnation of many sacred middle-class values.

From time to time academic critics, when not analysing fascinating symbols in the novels, such as the frequent appearance of twins, or her liking for dramas set by the sea, tend to complain that Iris Murdoch plays with themes and problems, taking no one or nothing seriously enough for very long. This apparent lack of depth, and I am convinced it is only apparent, is of course part of her indirect approach and her direct insistence that the reader must be entertained with a genuine narrative. Many earnest novelists would be better employed writing educational non-fiction because they will not accept Iris Murdoch's own soundly reasoned exhortations 'against dryness', which she wrote in a much-quoted essay. Nearly all her books are illuminated from within by a light which is not easily defined, it is not merely 'humour' or 'artistry', it is a sense of all that is vivid and dramatic, a quality in one way quite new: one feels that she has absorbed all the surprise element of surrealism and then grafted or welded it to the conventional aspects of the English novel, which include such obvious elements as a preference for middle class settings and an acceptance of narrative form little changed from the way it was in the nineteenth century.

Of all the genuinely creative women's novels which have appeared in Britain since 1940 or so Iris Murdoch's books are the hardest to analyse and the hardest to put down, even when slightly too long. She seems to have made an effort now and then to write novels which are more 'straightforward', without the so-called 'fantasy' associated most closely with her – *The Sandcastle* (1957), *An Unofficial Rose* (1962), *The Italian Girl* (1964) but her value is clearest in the books nobody else could have written, which are in fact nearly all the others. Readers of novels written since the Second World War may see Iris Murdoch as one of the figures dominating the landscape, but despite her long-lasting appeal of over twenty years she may not please our grandchildren, except as an oddity of history. She will not please women readers of today devoted to the cause of feminism because she is no militant in this cause; although constantly aware of women's problems she is inclined to be conservative about their social role. Her contribution is through her artistry. Just as she is a tantalising writer herself it is equally tantalising to think of her future among the twentieth-century classics, for it is still far too early to decide it. Sometimes in her work one comes across a remark which indicates an ancestor – Rose Macaulay for instance – but mercifully she is not likely to be followed by any imitative progeny. It is worth remembering what she said in discussion with Brian Magee in 1978 (BBC 2): 'Literature is, very often, mystification – and, besides, literature is for fun, literature entertains.' Entertainer and enchantress as she is, her achievements are unique.

Since 1940 or so, fiction by women has been extraordinarily varied and so many names have earned so much praise that it is impossible to assess them all, especially when many of the writers, as this goes to press, are only half-way through their careers.

Some, sadly, did not live long enough to prove their talents. I regret very much Elizabeth Myers, whose 1943 book *A Well Full of Leaves* glittered with imagery and movement and awareness of social problems. Some have been oddly neglected, like Barbara Comyns, but her novel *The Vet's Daughter* (1959), based on a true story from Edwardian times, has now been revived.

Revived, too, are some rewarding names from the inter-war period: Fryniwyd Tennyson Jesse and Sylvia Townsend Warner, for instance. Who could ever forget the latter's *Lolly Willowes* of 1926? The same year saw Radclyffe Hall's novel *Adam's Breed*, probably her best. And it is a pity that women (and men, no doubt) will study every word of Victoria Sackville-West's excellent gardening books but forget to read *All Passion Spent* of 1931, about the woman who yearned to be a painter but chose instead to dwindle into a wife.

But neglected women novelists are nothing today compared with the numbers of neglected wives, and the latter have been lucky in some ways that so many competent writers have spoken up for them. This happened when the horrors of the domestic scene in the servantless post-war period began to occupy too much of middle-class time. Somebody had to write about the problem, and Penelope Mortimer's first novel *A Villa in Summer* (1954) was one of the first in Britain to dwell on the unbearable domestic chaos of family life. Women writers had to undertake this type of writing – in fact they could not have stopped themselves – because men simply left the house and banged the door behind them. The new type of novel was different from those presenting fairly obvious problems, such as keeping up with the Joneses, which occur in all so-called developed societies. Penelope Mortimer does not forget this side of life, but she is intent on showing how both husband and wife react, and how much the children matter. Domestic details did not preoccupy novelists too much until the novelists themselves suddenly realized how much they personally were affected by the servantless society. For 'novelists' we can read 'women novelists' because the majority of men novelists still had self-effacing wives who devoted their existence to their husbands. Other men novelists managed somehow and did not allow washing up – if they ever had meals at home – to stop production. But after the Second World War many strange things happened, including a baby-boom, and only sulky undomesticated continental *au pair* girls were there to take over from the fast-disappearing nannies, grandmothers and other helpers. It was obvious that this awkward transitional situation would be described in fiction by women, even if men were quite equal to writing 'kitchen sink' dramas for television. Men writers will deal with the atmosphere generated round the sink but they will not actually describe, as Esther McCracken did in one of her war-time plays, *No Medals*, what it feels like to pick the little bits out of the sink, after they had failed to go down the waste-pipe. This type of detail is more than boring in itself but since it has occupied so much of women's time they tend to dwell on it, for they have not men's capacity for ignoring it or cursing it.

Children are inseparable from the day-to-day details of domestic life and the women novelists of the late 1940s and after made both the children and the details into important elements in their books. No more fanciful idealism, no more Compton-Burnett children uttering profound psychological truths, for some time now it was to be all bath-time, push-chairs and play-schools. The very conception of children was desperately important in fiction as in life, and surely Penelope Mortimer created a minor classic of women's writing, of great relevance to men, in *The Pumpkin-Eater* (1962) about the woman who was obsessed with pregnancy as the means of justifying her existence. It has been described as a journalistic novel but it has a direct intensity of style which few of the so-called literary novelists have equalled. The dialogue moves fast, no word is wasted and the novel can be reread at any time without striking us as dated.

In case any reader thinks *The Pumpkin-Eater* is the one book which will always be identified with Penelope Mortimer I would advise them to read *Long Distance* (1974), the story of a woman undergoing psychiatric treatment after her life is broken at the centre. One is aware of nothing less than personal tragedy but also of immense courage, while the artistic success of the book lifts it miles away from the confession novel. It makes *The Ha-ha* by Jennifer Dawson seem very young indeed and Janet Frame's novels about life in a mental hospital diffuse. Penelope Mortimer has not survived as a cult figure, despite the success of *The Pumpkin-Eater*, but she was a pioneer novelist among the women writers who had grown up during the war, recorded the new society of the 'Forties and 'Fifties, and wasted no time, just as she wasted no words, in looking back.

In the *Penguin Companion to Literature*, the entry about Penelope Mortimer, written by P.J. Keating, states that 'her novels bring vividly alive a world of domesticity, child-bearing and broken marriages, a world that hovers continually on the edge of nightmare.' A world in fact that everyone would be glad to escape from, but far too many women feel trapped in it and do not seem to know what to do about it. Margaret Drabble, in the group of novels published in the 1960s and early 70s, gave another picture of this world. She created a series of young heroines, middle-class girls, who were all more or less the same, feckless, unpractical, earnest, somehow incapable of straightforward feeling and quite remarkably dull. There is no doubt that they appealed directly to endless young women readers whose lives, crowded with small children and empty of domestic help, were not much fun. The lives of the heroines tended to be empty of satisfactory husbands and lovers too, for frankly what man could be interested for long in such unamusing creatures? Strangely, Iris Murdoch's novels appear frivolous and are not, whereas Margaret Drabble's heroines appear responsible but are the reverse. In *The Millstone* (1965) for instance Rosamund accepts casual sex without love and has her baby with relative ease because she has an apartment to live in while her parents are safely thousands of miles away. She has none of the problems that beset the unmarried pregnant girl and I cannot see what she is being brave about.

As for Rose Vassiliou in *The Needle's Eye* (1972), the incompetent poor little rich girl, and Jane Grey the poet who accepts post-puerperal sex with little surprise (*The Waterfall*, 1969), they are a very odd and depressing bunch of young women, but interesting to the older generation who could not have borne to live this way; these lives do not appear to have anything to do with liberty. The women are in a muddle, confused about the difference between liberty and liberation, always waiting for someone or something external to themselves to decide things for them. They are in the grip of the life force and insist on having children. Fortunately these children give them some pleasure, which is just as well, for the children's fathers do not seem very welcome on the whole. The children of course reflect the mothers' intense concern with themselves, so intense that they cannot obviously take any serious interest in men.

These books, with their strangely invertebrate style, their editing as vague as their heroines, provide a curious chapter in the history of the post-war domestic novel. They have perpetuated a group of women who spend much time creating their own problems and they have certainly influenced many other writers: they have increased interest in mother-child relationships in fiction. Unlike Fay Weldon, Margaret Drabble does not offer any help to her readers on how to bring up children, especially girls, in the hope of improving their lot in the next generation. Women novelists ought to be outstanding in their presentation of children in fiction, but I must say I prefer the children described by the French novelists, such as Françoise Mallet-Joris, they learn some charm and wit early in life.

I imagine that after another decade or so women novelists will write more about adult behaviour and less about pregnancy, childbirth and intense mother-child relationships. Paddy Kitchen's *Lying-In* (1965), Verity Bargate's *No Mama No!* of 1977 and Fay Weldon's *Puffball* (1980) have briefed us, warned, depressed and amused us. It would be a mistake to say there can be nothing new for some woman novelist is undoubtedly writing it as this goes to press.

Novels set in the kitchen and the nursery are obviously inclined to be intense and like Sue Kaufmann's 'mad housewife' everyone is glad to escape, however briefly, into adult, coolly amusing novels like those written earlier by Elizabeth Taylor, who offers entertainment, subtlety of style and the plus quality of satire. There is also the elegant, classical work of Sybille Bedford. If the short, sharp novels of Caroline Blackwood or Helen Hodgman seem more suitable to late twentieth-century conditions a few women writers have obviously enjoyed the panoramic novel, which seems to be the current version of the family saga so popular in the 1930s. Maureen Duffy's *Microcosm*, a 1966 landscape of lesbian life, seems to me a fascinating social document, whereas A.S. Byatt no doubt aimed at a similar result with her immensely long work *The Virgin in the Garden* (1978). If only it were less soporific the older generation would no doubt find it absorbing, through sheer nostalgia, but they lack the author's stamina.

Among so many outstanding women novelists writing in the late twentieth century it seems invidious to mention only a few, but indeed only a few names are needed to rout those absurd commentators who periodically moan about the death of the novel. Over a period of twenty-five years for instance Brigid Brophy has published a series of novels in several different genres, from the still relevant fable *Hackenfeller's Ape* of 1953 through the Firbankian *Finishing Touch* of ten years later to the openly baroque type of writing she seems to prefer, such as *Palace without Chairs* (1974). If she were to concentrate on the writing of fiction there would be even more surprises and successes from her but she might then be lost to us as a critic and a tireless campaigner for authors' rights.

During the 1960s Nell Dunn proved in *Up the Junction* and *Poor Cow* that it *was* possible, if one's ear was good enough, to put lively working-class speech down on paper. At the same time, and during the earlier 1970s, Susan Hill wrote some successful and memorable novels but decided that she no longer wanted to be a novelist. At the time of writing Alice Thomas Ellis has published *The Sin Eater* (1977) offering much of the 'mystification' that Iris Murdoch has spoken about, together with light, telling brushwork of satiric subtlety; she followed it up three years later with *The Birds of the Air*. Margaret Forster has written ten novels, and none so intriguing as *Can you Hear Me Mother?* of 1979, about three generations of women. The central character, Angela, while trying to ensure that her daughter can be 'free', discovers she is far from 'free' herself. Less violent than Fay Weldon's books, it could be a primer for women in their forties who have just begun to think –

and there are such – about the whole question of 'liberation' and what it means.

Fortunately the list of writers is never-ending and by the time this book is published several more will have been added. Even if the Sex Discrimination Act of 1975 has reduced both women and men in Britain to the status of 'person' women writers at least do not now deny their sex. They have been particularly concerned with their women characters, and the best of them have thought hard about the way women live or want to live, even if they are not hard line feminists. Their humour is their own, so is their interest in experimental writing. Gamesmanship does not concern them as much as the concept of form. They have never lost that particular talent of women for loving and caring, they will destroy nothing except the urge to destroy. If some have tended to produce novels that grow continually shorter and terser, this does not mean they are incapable of thought. I do not see how acreage of words can be related to depth of meaning. The message of their work takes us towards the twenty-first century with the right degree of hope, for the true liberation of women is the liberation of the will to create.

In A.E. Baker's *History of the English Novel*, Volume XI, completed by Lionel Stevenson in 1967, a group of writers belonging to the era 'Yesterday and After' were considered together, and the title given to this chapter was adapted from that of a novel by Thomas Hardy. The chapter was called 'A Group of Able Dames'. Such a silly piece of editing would make any woman angry, feminist or not, but I think it is better to laugh it off and realize cheerfully that no literary history would dare use such a title now. The intensely nationalistic era for women may be approaching its end, thanks in no small way to the women novelists, and it is better to remember what Virginia Woolf wrote in *Three Guineas*: 'As a woman I have no country. . . . As a woman my country is the whole world.'

Select Bibliography

I   THE WOMEN'S MOVEMENT

JUDITH BARDWICK: *Women in Transition*, Brighton, 1980
SARA CLAYTON, Compiler, P.D. Gann, ed: *The Women's Movement, Books on Feminism*, London Borough of Bromley Library Service, 1977
JULIET MITCHELL and ANN OAKLEY, ed. and introd: *The Rights and Wrongs of Women*, Harmondsworth, 1976
NATIONAL BOOK LEAGUE: *Women and Women Writers in the Commonwealth*, Commonwealth Book Fair Catalogue, 1975
JANET RADCLIFFE: *The Sceptical Feminist*, London, 1980
JOANNA BUNKER ROHRBAUGH: *Women: Psychology's Puzzle*, Brighton, 1979
H.G. WELLS: *The Work, Wealth and Happiness of Mankind*, (Chapter XI, 'Women in the World's Work') London, 1932

II   LITERARY AND SOCIAL BACKGROUND

WALTER ALLEN: *The English Novel*, London, 1954
Tradition and Dream, A Critical Survey of British and American Fiction from the 1920's to the Present Day, London, 1964
A.E. BAKER, completed by Lionel Stevenson: *History of the English Novel*, Vol. XI, London, 1967
H.E. BATES: *The Modern Short Story. A Critical Survey*, London 1943
PHYLLIS BENTLEY: *The English Regional Novel*, London, 1941
RONALD BLYTHE: *The Age of Illusion, England in the Twenties and Thirties*, London, 1963
MALCOLM BRADBURY, ed: *The Novel Today*, London, 1977
ANTHONY BURGESS: *The Novel Today*, London, 1963
The Novel Now: A Student's Guide to Contemporary Fiction, London, 1967
MARY CADOGAN and WENDY CRAIG: *Women and Children First. Aspects of War and Literature*, London, 1978
RICHARD CHURCH: *The Growth of the English Novel* (Home Study Books), London, 1951

DAVID DAICHES, ed: *The Penguin Companion to English Literature*, Vol. I, Harmondsworth, 1971

AVROM FLEISHMAN: *The English Historical Novel*, Baltimore, 1971

G.S. FRASER: *The Modern Writer and his World*, rev. ed., London, 1964

DOUGLAS GOLDRING: *The Nineteen Twenties*, London, 1945

MARTIN GREEN: *Children of the Sun: A Narrative of 'Decadence' in England after 1918*. New York, 1976; London, 1977

R. BRIMLEY JOHNSON: *Some Contemporary Novelists (Women)*, London, 1920

HOLGER KLEIN, ed: *The First World War in Fiction*, London, 1976

MARGARET LAWRENCE: *We Write as Women*, London, 1937

JESSICA MANN: *Deadlier than the Male. An Investigation into Feminine Crime Writing*, Newton Abbot, 1981

ELLEN MOERS: *Literary Women. The Great Writers*, London, 1977

WILLIAM VAN O'CONNOR, ed: *Forms of Modern Fiction* (Midland Book) Bloomington, Indiana, 1959

E.D. PENDRY: *The New Feminism of English Fiction: a study in contemporary women novelists*, Tokyo, 1956

MARTIN SEYMOUR-SMITH: *Guide to Modern World Literature*, London, 1975
Who's Who in Twentieth Century Literature, London, 1976
Novels and Novelists, London, 1980

ELAINE SHOWALTER: *A Literature of their Own, British Women Novelists from Brontë to Lessing*, Princeton and London, 1977

PATRICIA MEYER SPACK: *Contemporary Women Novelists. A Collection of Critical Essays*. New Jersey, 1977

PATRICIA STUBBS: *Women and Fiction*, Brighton, 1979

JULIAN SYMONS: *The Detective Story in Britain*, London, 1962 rep, 1969
Bloody Murder: From the Detective Story to the Crime Novel, London, 1972

WILLIAM YORK TINDALL: *Forces in Modern British Literature, 1885–1956*, New York, 1947

III   INDIVIDUAL NOVELISTS

Selected titles written by and about individual novelists are set out below. As an indication of further reading various novelists are included whose names do not figure in the main text of this book.

Detailed bibliographies of major twentieth century novelists are best found in J.R. Willison, ed. *The New Cambridge Bibliography of English Literature*, Vol. 4, 1900–1950, Cambridge, 1972. Biographical information and critical interpretations are also available in current reference works such as Kunitz and Haycraft: *Twentieth Century Authors*, New York and

London, 1950, 1955, *Contemporary Novelists*, London and New York, 1976 *The Writer's Directory*, 1980–82, London, 1979.

PHYLLIS SHAND ALLFREY
  The Orchid House, London, 1953
E.M. VON ARNIM, Countess, 'Elizabeth' 1866–1941
  Elizabeth and her German Garden, London, 1898
  The Enchanted April, London, 1922
  Leslie De Charms: *Elizabeth of the German Garden*, London, 1958
DAISY ASHFORD 1881–1972
  The Young Visiters, London, 1919
SILVIA ASHTON-WARNER 1908–
  Spinster, London, 1958
  Teacher, London, 1963
MARGARET ATWOOD 1939–
  The Edible Woman, London, 1969
  Surfacing, London, 1972
  Lady Oracle, London, 1977
ENID BAGNOLD 1889–
  Serena Blandish, 1924
  National Velvet, 1935
  The Loved and Envied, 1951
BERYL BAINBRIDGE 1934–
  A Weekend with Claude, London, 1966
  Another Part of the Wood, London, 1968, new ed. 1979
  Harriet said . . . London, 1972
  The Dressmaker, London, 1973
  The Bottle-Factory Outing, London, 1974
  Sweet William, London, 1975
  A Quiet Life, London, 1976
  Injury Time, London, 1977
  Young Adolf, London, 1978
  Winter Garden, London, 1980
LYNNE REID BANKS 1929–
  The L-Shaped Room, London, 1960
  The Backward Shadow, London, 1970
  The Adventure of King Midas, London, 1974
VERITY BARGATE
  No Mama No!, London, 1977
  Children Crossing, London, 1979
  Tit for Tat, London, 1980
A.L. BARKER 1918–
  Lost upon the Roundabouts (stories), London, 1964

NINA BAWDEN 1925–
Tortoise by Candlelight, London, 1963
The Birds on the Trees, London, 1970
George Beneath a Paper Moon, London, 1974
Family Passions, London, 1979
SYBILLE BEDFORD 1911–
A Legacy, London, 1956
A Favourite of the Gods, London, 1962
A Compass Error, London, 1968
ROSALIND BELBEN 1941–
Dreaming of Dead People, Brighton, 1979
STELLA BENSON 1892–1933
I Pose, London, 1915, New York, 1916
The Poor Man, London, 1922, New York, 1923
The Far-away Bride, New York, 1930, London, 1931 (*Tobit Transplanted*)
PHYLLIS BENTLEY 1894–1977
The Spinner of the Years, London, 1928, New York, 1929
Carr, London, 1929, New York, 1933
Inheritance, London, 1932, New York, 1934
Freedom, farewell! London, 1936, New York, 1936
The Rise of Henry Morcar, London, 1946, New York, 1958
Crescendo, London, 1958, New York, 1958
ELIZABETH BERRIDGE 1921–
Across the Common, London, 1964
CAROLINE BLACKWOOD
For All that I Found There, London, 1973
The Stepdaughter, London, 1976
Great Granny Webster, London, 1977
The Fate of Mary Rose, London, 1980
PHYLLIS BOTTOME 1884–1963
The Mortal Storm, London, 1937, Boston, 1938
London Pride, London, 1941
ELIZABETH BOWEN 1899–1973
Encounters: stories, London, 1923
Ann Lee's and other stories, London, 1926, New York, 1928
The Hotel, London, 1927, New York, 1928
Joining Charles, and other stories, London, 1929, New York, 1929
The Last September, London, 1929, New York, 1929
Friends and Relations, London, 1931, New York, 1931
To the North, London, 1932, New York, 1933
The Cat Jumps, and other stories, London, 1934
The House in Paris, London, 1935, New York, 1936

The Death of the Heart, London, 1938, New York, 1939
Look at All those Roses: short stories, London, 1941, New York, 1941
The Demon Lover and other stories, London, 1945, New York, 1946 (*Ivy Gripped the Steps*)
The Heat of the Day, London, 1949, New York, 1949
A World of Love, London, 1955, New York, 1955
The Little Girls, London, 1964, New York, 1964
A Day in the Dark, and other stories, London, 1965, New York
Eva Trout, or Changing Scenes, New York, 1968, London, 1969
Victoria Glendinning: *Elizabeth Bowen, Portrait of a Writer*, Select bibliography. London, 1977
CAROLINE BOWDER Brighton
The Walled Landscape, London, 1980
MARJORIE BOWEN 1888–1952
The Viper of Milan, London, 1906
General Crack, London, 1928 as 'George Preedy'
VERA BRITTAIN 1896–1970
The Dark Tide, London, 1923
Account Rendered, London, 1945
Born 1925: A Novel of Youth, London, 1948
ROSALIND BRACKENBURY 1942–
The Coelacanth, Brighton, 1979
CHRISTINE BROOKE-ROSE 1926–
Out, London, 1964
Between, London, 1968
Thru, London, 1975
BRIGID BROPHY 1929–
Hackenfeller's Ape, London, 1953, New York, 1954
The King of a Rainy Country, London, 1956, New York, 1957
Flesh, London, 1962, New York, 1963
The Snow Ball, London, 1964
Palace without Chairs, London, 1978
D.K. BROSTER d.1950
The Flight of the Heron, London, 1925
The Gleam in the North, London, 1927
The Dark Mile, London, 1929
'BRYHER' (Winifred Elliman) 1894–
The Fourteenth of October, New York, 1952, London, 1954
The Player's Boy, New York, 1953, London, 1957
Roman Wall, New York, 1954, London, 1955
Gate to the Sea, New York, 1958, London, 1959
Ruan, New York, 1960, London, 1961
The Coin of Carthage, New York, 1963, London, 1964

This January Tale, New York, 1966, London, 1968
MARY BUTTS 1893–1937
Death of Felicity Taverner, London, 1932
A.S. BYATT 1936–
Shadow of a Sun, London, 1964
The Game, London, 1967
The Virgin in the Garden, London, 1978
CATHERINE CARSWELL 1870–1946
Open the Door! London, 1920
ANGELA CARTER 1940–
Shadow Dance, London, 1966 later republished as *Honeybuzzard*
The Magic Toyshop, London, 1967
Several Perceptions, London, 1968
Heroes and Villains, London, 1969
MARY CHOLMONDELEY 1859–1925
Red Pottage, London, 1898
AGATHA CHRISTIE 1891–1976
The Murder of Roger Ackroyd, 1926
ISOBEL COLEGATE
Orlando King, London, 1968
Orlando at the Brazen Threshold, London, 1971
Agatha, London, 1973
The Shooting Party, London, 1981
IVY COMPTON-BURNETT 1884–1969
Dolores, Edinburgh and London, 1911
Pastors and Masters: A Study, London, 1925
Men and Wives, London, 1931, New York, 1931
More Women than Men, London, 1933
A House and its Head, London and Toronto, 1935
Daughters and Sons, London, 1937, New York, 1938
A Family and a Fortune, London, 1939
Parents and Children, London 1941
Elders and Betters, London, 1944
Manservants and Maidservants, London, 1947, New York, 1948 (*Bullivant and the Lambs*)
Two Worlds and their Ways, London, 1949, New York, 1949
Darkness and Day, London, 1951, New York, 1951
The Present and the Past, London, 1953, New York, 1953
Mother and Son, London, 1955, New York, 1955
A Father and his Fate, London, 1957, New York, 1958
A Heritage and its History, London, 1959, New York, 1959
The Mighty and their Fall, London, 1961, New York, 1962
A God and his Gifts, London, 1963, New York, 1963

The Last and the First, London, 1971 (posthumous and uncorrected), New York, 1971

Charles Burkhardt: *Ivy Compton-Burnett*, London, 1964, New York, 1965

Elizabeth Sprigge: *Ivy Compton-Burnett*, London, 1971, New York, 1973

Hilary Spurling: *A Critical Biography of Ivy Compton-Burnett*, London, 1971

R. Glynn-Grylls: *I. Compton-Burnett*, London, 1971 (Writers and their Work)

BARBARA COMYNS 1909–
   The Vet's Daughter, London, 1959

LETTICE COOPER 1897–
   National Provincial, London, 1938, New York, 1938
   Fenny, London, 1953
   A Certain Compass, London, 1960

MARIE CORELLI 1854–1924
   Boy, London, 1900, Philadelphia, 1901
   Brian Masters: *Now Barabbas was a Rotter . . .*, London, 1978

ELSPETH DAVIE
   Providings, London, 1965
   The Spark and other Stories, London, 1968

JENNIFER DAWSON
   The Ha-ha, London, 1961, Boston, 1961
   Fowler's Snare, London, 1963
   The Cold Country, London, 1966

ANITA DESAI 1937–
   Cry, the Peacock, London, 1963
   Voices in the City, London, 1965
   Bye-bye, Blackbird, London, 1971
   The Clear Light of Day, London, 1980

MARGARET DRABBLE 1939–
   A Summer Bird-cage, London, 1963, New York, 1964
   The Garrick Year, London, 1964, New York, 1965
   The Millstone, London, 1965, New York, 1966
   Jerusalem the Golden, London, 1967, New York, 1968
   The Waterfall, London, 1969, New York, 1969
   The Needle's Eye, London, 1972, New York, 1972
   The Realms of Gold, London, 1975, New York, 1975
   The Ice Age, London, 1977, New York, 1977

MAUREEN DUFFY 1933–
   That's How it Was, London, 1962
   The Single Eye, London, 1964
   The Microcosm, London, 1966, New York, 1966
   The Paradox Players, London, 1967, New York, 1968

Wounds, London, 1969, New York, 1969
Love Child, London, 1970, New York, 1971
NELL DUNN 1936–
    Up the Junction, London, 1963, New York, 1966
    Poor Cow, London, 1967, New York, 1967
    The Only Child, London, 1979
CATHERINE DUPRE
    The Chicken Coop, London, 1967
    Jelly Baby, London, 1968
    A Face full of Flowers, London, 1969
JANICE ELLIOTT 1931–
    The Buttercup Chain, London, 1967
    Heaven on Earth, London, 1975
ALICE THOMAS ELLIS
    The Sin Eater, London, 1977
    The Birds of the Air, London, 1980
'MARGIAD EVANS' Williams, Peggy Eileen 1909–58
    Country Dance, London, 1932
    The Wooden Doctor, Oxford 1933, Boston, 1933
    Turf or Stone, Oxford, 1934
    Creed, Oxford, 1936
    The Old and the Young, London, 1948
D.S. Savage: *The Withered Branch*, London, 1950, pp. 106–128.
Moira Dearnley, *Margiad Evans*, 'Writers of Wales' series. Forthcoming
VIRGINIA FASSNIDGE 1939–
    Finding Out, London, 1979
EVA FIGES 1932– (b. Germany)
    Winter Journey, London, 1967, New York, 1968
    B, London, 1972
    Days, London, 1974
PENELOPE FITZGERALD
    The Golden Child, London, 1977, New York, 1978
    The Bookshop, London, 1978
    Offshore, London, 1979
    Human Voices, London, 1980
MARGARET FORSTER 1938–
    Can You Hear Me, Mother? London, 1979
JANET FRAME 1924–
    Owls do Cry, London, 1957, New York, 1960
    Faces in the Water, London, 1962, New York, 1961
    The Edge of the Alphabet, London, 1962, New York, 1962
    Scented Gardens for the Blind, London, 1963, New York, 1964
    Daughter Buffalo, London, 1973, New York, 1972

MILES FRANKLIN 1879–1954
   My Brilliant Career, Sydney, 1901, New York, 1980
   All that Swagger, Sydney, 1936
   My Career goes Bung, Sydney, 1942
MAVIS GALLANT 1922–
   The Other Paris, Boston, 1946, London, 1957
   Green Water, Green Sky, Boston, 1959, London, 1960
   My Heart is Broken: Eight Stories and a Short Novel, New York and
      Toronto, 1964. London, 1965 (An Unmarried Man's Summer)
   A Fairly Good Time, London, 1970, New York, 1970
STELLA GIBBONS 1902–
   Cold Comfort Farm, London, 1932, New York, 1933
PENELOPE GILLIATT 1924–
   What's it Like Out? and Other Stories, London, 1968
   Nobody's Business, Stories, London, 1972, New York, 1972
ELINOR GLYN 1864–1943
   The Visits of Elizabeth, London, 1900, New York, 1901
   Three Weeks, London, 1907, New York, 1907, With intro. by Cecil
      Beaton, London, 1974
   Elizabeth visits America, London, 1909, New York, 1909
   His Hour, London, 1910, New York, 1910 (Later known as *When the
      Hour Came*)
Anthony Glyn: *Elinor Glyn*, London, 1955
RUMER GODDEN 1907–
   Black Narcissus, London, 1939, New York, 1968
   The Greengage Summer, London, 1958, New York, 1958
   In this House of Brede, London, 1969, New York, 1969
NADINE GORDIMER 1923–
   The Lying Days, London, 1953
   Friday's Footprint, London, 1960, New York, 1960
   Occasion for Loving, London, 1963, New York, 1963
   The Late Bourgeois World, London, 1966, New York, 1966
   A Guest of Honour, London, 1970, New York, 1970
   The Conservationist, London, 1974, New York, 1975
   Burger's Daughter, London, 1979, New York, 1979
SARAH GRAND 1854–1943
   The Heavenly Twins, London, 1893, New York, 1893
   The Beth Book, London, 1897, New York, 1897
   Emotional Moments, London, 1908
Frederic Whyte: *William Heinemann, A Memoir*, London, 1928, Garden
   City, New York, 1929
RADCLYFFE HALL 1883–1943
   The Unlit Lamp, London, 1924, New York, 1929

A Saturday Life, London, 1925, New York, 1930
Adam's Breed, London, 1926, New York, 1926
The Well of Loneliness, London, 1928, (withdrawn), Paris, 1928, New
   York, 1928
GERALDINE HALLS
The Silk Project, London, 1965
The Cats of Benares, London, 1967, New York, 1967
The Cobra Kite, London, 1971
The Last Summer of the Men Shortage, London, 1976
EVA HANAGAN
In Thrall, London, 1977
Playmates, London, 1978
The Upas Tree, London, 1979, New York, 1980
Holding On, London, 1980
SUSAN HILL 1942–
I'm the King of the Castle, London, 1970, New York, 1977 (paper)
Strange Meeting, London, 1971, New York, 1972
The Bird of Night, London, 1972, New York, 1973
The Springtime of the Year, London, 1974, New York, 1974
HELEN HODGMAN
Blue Skies, London, 1977
Jack and Jill, London, 1978
CONSTANCE HOLME 1880–1955
Crump Folk Going Home, London, 1913
The Lonely Plough, London, 1914
The Old Road from Spain, London, 1916
Beautiful End, London, 1918
The Splendid Fairing, London, 1919
The Trumpet in the Dust, London, 1921
The Things which belong . . . London, 1925
He-who-came? London, 1930
WINIFRED HOLTBY 1898–1935
Anderby Wold, London, 1923
The Crowded Street, London, 1924
The Land of Green Ginger, London, 1927, New York, 1928
Poor Caroline, London, 1931, New York, 1931
Mandoa! Mandoa!, London, 1933, New York, 1933
South Riding, London, 1936, New York, 1936
Vera Brittain: *Testament of Friendship*, London, 1940, New York, 1940
VIOLET HUNT 1866–1942
The House of Many Mirrors, London, 1915, New York, 1915
Douglas Goldring: *South Lodge*, London, 1943
ANGELA HUTH 1938–

Monday Lunch in Fairyland (stories), London, 1978
MARGARET IRWIN d. 1967
  Still She Wished for Company, London, 1924
  Royal Flush, London, 1932, New York, 1932
  The Proud Servant, London, 1934, New York, 1934
  The Stranger Prince, London, 1937, New York, 1934
  The Bride, London, 1939, New York, 1939
  The Gay Galliard, London, 1941, New York, 1942
  Young Bess, London, 1944, New York, 1945
  Elizabeth, Captive Princess, London, 1948, New York, 1948
  Elizabeth and the Prince of Spain, London, 1953, New York, 1953
F. TENNYSON JESSE 1888–1958
  The Lacquer Lady, London, 1929, New York, 1930
  A Pin to See the Peepshow, London, 1934, Garden City, New York, 1934
RUTH PRAWER JHABVALA 1927– (b. Germany)
  Esmond in India, London, 1958, New York, 1958
  The Householder, London, 1960, New York, 1977 (paper)
  A New Dominion, London, 1973
  Heat and Dust, London, 1975, New York, 1976
PAMELA HANSFORD JOHNSON 1912–
  Too Dear for My Possessing, London, 1940
  An Avenue of Stone, London, 1947, New York, 1948
  A Summer to Decide, London, 1948, New York, 1975
  The Holiday Friend, London, 1972, New York, 1973
JENNIFER JOHNSTON 1930–
  The Captains and the Kings, London, 1972
  The Gates, London, 1973
  How Many Miles to Babylon, London, 1974, New York, 1975 (paper)
  Shadows on our Skins, London, 1977, New York, 1978
'ANNA KAVAN' Mrs Helen Edmonds 1901–1968
  Let Me Alone (Helen Ferguson) 1930, 1974
  Asylum Piece, London, 1940, Garden City, New York, 1946
  I am Lazarus, London, 1945
  Sleep Has His House, London, 1948, *The House of Sleep*, Garden City, New York, 1947
  A Scarcity of Love, London, 1956, New York, n.d.
  Eagle's Nest, London, 1957
  A Bright Green Field, and other stories London, 1958
  Who Are You? London, 1963
  Ice, London, 1967, New York, 1971
  Julia and the Bazooka, London, 1970, New York, 1975
SHEILA KAYE-SMITH 1887–1955
  The Tramping Methodist, London, 1908, New York, 1922

Starbrace, London, 1909, New York, 1926
Sussex Gorse, London, 1916, New York, 1916
Tamarisk Town, London, 1919, New York, 1920
Green Apple Harvest, London, 1920, New York, 1921
Joanna Godden, London, 1921, New York, 1922
The End of the House of Alard, London, 1923, New York, 1923
MARGARET KENNEDY 1896–1967
The Constant Nymph, London, 1924, New York, 1969 (paper)
Troy Chimneys, London, 1953, New York, 1952
PADDY KITCHEN 1934–
Lying-in, London, 1965
The Fleshly School, London, 1970
MARGARET LANE 1907–
A Night at Sea, London, 1964, New York, 1965
A Smell of Burning, London, 1965, New York, 1966
MARGARET LAURENCE, 1926–
The Stone Angel, Toronto, 1964, New York, 1964, London, 1964
A Jest of God, Toronto, 1966
The Diviners, New York, 1974
MARY LAVIN, 1912–
The House in Clewe Street, London, 1945, New York, 1946
Mary O'Grady, London, 1950
The Stories of Mary Lavin, London, 2 vols., 1964, 1974
PATRICIA LEDWARD, 1921–
A Root of Grace, London, 1969
ROSAMOND LEHMANN 1903–
Dusty Answer, London, 1927, New York, 1927
A Note in Music, London, 1930, New York, 1930
Invitation to the Waltz, London, 1932, New York, 1932
The Weather in the Streets, London, 1936, New York, 1936
The Ballad and the Source, London, 1944, New York, 1945
The Gypsy's Baby, and other stories, London, 1946, New York, 1946
The Echoing Grove, London, 1953, New York, 1953
A Sea-Grape Tree, London, 1976
DORIS LESSING 1919–
The Grass is Singing, London, 1950, New York, 1950
This was the Old Chief's Country, short stories, London, 1951, New York 1952
Martha Quest, London, 1952 (Children of Violence, I) New York, 1970 (paper)
Five: Short Novels – A Home for the Highland Cattle, The Other Woman, Eldorado, The Antheap, Hunger, London, 1953

A Proper Marriage, London, 1954 (Children of Violence, II) New
York, 1970, (paper)
Retreat to Innocence, London, 1956
The Habit of Loving, (short stories), London, 1957, New York, repr.
1974
A Ripple from the Storm, London, 1958 (Children of Violence, III) New
York, 1970 (paper)
The Golden Notebook, London, 1962, New edition, with author's
preface, 1972, New York, 1962
A Man and Two Women, (short stories), London, 1963, New York, 1963
Landlocked, London, 1965 (Children of Violence, IV) New York, 1970
(paper)
The Four-Gated City, London, 1969 (Children of Violence, V) New
York, 1969
Briefing for a Descent into Hell, London, 1971, New York, 1971
The Story of a Non-Marrying Man, (short stories), London, 1972
The Summer before the Dark, London, 1973, New York, 1973
D. Brewster: *Doris Lessing*, New York, 1965
Michael Thorpe: *Doris Lessing*, London, 1973, (Writers and their Work)
Elmsford, New York, 1973
Paul Schlueter: *The Novels of Doris Lessing*. With a preface by Harry T.
Moore, Carbondale, Illinois, 1973
ADA LEVERSON 1862–1933
The Twelfth Hour, London, 1907
*Love's Shadow, London, 1908
The Limit, London, 1911, New York, 1951
*Tenterhooks, London, 1912
Bird of Paradise, London, 1914, New York, 1952
*Love at Second Sight, London, 1916
*These are published together in *The Little Ottleys*, with a foreword by
Colin MacInnes. London, 1962, New York, 1962
PENELOPE LIVELY 1933–
Treasures of Time, London, 1979
ROSE MACAULAY 1881–1958
Abbots Verney, London, 1906
Potterism: A Tragi-farcical Tract, London, 1920, New York, 1920
Dangerous Ages, London, 1921, New York, 1921
Told by an Idiot, London, 1923, New York, 1923
Orphan Island, London, 1924, New York, 1925
Crewe Train, London, 1926, New York, 1926
Keeping up Appearances, London, 1928
Staying with Relations, London, 1930, New York, 1930
They were Defeated, London, 1932

The World My Wilderness, London, 1950, Boston, 1950
The Towers of Trebizond, London, 1956
Constance Babington-Smith: *Rose Macaulay*, London, 1972
With checklist.
SHEILA MACLEOD 1939–
Circuit Breaker, London, 1978
ETHEL MANNIN 1900–78
Sounding Brass, London, 1925, New York, 1926
OLIVIA MANNING 1915–1980
The Wind Changes, London, 1937, New York, 1938
Artist among the Missing, London, 1949
School for Love, London, 1951
A Different Face, London, 1953, New York, 1957
The Doves of Venus, London, 1955, New York, 1956
The Great Fortune, London, 1960, New York, 1961 ⎫
The Spoilt City, London, 1962, New York, 1962 ⎬ The Balkan Trilog
Friends and Heroes, London, 1965, New York, 1966 ⎭
The Play Room, London, 1969, New York, 1969, (*The Camperlea Girls*)
The Rain Forest, London, 1974
The Danger Tree, London, 1977
The Battle Lost and Won, London 1978
The Sum of Things, London, 1980
KATHERINE MANSFIELD 1888–1923
In a German Pension, London, 1911, New York, 1926
Prelude, London, 1918
Je ne parle pas français, London, 1918
Bliss and other stories, London, 1920, New York, 1921
The Garden Party, and other stories, London, 1922, New York, 1922
The Dove's Nest, and other stories, London, 1924, New York, 1923
Something Childish, and other stories, London, 1924, New York, (*The Little Girl*)
The Aloe, London, 1930 (original form of *Prelude*, 1918), New York, 1930 (reprint)
A. Alpers: *Katherine Mansfield*, New York, 1953, London, 1954
A. Alpers: *The Life of Katherine Mansfield*, London, 1979
John Carswell: *Lives and Letters*, London, 1978
Ian A. Gordon: *Katherine Mansfield*, London, 1954, revised 1963, 1971 (Writers and their Work). Contains a useful Index of Short stories. Elmsford, New York, n.d.
KAMALA MARKANDAYA 1924–
A Silence of Desire, London, 1960, New York, 1960
The Two Virgins, London, 1974, New York, 1975

NAOMI MAY
  At Home, London, 1969
  The Adventurer, London, 1970
  Troubles, London, 1976
F.M. MAYOR 1872–1932
  The Third Miss Symons, London, 1913
  The Rector's Daughter, London, 1924, New York, 1930
VIOLA MEYNELL 1886–1956
  Follow thy Fair Sun, London, 1933 (rev. as *Lovers*, 1944)
YVONNE MITCHELL 1919–1979
  Martha on Sunday, London, 1970
  God is Inexperienced, London, 1974
  But Answer Came There None, London, 1977
NAOMI MITCHISON 1897–
  The Conquered, London, 1923, New York, 1923
  The Corn King and the Spring Queen, London, 1931, New York, 1931
  Memoirs of a Space Woman, London, 1962
NANCY MITFORD 1904–1973
  Highland Fling, London, 1931
  Christmas Pudding, London, 1932
  Wigs on the Green, London, 1935
  The Pursuit of Love, London, 1945, New York, 1946
  Love in a Cold Climate, London, 1949, New York, 1949
  The Blessing, London, 1951, New York, 1951
  Don't Tell Alfred, London, 1960, New York, 1961
PENELOPE MORTIMER 1918–
  A Villa in Summer, London, 1954, New York, 1955
  The Pumpkin Eater, London, 1962, New York, 1963
  Long Distance, London, 1974, New York, 1974
ALICE MUNRO 1931–
  Lives of Girls and Women, Toronto, 1971, London, 1973, New York, 1974 (paper)
  The Beggar Maid, London, 1979, New York, 1979
HOPE MUNTZ 1907–
  The Golden Warrior, London, 1948, New York, 1949
IRIS MURDOCH 1919–
  Under the Net, London, 1954, New York, 1954
  The Flight from the Enchanter, London, 1956, New York, 1956
  The Sandcastle, London, 1957, New York, 1957
  The Bell, London, 1958, New York, 1958
  A Severed Head, London, 1961, New York, 1961
  An Unofficial Rose, London, 1962, New York, 1962
  The Unicorn, London, 1963, New York, 1963

The Italian Girl, London, 1964, New York, 1964
The Red and the Green, London, 1965, New York, 1965
The Time of the Angels, London, 1966, New York, 1966
The Nice and the Good, London, 1968, New York, 1968
Bruno's Dream, London, 1969, New York, 1969
A Fairly Honourable Defeat, London, 1970, New York, 1970
An Accidental Man, London, 1971, New York, 1971
The Black Prince, London, 1973, New York, 1973
The Sacred and Profane Love Machine, London, 1974, New York, 1974
A Word Child, London, 1975, New York, 1975
Henry and Cato, London, 1976, New York, 1977
The Sea, the Sea, London, 1978, New York, 1978
Nuns and Soldiers, London, 1980, New York, 1981
A.S.Byatt: *Degrees of Freedom*, London, 1965, New York, 1965
A.S. Byatt: *Iris Murdoch*, London, 1976 (Writers and their Work)
ELIZABETH MYERS 1912–47
   A Well Full of Leaves, London, 1943, New York, 1944
   The Basilisk of St James's, London, 1945
   Mrs Christopher, London, 1946
EDNA O'BRIEN 1932–
   The Country Girls, London, 1960, New York, 1960
JULIA O'FAOLAIN
   We Might see Sights! and Other Stories, London, 1968
   Godded and Codded, London, 1970, New York, 1971 (*Three Lovers*)
   Man in the Cellar, London, 1974
   Women in the Wall, London, 1975, New York, 1975
   No City for Young Men, London, 1980
'OLIVIA' (Dorothy Bussy)
   Olivia, London, 1949, New York, 1949
EDITH OLIVIER 1874–1948
   The Love Child, London, 1927, New York, 1927
BARONESS ORCZY 1865–1947
   The Scarlet Pimpernel, London, 1905, New York, 1905
RUTH PARK
   The Harp in the South, Sydney, London, 1948, Boston, 1948
   Poor Man's Orange, Sydney, 1950
WINIFRED PECK
   House Bound, London, 1942
KATHARINE SUSANNAH PRICHARD 1884–1972
   Coonardoo, London, 1929, New York, 1930
   Haxby's Circus, London, 1930
   The Roaring Nineties, London, 1946
   Golden Miles, London, 1948

BARBARA PYM 1913–1980
Some Tame Gazelle, London, 1950
Excellent Women, London, 1952, New York, 1978
Jane and Prudence, London, 1953
Less than Angels, London, 1955, New York, 1957
A Glass of Blessings, London, 1958
No Fond Return of Love, London, 1961
Quartet in Autumn, London, 1977, New York, 1980
A Few Green Leaves, London, 1980 (posthumous)

ANN QUIN 1936–1973
Berg, London, 1964
Three, London, 1966, New York, 1966
Passages, London, 1969
Tripticks, London, 1972

MARY RENAULT 1905–
North Face, London, 1949, New York, 1949
The Charioteer, London, 1953
The Last of the Wine, London, 1956, New York, 1956
The King must Die, London, 1958, New York, 1958
The Bull from the Sea, London, 1962, New York, 1962
The Persian Boy, London, 1972, New York, 1972
The Praise Singer, London, 1974, New York, 1978

DOROTHY RICHARDSON 1873–1957
Pilgrimage, 11 separate vols, London, 1915–1935
Collected edition, with final section, *Dimple Hill*, London, 1938, New York, 1938. Republished 1967 with *March Moonlight*.
Gillian E. Hanscombe. *The Art of Life: Dorothy Richardson and the Development of Feminist Consciousness*, London, (forthcoming)
John Rosenberg: *Dorothy Richardson: the genius they forgot*, London, 1973
H.G. Wells: *Experiment in Autobiography*, London, 1934, New York, 1934

JEAN RHYS 1894–1979
The Left Bank and other stories, with a preface by F.M. Ford, London, 1927
Postures, London, 1928, New York, 1929 (*Quartet*)
After Leaving Mr Mackenzie, London, 1931, New York, 1931
Voyage in the Dark, London, 1934, New York, 1935
Good morning, Midnight, London, 1939
Wide Sargasso Sea, London, 1966, New York, 1967
Tigers are Better Looking, London, 1968

HENRY HANDEL RICHARDSON 1870–1946
Maurice Guest, 1908
Australia Felix, 1917 ⎫ published as
The Way Home, 1925 ⎬ *The Fortunes of Richard Mahoney*, London, 1930
Ultima Thule, 1929 ⎭

E. ARNOT ROBERTSON 1903–
  Cullum, London, 1928
  Three Came Unarmed, London, 1929
  Four Frightened People, London, 1931
  Ordinary Families, London, 1933
DAPHNE ROOKE 1914
  Mittee, London, 1951, Boston, 1952
  A Lover for Estelle, London, 1961, Boston, 1961
  The Greyling, London, 1962, New York, 1963
NAOMI ROYDE-SMITH d. 1964
  The Tortoiseshell Cat, London, 1925, New York, 1925
  The Island, London, 1930, New York, 1930
BERNICE RUBENS 1927–
  The Elected Member, London, 1969, New York, (*The Chosen People*)
  Set on Edge, London, 1972
  I sent a Letter to my Love, London, 1975
  Favours, London, 1979
VICTORIA SACKVILLE-WEST 1892–1962
  Challenge, New York, 1923
  The Edwardians, London, 1930, Garden City, N.Y., 1930
  All Passion Spent, London, 1931, Garden City, N.Y., 1932
DOROTHY L. SAYERS 1893–1957
  Murder Must Advertise, London, 1933, New York, 1933
  The Nine Tailors, London, 1934, New York, 1934
  Gaudy Night, London, 1935, New York, 1936
James Brabazon: *Dorothy L. Sayers*, London, 1981
BEATRICE KEAN SEYMOUR d. 1955
  Three Wives, London, 1927, New York, 1927
  Maids and Mistresses, London, 1932, New York, 1932
  Frost at Morning, London, 1935, Boston, 1935
  Summer of Life, London, 1936, Boston, 1936
  Buds of May, London, 1943
  The Painted Lath, London, 1955
BAPSI SIDHWA
  The Crow-Eaters, London, 1980
MAY SINCLAIR 1870–1942
  The Divine Fire, London, 1904, New York, 1904
  The Combined Maze, London, 1913, New York, 1913
  The Three Sisters, London, 1914, New York, 1914
  The Tree of Heaven, London, 1917, New York, 1917
  Mary Olivier, A Life, London, 1919, New York, 1919
  Life and Death of Harriet Frean, London, 1922, New York, 1922
  Arnold Waterlow; A Life, London 1924, New York, 1924

EDITH SITWELL 1887–1964
I Live under a Black Sun, London, 1937
ELIZABETH SMART
By Grand Central Station I Sat Down and Wept, London, 1945
Assumption of the Rogues and Rascals, London, 1978
EMMA SMITH 1923–
Maiden's Trip, London, 1948
The Far Cry, London, 1949, New York, 1950
STEVIE SMITH 1902–1971
Novel on Yellow Paper, London, 1936
Over the Frontier, London, 1938
The Holiday, London, 1949
'SOMERVILLE AND ROSS'
Edith A.O. Somerville, 1858–1949 and Violet Florence Martin, 1862–1915
The Real Charlotte, London, 1894
The Silver Fox, London, 1897
Some Experiences of an Irish R.M. London, 1899
Further Experiences of an Irish R.M., London, 1908
In Mr Knox's Country, London, 1915
MURIEL SPARK 1918–
The Comforters, London, 1957, New York, 1964, (paper)
Robinson, London, 1958, New York, 1964, (paper)
Memento Mori, London, 1959, New York, 1959
The Bachelors, London, 1960, New York, 1961
The Ballad of Peckham Rye, London, 1960, New York, 1960
The Prime of Miss Jean Brodie, London, 1961, New York, 1962
The Mandelbaum Gate, London, 1965, New York, 1965
CHRISTINA STEAD 1902–
The Salzburg Tales, London, 1934, New York, 1934
Seven Poor Men of Sydney, London, 1934, New York, 1935
The Man who Loved Children, New York, 1940, London, 1941
For Love Alone, New York, 1944, London, 1945
Letty Fox, Her Luck, New York, 1946, London, 1947
Dark Places of the Heart, New York, 1966, London, 1967, (*Cotters' England*)
The Puzzle-Headed Girl: Four novellas, New York, 1967
Miss Herbert, New York, 1976, London, 1979
FLORA ANNIE STEEL 1847–1929
The Hosts of the Lord, London, 1900, New York, 1900
JEAN STUBBS 1926–
The Rose-Grower, London, 1962, New York, 1963

KATHLEEN SULLY
  A Man Talking to Seagulls, London, 1959
  A Breeze on a Lonely Road, London, 1969
ROSEMARY SUTCLIFF 1920–
  Sword at Sunset, London, 1963, New York, 1963
ELIZABETH TAYLOR 1912–75
  A View of the Harbour, London, 1947, New York, 1947
  At Mrs Lippincote's, London, 1948, New York, 1948
  In a Summer Season, London, 1961, New York, 1961
  The Wedding Group, London, 1968, New York, 1968
EMMA TENNANT
  The Time of the Crack, London, 1973
  The Last of the Country House Murders, London, 1975
  Hotel de Dream, London, 1976
JOSEPHINE TEY 1897–1952 Mackintosh, Elizabeth
  The Franchise Affair, London, 1948, New York, 1949
  The Daughter of Time, London, 1951, New York, 1951
ANGELA THIRKELL 1890–1960
  Ankle Deep, London, 1932
  High Rising, London, 1933, New York, 1951
  Wild Strawberries, London, 1934, New York, 1934
  Pomfret Towers, London, 1938, New York, 1938
  Miss Bunting, London, 1946, New York, 1946
  Peace Breaks Out, London, 197?, New York, 1947
  What Did it Mean? London, 1954, New York, 1954
  Love at all Ages, London, 1959
Margot Strickland: *Portrait of a Lady Novelist*, London, 1977, with
  bibliography
SYLVIA TOWNSEND WARNER 1893–1978
  Lolly Willowes: or, the Loving Huntsman, London, 1926, New York,
    1926
  Mr Fortune's Maggot, London, 1927, New York, 1927
  Summer Will Show, London, 1936, New York, 1936
  The Corner that Held Them, London, 1948
  A Spirit Rises, London, 1962, New York, 1962
HILDA VAUGHAN
  Here are Lovers, London, 1926, New York, 1926
  Iron and Gold, London, 1948
HELEN WADDELL 1899–1965
  Peter Abelard, London, 1933, New York, 1933
M.T. WADEY
  Sleight of Heart, London, 1975

MRS HUMPHRY WARD 1851–1920 (Mary Augusta Ware)
  Robert Elsmere, London, 1888, New York, 1888
  The Marriage of William Ashe, London, 1905, New York, 1905
  The Coryston Family, London, 1913, New York, 1913
MARY WEBB 1881–1927
  The Golden Arrow, London, 1916, New York, 19??
  Gone to Earth, London, 1917, New York, 1917
  The House in Dormer Forest, London, 1920, New York, 1921
  Seven for a Secret, London, 1922, New York, 1923
  Precious Bane, London, 1924, New York, 1926
  Armour Wherein He Trusted, London, 1928, (posthumous) New York,
    1929
Gladys Mary Coles: *The Flower of Light: a Biography of Mary Webb*
  London, 1978
FAY WELDON 1933–
  Down Among the Women, London, 1971, New York, 1972
  Female Friends, London, 1975, New York, 1974
  Remember Me, London, 1976, New York, 1976
  Little Sister, London, 1978
  Praxis, London, 1979, New York, 1978
  Puffball, London, 1980
REBECCA WEST 1892–
  The Return of the Soldier, London, 1918, New York, 1918
  The Judge, London, 1922, New York, 1922
  The Thinking Reed, London, 1936, New York, 1936
  The Fountain Overflows, London, 1957, New York, 1956
  The Birds Fall Down, London, 1966, New York, 1966
ANTONIA WHITE 1899–1980
  Frost in May, London, 1933, New York, 1934
  The Lost Traveller, London, 1950, New York, 1950
  The Sugar House, London, 1952
  Beyond the Glass, London, 1955, New York, 1955
ETHEL WILSON 1890–
  Hetty Forval, London, 1947
  Equations of Love, London, 1952
  Swamp Angel, London, 1954, New York, 1954
  Love and Salt Water, London, 1950
  Mrs Golightly, London, 1961
VIRGINIA WOOLF 1882–1941
  The Voyage Out, London, 1915, New York, 1920
  The Mark on the Wall, Richmond, Surrey, 1919
  Kew Gardens, Richmond, Surrey, 1919

Night and Day, London, 1919, New York, 1920
Monday or Tuesday, Richmond, Surrey, 1921, New York, 1921
Jacob's Room, London, 1922, New York, 1923
Mrs Dalloway, London, 1925, New York, 1928
To the Lighthouse, London, 1927, New York, 1927
Orlando, London, 1928, New York, 1928 (limited edition)
The Waves, London, 1931, New York, 1931
The Years, London, 1937, New York, 1937
Between the Acts, London, 1941, New York, 1941
A Haunted House and other short stories, London, 1943, New York, 1944
B.J. Kirkpatrick: *A Bibliography of Virginia Woolf*, London, 1957, 1967 (revised)
Bernard Blackstone: *Virginia Woolf*, London, 1952, rev. 1962 (Writers and their Work)
Herbert Marder: *Feminism and Art: A study of Virginia Woolf*, Chicago, 1968
Nancy Topping Bazin: *Virginia Woolf and the Androgynous Vision*, New Brunswick, 1973
Joan Russell Noble ed. and intro.: *Recollections of Virginia Woolf by her contemporaries*, London, 1972, New York, 1972
E.H. YOUNG 1880–1949
Moor Fires, London, 1916, New York, 19??
The Bridge Dividing, London, 1922 (later republished as *The Misses Mallett*, 1927) *The Malletts*, New York, 1927
William, London, 1925, New York, 1926
The Vicar's Daughter, London, 1928, New York, 1928
Miss Mole, London, 1930, New York, 1931
Chatterton Square, London, 1947, New York, 1947

Index